# WHAT YOUR COLLEAGUE

Multitasking mentor texts are beloved favorites and exciting new titles that can help students learn about reading and writing! Multitasking texts are worthy of revisiting. They are learning tools in a student-centered classroom that invite teachers to model and students to practice then reflect on their learning experiences. Pamela Koutrakos's voice is powerful, and she quickly draws you into her book. Every page returns to a central point: It's you, the teacher, who makes a huge difference in students' learning. Using compelling examples, this book shows you how multitasking mentor text lessons motivate and engage students in their learning and make you want to implement instructional ideas immediately. You'll learn how to use diverse genres and formats across grades and students' learning stages as Pam helps you make this important work your own. Along with guidelines for creating mentor text sets, you'll explore how to develop units with outstanding culturally relevant texts. The book opens with a matrix of featured texts and text pairings, as well as a chart of recurring features in the lessons. I guarantee that *Mentor Texts That Multitask* will become one of your most valued and helpful professional books—one you'll return to again and again!

—Laura Robb, Author
*Guided Practice for Reading Growth*

When I am thinking through a classroom challenge or looking for insight, Pamela Koutrakos is one of the people that I turn to. *Mentor Texts That Multitask* resonates with Pam's characteristic wisdom, and it is imbued with her unshakable belief in young learners. This is not just a professional text; this is a transformative conversation with a powerfully capable friend.

—Cornelius Minor, Educator and Author
*We Got This: Equity, Access, and the Quest to Be Who Our Students Need Us to Be*

While reading *Mentor Texts That Multitask*, I found myself agreeing over and over again with Pamela Koutrakos and thinking about all the ways we can become more efficient through the use of smaller, strategically chosen collections of texts. The "day in and day out" work we do as educators is complex and multifaceted. In this beautiful book, Pam offers us ways to maximize time and find quality resources that enhance instruction with a "less is more" approach. This book will be a staple on my bookshelf and as I work alongside teachers.

—Valentina Gonzalez, Coauthor
*Reading and Writing With English Learners: A Framework for K–5*

Mentor texts that multitask?! This is what all educators need. I am thrilled this playful and thoughtful book exists in the world as a practical yet inspirational springboard for using books teachers love over and over again for a variety of instructional, holistic instructional purposes! Pamela Koutrakos shares tons of ideas for integrated literacy lessons *and* shows us why it all matters. From the text pairings to the inquiry ideas to the high-quality (and cross-genre!) text titles, I know educators with this book in their hands will feel more confident *and* excited about the possibilities. It is invaluable.

—Nawal Q. Casiano, Educator, Author, and Staff Developer

The moment you open *Mentor Texts That Multitask*, it's clear that you are in the company of a passionate professional who loves books, respects learners, and delights in bringing the two together. In this dynamic resource, you'll benefit from Pamela Koutrakos's asset-based approach as she charts a path for redefining the role of mentor texts in your learning space. The flexible lesson sets offer infinite learning possibilities to illuminate and integrate the essential aspects of literacy. Pam will cheer you on as you make multitasking mentor texts work for the students in your care.

—Maria Walther, Traveling Teacher, Author, and Literacy Consultant
*Shake Up Shared Reading: Expanding on Read Alouds to Encourage*
*Student Independence*

Pamela Koutrakos's passion for kid-lit, middle-grade, and YA books is matched only by her passion for supporting teachers. *Mentor Texts That Multitask* is a gorgeous marriage of the two. Pam has taken wonderfully rich books and designed lessons to support and grow student thinking, talking, reading, and writing. This is a book that I wish was around when I was a literacy coach working with teachers. Now as a current classroom teacher, I can't wait to use it to inform my own classroom practice during reading and writing instruction!

—Christina Nosek, Classroom Teacher and Author

*Mentor Texts That Multitask* helps teachers connect different parts of the curriculum to create a more cohesive and connected set of learning experiences. Pamela Koutrakos's model has the benefit of saving teachers time as well as supporting depth of thinking for students. It is grounded in research and classroom practice and is the type of book that teachers can return to again and again for ideas to try right away. After reading this book, teachers will know how to shift to a more student-centered and inquiry-based way of using mentor texts throughout the day that brings joy, engagement, and deep learning.

—Gravity Goldberg, Author
*Teach Like Yourself* and *Mindsets and Moves*

With an emphasis and deep commitment toward asset-based instruction that is unwaveringly responsive to students, Pamela Koutrakos invites readers into the endless possibilities for learning that exist within the pages of books. While Pam provides replicable lessons and resources based on specific texts, she also empowers readers to be able to select their own mentor texts and develop their own lessons. *Mentor Texts That Multitask* weaves research, resources, and practicality, inspiring teachers with lessons they can use right away, as well as approaches to take within classrooms that maximize minutes, learning, and joy.

—Melanie Meehan, Author
*Every Child Can Write and Coauthor, The Responsive Writing Teacher*

This book is not a collection of texts or an anthology of stand-alone activities. Instead, it meets students and teachers where they are and helps them grow. Pamela Koutrakos shows how simple, well-chosen texts can serve in so many ways, but she also fills the air with rich teaching practice, modeling how to embed humanity, compassion, and understanding into the standards. It's a book that should go into every teacher's tool belt.

—Gretchen Bernabei, Teacher, Consultant, and Author
*Text Structures From Poetry, Grades 4-12: Lessons to Help*
*Students Read, Analyze, and Create Poems They Will Remember*

Nothing (not even the greatest of books) can replace the human genius of a teacher; a teacher with a great *multitasking mentor text* and a practical set of tools in their hands is a force to reckon with. Pamela Koutrakos sets us up for success by reminding us of the importance of seeing the brilliance of students through an asset-based lens, and the way she guides us through our decision-making process by setting up frameworks for us to think about the student process as emerging, developing, and extending is not only a refreshing way of thinking, but a necessary one. Pam invites us to think about practical ways in which we can reduce our decision fatigue by leaning into our love of books and integrating those books across our curriculum all while centering students at the heart of our classrooms. As I scan the books on my bookshelves, I can imagine how to employ them as trusted *mentor texts that multitask* by integrating them across the elements of curriculum. From one obsessed book fan to another, thank you, Pam, for giving us the gift *Mentor Texts That Multitask*!

—Renee Houser, **Consultant and Co-Author**
*What Do I Teach Readers Tomorrow?*

Mentor texts have been a favorite for teachers and students as a touchstone for deep learning. A big thank-you to Pamela Koutrakos for revealing to us an even more expansive potential of what a few carefully selected mentor texts can hold *across* learning contexts. What this book teaches us is a paramount implementation of responsive teaching, in a streamlined, learner-centered way. Pam's deep pedagogical knowledge paired with a love of books of all sorts (yes, even some books we may not imagine!) brings us this seminal book that will only evolve our instruction in the most joyful and impactful ways. Pam does so through favorite text selections, ways to use those texts to teach, and a pathway for educators and students to multitask *their* favorite mentor texts.

—Patty McGee, Author
*Feedback That Moves Writers Forward*

This book deserves a space on every educator's bookshelf. In *Mentor Texts That Multitask*, Pamela Koutrakos understands that the never-ending search for "perfect" mentor texts can eat up time that educators could use to prepare for student-centered responsive literacy instruction. Her carefully chosen texts and thoughtfully crafted lesson sets leave the reader inspired to try them out with learners. Thank you, Pam, for ensuring that we feel confident enough to curate our own stack of multitasking texts, facilitate affirming and integrated literacy learning experiences, and engage students in the process!

—Heather Frank, Literacy Consultant

*Mentor Texts That Multitask* gives educators access to one of the most authentic voices and thought leaders in literacy practices. With all angles and lenses considered, and the face of every potential student honored, Pamela Koutrakos gives teachers the tools to be intentional about their use of powerful mentor texts. This gift for teachers offers a strong and manageable platform on which to build community and enhance literacy instruction in their classrooms utilizing some of the most meaningful mentor texts.

—Kathy Pina, Principal
*Mary A. Hubbard Elementary School*

One thing I often hear from educators is they wish they had more time—more time to plan, more time to play and practice, more time to read! Pamela Koutrakos's *Mentor Texts That Multitask* tackles this challenge of time with thoughtfulness, innovation, and clarity. This text not only provides teachers with a rich list of student-centered learning experiences, but also shares a road map of how to implement these experiences in conjunction with authentic, engaging texts. The strategies Pam gives teachers have the beautiful balance of being supported by research while also being practical and adaptable for the classroom. You can read through a chapter, select a text type, choose which lesson(s) best match students' next steps, and implement that lesson the following day. A true gift. Pam has shown us that less can be more. We don't have to select a new text every lesson, and there is real power in revisiting a mentor text through various lenses and focuses. While there is no "best" or "perfect" book, this resource certainly comes close to being the best time-saving gift for educators to select and plan lessons with rich texts at the center.

—Katie McGrath, Instructional Facilitator
*Loudoun County Public Schools*

*Mentor Texts That Multitask* is a must-read for every educator, instructional coach, and literacy leader! Pamela Koutrakos's latest book shares limitless possibilities on simplifying instruction into smaller collections of strategies that are layered with multidimensional texts! Her work is both student centered and teacher supportive. She eliminates the myth of "more books" by outlining a framework where books can be used in a variety of ways through flexible design and multifaceted learning. This book is an educator's dream!

—Jigisha Vyas, Instructional Coach
*Wyckoff School District, NJ*

Classroom teachers at the elementary level, middle school teachers, and literacy coaches (*especially* literacy coaches!) will feel equipped to teach in a meaningful and comprehensive way with a mentor text that multitasks. Gone are the totes loaded with books when traveling from classroom to classroom. Pamela Koutrakos invites teachers to open a book, any book, and list the learning possibilities that can be pulled out of it.

—Viviana Tamas, Instructional Coach
*Ward Elementary School, New Rochelle, NY*

# Mentor Texts That Multitask

To all teachers—

I am honored to learn from you and work alongside you. Thank you for the creativity, imagination, and heart you infuse into each day.

# Mentor Texts That Multitask

## A Less-Is-More Approach to Integrated Literacy Instruction

Pamela Koutrakos

**FOR INFORMATION:**

Corwin

A SAGE Company

2455 Teller Road

Thousand Oaks, California 91320

(800) 233-9936

www.corwin.com

SAGE Publications Ltd.

1 Oliver's Yard

55 City Road

London EC1Y 1SP

United Kingdom

SAGE Publications India Pvt. Ltd.

B 1/I 1 Mohan Cooperative Industrial Area

Mathura Road, New Delhi 110 044

India

SAGE Publications Asia-Pacific Pte. Ltd.

18 Cross Street #10-10/11/12

China Square Central

Singapore 048423

President: Mike Soules

Associate Vice President
and Editorial Director: Monica Eckman

Executive Editor: Tori Mello Bachman

Associate Content
Development Editor: Sharon Wu

Editorial Assistant: Nancy Chung

Project Editor: Amy Schroller

Copy Editor: Melinda Masson

Typesetter: C&M Digitals (P) Ltd.

Proofreader: Susan Schon

Indexer: Sheila Hill

Cover Designer: Gail Buschman

Marketing Manager: Margaret O'Connor

Printed in the United States of America

*Library of Congress Cataloging-in-Publication Data*

Names: Koutrakos, Pamela, author.

Title: Mentor texts that multitask: a less-is-more approach to integrated literacy instruction / Pamela A. Koutrakos.

Description: Thousand Oaks, California : Corwin, 2022. | Series: Corwin literacy | Includes bibliographical references and index.

Identifiers: LCCN 2021043582 | ISBN 9781071836132 (paperback) | ISBN 9781071859254 (epub) | ISBN 9781071859292 (epub) | ISBN 9781071859285 (pdf)

Subjects: LCSH: English language—Composition and exercises—Study and teaching (Elementary) | English language—Composition and exercises—Study and teaching (Middle school) | Mentor texts (Language arts)

Classification: LCC LB1576 .K647 2022 | DDC 372.62/3044—dc23/eng/20211012
LC record available at https://lccn.loc.gov/2021043582

This book is printed on acid-free paper.

21 22 23 24 25 10 9 8 7 6 5 4 3 2 1

# Contents

## 8   POETRY   182

# Matrix of Featured Texts and Text Pairings

| | EMERGING | DEVELOPING | EXTENDING |
|---|---|---|---|
| **Chapter 3**<br><br>**Featured Wordless Texts and Images** | *Another* by Christian Robinson (2019) | *Brave Molly* by Brooke Boynton-Hughes (2019) | *Sanjay's Super Team* by Sanjay Patel (2015) |
| **Pairings** | *Anno's Journey* by Mitsumasa Anno (1997)<br><br>*Journey* and *Quest* by Aaron Becker (2013, 2014)<br><br>*Harold and the Purple Crayon* by Crockett Johnson (1955)<br><br>*The Red Book* and *The Secret Box* by Barbara Lehman (2004, 2011)<br><br>*Chalk* and *Fossil* by Bill Thomson (2010, 2013) | *Wemberly Worried* by Kevin Henkes (2000)<br><br>*The Girl Who Never Made Mistakes* by Mark Pett and Gary Rubenstein (2011)<br><br>*Guts* by Reina Telgemeier (2019)<br><br>*What Do You Do With a Problem?* and *What Do You Do With a Chance?* by Kobi Yamada (2016, 2018)<br><br>**Online Resource:**<br><br>*Piper*, a wordless animated short by Pixar, directed by Alan Barillaro (2016) | *A Movie in My Pillow / Una pelicula en mi almohada* by Jorge Argueta (2001), with art by Elizabeth Gómez<br><br>*Inside Out and Back Again* by Thanhhà Lại (2011)<br><br>*The Year of the Dog* by Grace Lin (2005)<br><br>*The Art of Sanjay's Super Team* by Sanjay Patel (2015)<br><br>*Other Words for Home* by Jasmine Warga (2019)<br><br>**Online Resources:**<br><br>Select clips from *Never Have I Ever*, created and directed by Mindy Kaling and Lang Fisher (2020)<br><br>*Sanjay's Super Team: The Backstory*, interview by Christopher J. Farley (2015) and video created by *The Wall Street Journal* |

*(Continued)*

| | EMERGING | DEVELOPING | EXTENDING |
|---|---|---|---|
| **Chapter 4** | | | |
| **Featured Graphic Texts** | *Little Robot* by Ben Hatke (2015) | *Red Panda and Moon Bear* by Jarod Roselló (2019) | *New Kid* by Jerry Craft (2019) |
| **Pairings** | *Peter and Ernesto: The Lost Sloths* by Graham Annable (2019)<br><br>*The Flying Beaver Brothers* (series) by Maxwell Eaton III (2012)<br><br>*The Great Pet Escape* by Victoria Jamieson (2016)<br><br>*The Shark King* by R. Kikuo Johnson (2012)<br><br>*Owly* (series) by Andy Runton (2004)<br><br>*Binky the Space Cat* (series) by Ashley Spires (2009)<br><br>*Sleepless Knight* by James Sturm, Andrew Arnold, and Alexis Frederick-Frost (2015)<br><br>*Hamster and Cheese* by Colleen A. F. Venable and Stephanie Yu (2010) | *Giants Beware!* by Jorge Aguirre (2012), with art by Rafael Rosado<br><br>*Dinosaurs in Space: Out of This World!* by Pranas T. Naujokaitis (2017)<br><br>*Hilda and the Troll* by Luke Pearson (2015)<br><br>*Panda roja y oso lunar* by Jarod Roselló (2020)<br><br>*Sidekicks* by Dan Santat (2011)<br><br>*The Cardboard Kingdom* by Chad Sell (2018)<br><br>*Stargazing* by Jen Wang (2019) | *Be Prepared* by Vera Brosgol (2018)<br><br>*Class Act* by Jerry Craft (2020)<br><br>*Real Friends* and *Best Friends* by Shannon Hale (2017, 2019)<br><br>*Sunny Rolls the Dice* by Jennifer L. Holm (2019), with art by Matthew Holm<br><br>*When Stars Are Scattered* by Victoria Jamieson and Omar Mohamed (2020)<br><br>*Hey, Kiddo* by Jarrett Krosoczka (2018)<br><br>**Online Resources:**<br><br>*New Kid With Jerry Craft* by #HarperKids (HarperCollins Publishers, 2021)<br><br>*The Writer's Block: An Interview With Jerry Craft* by Kevin Springer (2019)<br><br>*Jerry Craft Breaks Barriers With Historic 2020 Newbery Win* by Kara Yorio (2020) |
| **Chapter 5** | | | |
| **Featured Realistic Fiction Texts** | *The Invisible Boy* by Trudy Ludwig (2013), with art by Patrice Barton | *The Proudest Blue: A Story of Hijab and Family* by Ibtihaj Muhammad (2019), with S.K. Ali and art by Hatem Aly | *Mango Moon* by Diane de Anda (2019), with art by Sue Cornelison |
| **Pairings** | *The Sandwich Swap* by Queen Rania Al Abdullah (2010), with Kelly DiPuccio and art by Tricia Tusa<br><br>*The Big Umbrella* by Amy June Bates (2018)<br><br>*Will I Have a Friend?* by Miriam Cohen (1967), with art by Lillian Hoban<br><br>*The Day You Begin* by Jacqueline Woodson (2018), with art by Rafael López<br><br>*Be a Friend* by Salina Yoon (2016) | *The Name Jar* by Yangsook Choi (2001)<br><br>*Sheila Rae, The Brave* by Kevin Henkes (1987)<br><br>*Ling and Ting* (series) by Grace Lin (2010)<br><br>*Ish* by Peter H. Reynolds (2004)<br><br>*Exclamation Mark* by Amy Krouse Rosenthal (2013) | *Two White Rabbits* by Jairo Buitrago (2015)<br><br>*Like the Moon Loves the Sky* by Hena Khan (2020), with art by Saffa Khan<br><br>*La frontera: El viaje con papa / My Journey With Papa* by Deborah Mills (2018)<br><br>*Dreamers* by Yuyi Morales (2018) |

| | EMERGING | DEVELOPING | EXTENDING |
|---|---|---|---|
| | *Be Kind* by Pat Zietlow Miller (2018), with art by Jen Hill | **Online Resource:**<br>*Hair Love*, an animated short film written by Matthew A. Cherry (Cherry et al., 2019) | **Online Resources:**<br>*California Teen Leads Lawsuit to Keep Immigrant TPS Recipients in the U.S.* by Public Radio International, adapted by Newsela staff (2019)<br><br>*Children Immigrating From Central America Face Long Road to U.S.* by Washington Post, adapted by Newsela staff (2019) |
| **Chapter 6**<br>**Featured Creative Nonfiction Texts** | *Planting Stories: The Life of Librarian and Storyteller Pura Belpré* by Anika Aldamuy Denise (2019), with art by Paola Escobar | *All the Way to the Top: How One Girl's Fight for Americans With Disabilities Changed Everything* by Annette Bay Pimentel (2020), with art by Nabi H. Ali and a Foreword by Jennifer Keelan-Chaffins | *Pride: The Story of Harvey Milk and the Rainbow Flag* by Rob Sanders (2018), with art by Steven Salerno |
| **Pairings** | *Sembrando historias: Pura Belpré: bibliotecaria y narradora de cuentos* by Anika Aldamuy Denise (2019), with art by Paola Escobar<br><br>*Digging for Words: José Alberto Gutiérrez and the Library He Built* by Angela Burke Kunkel (2020), with art by Paola Escobar<br><br>*Queen of Physics: How Wu Chien Shiung Helped Unlock the Secrets of the Atom* by Teresa Robeson (2019), with art by Rebecca Huang<br><br>*Frida* by Jonah Winter (2002), with art by Ana Juan<br><br>*Mae Among the Stars* by Roda Ahmed and Stasia Burrington (2020), with art by Stasia Burrington<br><br>**Online Resources:**<br>*Carmen Agra Deedy: Family Stories From a Master Storyteller* (and other select videos) from the Library of Congress (2020) | *Greta's Story: The Schoolgirl Who Went On Strike To Save The Planet* by Valentina Camerini (2019)<br><br>*The Girl Who Thought in Pictures: The Story of Dr. Temple Grandin* written by Julia Finley Mosca (2017), with art by Daniel Rieley<br><br>*All Are Welcome* by Alexandra Penfold (2018), with art by Suzanne Kaufman<br><br>*Just Ask!* By Sonia Sotomayor (2019), with art by Rafael López<br><br>*Emmanuel's Dream: The True Story of Emmanuel Ofosu Yeboah* by Laurie Ann Thompson (2015), with art by Sean Qualls<br><br>**Online Resources:**<br>Excerpts from *Young Advocate Webinar: Jennifer Keelan* by The Ability Center of Greater Toledo (2020) | *Queer Icons From Gay to Z: Activists, Artists, and Trailblazers* by Patrick Boyle (2019), with art by Antoine Corbineau<br><br>*Becoming RBG: Ruth Bader Ginsburg's Journey to Justice* by Debbie Levy (2019), with art by Whitney Gardner<br><br>*Queer Heroes: Meet 52 LGBTQ Heroes From Past and Present* by Arabelle Sicardi (2019), with art by Sarah Tanat-Jones<br><br>**Online Resources:**<br>*Merriam-Webster Declares "They" Its 2019 Word of the Year* by Associated Press (2020), Adapted by Newsela Staff<br><br>*Opinion: By Being Kind, We Can All Become Better People* by Arthur C. Brooks (2019), Originally Published in *The Washington Post* and Adapted by Newsela |

*(Continued)*

| | EMERGING | DEVELOPING | EXTENDING |
|---|---|---|---|
| | *Storytime Video [en Español]: Planting Stories: The Life of Librarian and Storyteller Pura Belpré* by WeAreTeachers (2019) | *Sprinter Marissa Papaconstantinou on What It Means to Be an Influencer On and Off the Track* by Jonathan Yue (2019)<br><br>*You Can't Stop Us* Commercial by Nike (Diaz, 2020)<br><br>*YouTube Creators Use Platform to Show What Life Is Like With Disabilities* by the Washington Post, Adapted by Newsela Staff (2019) | *This Is the History of the Rainbow Flag* (video) by Time (2015) |
| **Chapter 7**<br><br>**Featured Informational Texts** | *Hey, Water!* by Antoinette Portis (2019) | *Gross as a Snot Otter* by Jess Keating (2019), with art by David DeGrand | *Bringing Back the Wolves: How a Predator Restored an Ecosystem* by Jude Isabella (2020), with art by Kim Smith |
| **Pairings** | *I Wonder* by Tana Hoban (2003)<br><br>*We Are Water Protectors* by Carole Lindstrom (2020), with art by Michaela Goade<br><br>*Over and Under the Pond* by Kate Messner (2017), with art by Christopher Silas Neal<br><br>*Nibi Emosaawdang / The Water Walker (English and Ojibwa Edition)* by Joanne Robertson (2019), translated by Shirley Williams and Isadore Toulouse<br><br>*Water* by Melissa Stewart (2014) | *Pink as a Blobfish, What Makes a Monster?,* and *Cute as an Axolotl* by Jess Keating (2016, 2017, 2018)<br><br>*Animals Nobody Loves* by Seymour Simon (2001)<br><br>**Online Resources:**<br><br>*The World's Ugliest Animal* (video) by SciShow Kids (2015) | **Online Resources:**<br><br>*Scientists Debunk Myth That Yellowstone Wolves Changed Entire Ecosystem, Flow of Rivers* by Michael Kuhne (2019) of AccuWeather<br><br>*How Wolves Change Rivers* (video) by Sustainable Human (2014a)<br><br>*How Whales Change Climate* (video) by Sustainable Human (2014b) |

| | EMERGING | DEVELOPING | EXTENDING |
|---|---|---|---|
| **Chapter 8**<br><br>Featured **Poetry Texts** | *A Stick Is an Excellent Thing: Poems Celebrating Outdoor Play* by Marilyn Singer (2012), with art by LeUyen Pham | *Fry Bread: A Native American Family Story* by Kevin Noble Maillard (2019), with art by Juana Martinez-Neal | *Out of Wonder: Poems Celebrating Poets* by Kwame Alexander (2017), With Chris Colderley and Marjory Wentworth, and art by Ekua Holmes |
| **Pairings** | *Just Like Me* by Vanessa Brantley-Newton (2020)<br><br>*Wonderful Words: Poems About Reading, Writing, Speaking, and Listening* by Lee Bennett Hopkins (2004), with art by Karen Barbour<br><br>*All Are Welcome* by Alexandra Penfold (2018), with art by Suzanne Kaufman<br><br>*Feel the Beat: Dance Poems That Zing From Salsa to Swing* by Marilyn Singer (2017), with art by Kristi Valiant (audiobook also available)<br><br>*Forest Has a Song* by Amy Ludwig VanDerwater (2013), with art by Robin Gourley<br><br>*The Day You Begin / El día en que descubres quién eres* by Jacqueline Woodson (2018), with art by Rafael López | *The Arabic Quilt* by Aya Khalil (2020), with art by Anait Semirdzhyan<br><br>*Ohana Means Family* by Ilima Loomis (2020), with art by Kenard Pak<br><br>*This Day in June* by Gayle E. Pitman (2014), with art by Kristyna Litten<br><br>*Festival of Colors* by Kabir Sehgal and Surishtha Sehgal (2018), with art by Vashti Harrison<br><br>*Too Many Tamales* by Gary Soto (1996), with art by Ed Martinez<br><br>**Online Resources:**<br><br>*Off-the-Radar Foods: What Is Frybread? Made in the USA: Episode 7* (video) by Zagat (2015) | Any other poetry by the 20 poets featured in Alexander (2017)<br><br>*The Poet X* by Elizabeth Acevedo (2018)<br><br>*The Hill We Climb* by Amanda Gorman (2021)<br><br>*Thanku: Poems of Gratitude* by Miranda Paul (2019), with art by Marlena Myles<br><br>*Martin Rising: Requiem for a King* by Andrea Davis Pinkney (2018), with art by Brian Pinkney<br><br>*Write! Write! Write!* by Ludwig VanDerwater (2020), with art by Ryan O'Rourke<br><br>**Online Resources:**<br><br>Select videos of spoken word poetry (specifically check out youth and teen poets performing through Get Lit, Brave New Voices, and Poetry Out Loud) |

*(Continued)*

(Continued)

| | EMERGING | DEVELOPING | EXTENDING |
|---|---|---|---|
| **Online Bonus Chapter** <br><br> **Fantasy Fiction** | *Neither* by Airlie Anderson (2018) | *Interstellar Cinderella* Retold by Deborah Underwood (2015), with art by Meg Hunt | *Dragon Pearl* by Yoon Ha Lee (2019) |
| **Pairings** | *Giraffes Can't Dance* by Giles Andreae (2001), with art by Guy Parker-Rees <br><br> *I Will Be Fierce!* by Bea Birdsong (2019), with art by Nidhi Chanani <br><br> *I Am Enough* by Grace Byers (2018), with art by Keturah A. Bobo <br><br> *Mixed: A Colorful Story* by Arree Chung (2018) <br><br> *Pink Is for Boys* by Robb Pearlman (2018), with art by Eda Kaban | *The Egyptian Cinderella* and *The Korean Cinderella* by Shirley Climo (1992, 1996), Both with art by Ruth Heller <br><br> *Adelita: A Mexican Cinderella Story* by Tomie dePaola (2002) <br><br> *Yeh-Shen: A Cinderella Story From China* by Ai-Ling Louie (1996), with art by Ed Young <br><br> *The Rough-Face Girl* by Rafe Martin (1998), with art by David Shannon <br><br> *Sootface: An Ojibwa Cinderella Story* by Robert D. San Souci (1997), with art by Daniel San Souci <br><br> *Cendrillon: A Caribbean Cinderella* by Robert D. San Souci (1998), with art by Brian Pinkney <br><br> *Vasilisa the Wise and Tales of Other Brave Young Women* Retold by Kate Forsyth (2017), with art by Lorena Carrington <br><br> *Fiesta Femenina: Celebrating Women in Mexican Folklore* by Mary-Joan Gerson (2018), with art by Maya Christina Gonzalez <br><br> *Cinderella Liberator* by Rebecca Solnit (2019), with art by Arthur Rackham | *The Storm Runner* (series) by J. C. Cervantes (2018) <br><br> *Aru Shah* (series) by Roshani Chokshi (2018) <br><br> *The Fox Wife* by Beatrice Deer (2019), with art by D. J. Herron <br><br> *Tristan Strong* (series) by Kwame Mbalia (2019) <br><br> *The Scourge* by Jennifer A. Nielsen (2016) <br><br> **Online Resource:** <br><br> *Rick Riordan Interviews Yoon Ha Lee* (Read Riordan Staff, 2018) |

# Matrix of Instructional Concepts

|  | EMERGING | DEVELOPING | EXTENDING |
|---|---|---|---|
| **Chapter 3: Wordless Texts and Images** | • Predicting<br>• Academic vocabulary<br>• Conventional writing<br>• Retelling<br>• Speaking, listening, conversation, and collaboration | • Using precise language<br>• Academic vocabulary<br>• Conventional writing<br>• Noticing patterns while reading<br>• Using text evidence to support ideas<br>• Developing theories about characters<br>• Speaking, listening, conversation, and collaboration | • Format and structure analysis<br>• Academic vocabulary<br>• Conventional writing<br>• Noticing and thinking about character relationships<br>• Noticing, thinking about, and discussing significant moments<br>• Speaking, listening, conversation, and collaboration |
| **Chapter 4: Graphic Texts** | • Structure study<br>• Reading processes<br>• Jotting while reading<br>• Growing ideas while reading<br>• Partner reading<br>• Speaking, listening, conversation, and collaboration | • Structure study<br>• Reading responses<br>• Comparing and contrasting characters<br>• Partner coaching and feedback<br>• Speaking, listening, conversation, and collaboration | • Structure study<br>• Domain-specific vocabulary<br>• Reading responses<br>• Noting and thinking about author craft<br>• Partner coaching and feedback<br>• Speaking, listening, conversation, and collaboration |
| **Chapter 5: Realistic Fiction** | • Adjectives<br>• Retelling sequentially<br>• High-frequency words<br>• Inferring character feelings<br>• Fluency<br>• Speaking, listening, conversation, and collaboration | • Apostrophes<br>• Retelling sequentially<br>• Homophones<br>• Compound words<br>• Inferring<br>• Thinking about lessons/takeaways<br>• Speaking, listening, conversation, and collaboration | • Commas<br>• Figurative language<br>• Open and closed syllables<br>• Auxiliary verbs<br>• Considering perspectives and bias<br>• Speaking, listening, conversation, and collaboration |

*(Continued)*

(Continued)

| | EMERGING | DEVELOPING | EXTENDING |
|---|---|---|---|
| **Chapter 6: Creative Nonfiction** | • Supported research<br>• Literal comprehension<br>• Rehearsing and planning for writing<br>• Speaking, listening, conversation, and collaboration | • Supported research<br>• Inferring character feelings<br>• Exploring "takeaways" from reading<br>• Generating ideas for writing<br>• Speaking, listening, conversation, and collaboration | • Research<br>• Active reading (thinking, wondering, and feeling while reading)<br>• Writing leads<br>• Speaking, listening, conversation, and collaboration |
| **Chapter 7: Informational Texts** | • Supported research<br>• Writing processes<br>• Editing strategies<br>• Speaking, listening, conversation, and collaboration | • Research<br>• Writing processes<br>• Content-area vocabulary<br>• Word choice<br>• Speaking, listening, conversation, and collaboration | • Research<br>• Writing processes<br>• Presenting<br>• Teaching others<br>• Speaking, listening, conversation, and collaboration |
| **Chapter 8: Poetry** | • Visualizing<br>• Predicting<br>• Rhyming<br>• Consonant digraphs<br>• Fluency<br>• Writing craft<br>• Setting goals and making plans<br>• Speaking, listening, conversation, and collaboration | • Figurative language<br>• Author craft<br>• Synthesis<br>• Syllabification<br>• Subject–verb agreement<br>• Word choice<br>• Speaking, listening, conversation, and collaboration | • Genre study<br>• Structural analysis<br>• Synthesis<br>• Word choice<br>• Cross-text thinking<br>• Responding to reading<br>• Figurative language<br>• Revising strategies<br>• Speaking, listening, conversation, and collaboration |
| **Online Bonus Chapter: Fantasy Fiction** | • Common and proper nouns<br>• Retelling (five *W*s)<br>• Blends vs. consonant digraphs<br>• End-of-sentence punctuation<br>• Fluency<br>• Speaking, listening, conversation, and collaboration | • Punctuation<br>• Character relationships<br>• Ambiguous vowels<br>• Punctuating dialogue<br>• Cross-text thinking<br>• Speaking, listening, conversation, and collaboration | • Mood and tone<br>• Character traits<br>• Comparatives<br>• Subordinating conjunctions and complex sentences<br>• Exploring power dynamics<br>• Speaking, listening, conversation, and collaboration |

**NOTE:** These instructional concepts were intentionally designed and chosen to nurture common learning goals of students across the grades. The inherent skills (along with the abundant *What Else?* suggestions included with each lesson) align with and build proficiency toward state standards. Additionally, in Part III, readers learn a process for preparing similar lesson sets that spotlight the skills and concepts they intend to teach.

# Acknowledgments

## GRATITUDE FOR THOSE WHO BRING PROFESSIONAL JOY

The benefits of partnering with people who actively and consistently seek opportunities to lift others up are infinite. To my friends and colleagues at Gravity Goldberg LLC, having the chance to collaborate with such dedicated and passionate educators is a true gift! Aimee and Viviana, your feedback on an early draft of this manuscript guided me toward making thoughtful and needed improvements. I *always* look forward to collaborating with you and learning from you. Elaine, Katie, and Kristin, I was thrilled when you agreed to "field-test" some of the lessons included in this book. You all share a love of teaching (and deep pedagogical knowledge) that I admire and respect. Thank you for your time and thoughtful feedback. I also greatly appreciate the input and classroom artifacts from Rebecca and Christina. My friends and colleagues at #Here4Teachers and the "Writing Zone" have also been an unexpected gift in my life. Your talents serve as a model, and your insightful feedback has greatly influenced my writing.

Many colleagues and mentors have made a lasting imprint on my heart and teaching practice: Pat, Deirdre, Patti, Wendy, Brad, Mike, and so many more—thanks for serving as role models and nurturing my growth as an educator. Additionally, I have been so fortunate to meet, partner with, and learn from so many teachers and administrators in districts across the country. To *all* those I have had the chance to collaborate with, you bring not only professional joy, but personal joy as well.

## GRATITUDE FOR THOSE WHO BRING WRITING JOY

To the entire Corwin Literacy team, led by Lisa Luedeke, thanks for your belief and support. Tori Bachman, where can I even begin? Thank goodness for your professional expertise and wisdom—and the patience you possess as you make sense of what's in my head and heart. It's no secret that my favorite parts of writing are connected to our emails and conversations. Your compassion and contributions serve as a powerful example of how we can all work toward a more humane tomorrow.

Sharon Wu, you make the entire process of writing more enjoyable, efficient, and successful. I am so grateful for your knowledge and grace. Many thanks to Nancy Chung who stepped in and kept this project organized and on track from day one. Project Editor Amy Schroller, Copy Editor Melinda Masson, and Cover Designer Gail Buschman, your creativity and professionalism are so very appreciated! Margaret O'Connor, thank you for your time, imagination, and efforts, which all help get needed books into the hands of educators.

## GRATITUDE FOR THOSE WHO BRING PERSONAL JOY

The last couple years have only highlighted the importance of family. I am so very grateful for the chance I've had to grow up—and now grow older—with Ike, who has been by my side through every monumental and mundane event life has brought. I am humbled by your commitment to our family. Moreover, your belief in me and support of this process made it all possible. Colby, your contemplative spirit, insights, and sensitivity encourage me to see the world in new and important ways. My heart swells with pride as I witness the man you are becoming. Your pep talks and belief guided me through the days I was not sure I wanted to write or had anything valuable to share. Peyton, your strength, courage, and creativity inspire me. Writing alongside you brought such happiness to our time at home! Your example, partnership, and cheerleading got me to the finish line. Michele, Tim, Liam, and Ron, your generous support is extremely appreciated. Additionally, the laughter and lightheartedness you have shared propelled me (and this project) forward. I am especially grateful for Linda. You have supported me throughout my life and taken an active role in helping me become an author. From being a thinking partner to a classroom photographer to a graphic artist . . . it brings me great joy to flip through my books and see tracks of your love throughout. I am a truly lucky person!

## PUBLISHER'S ACKNOWLEDGMENTS

Corwin gratefully acknowledges the contributions of the following reviewers:

Melissa Black, Teacher
District of Columbia Public Schools in Washington, DC

Aimée Carroll-Matos, Instructional Coach
East Brook Middle School in Paramus, NJ

Kate Ferguson, Resident Teacher Program Director
Hillbrook School in Los Gatos, CA

Viviana Tamas, Instructional Coach
Ward Elementary School in New Rochelle, NY

Maria Walther, Traveling Teacher and Literacy Consultant
Author in Aurora, IL

# About the Author

Pamela Koutrakos is an experienced and enthusiastic educator who currently works as a middle school instructional coach. She also writes, presents, and works directly with PreK–12 teachers, coaches, and administrators as a consultant. Pam is the author of *Word Study That Sticks: Best Practices K–6* (Corwin, 2018), *The Word Study That Sticks Companion: Classroom-Ready Tools for Teachers and Students, K–6* (Corwin, 2019), and *Mentor Tasks That Multitask: A Less-Is-More Approach to Integrated Literacy Instruction, K–8,* (Corwin, 2022). Connect with Pam on Twitter (@PamKou), Instagram (@Pam.Kou), and LinkedIn.

For downloadable lists, templates, forms, suggestions, and other materials related to *Mentor Texts That Multitask*—including bonus lesson sets—visit the companion website at **resources.corwin.com/mttm.**

# Introduction

## THREE CONFESSIONS

Let's start with some unfiltered honesty:

*Confession 1:* My passion for books borders on obsession. A student once decided to calculate the amount of money I spent on the books currently in the classroom (a small sample of the books I actually owned). The sum was truly astounding! Like an I-could-have-bought-a-brand-new-vehicle-or-felt-better-prepared-for-my-kids'-college-education kind of sum. On the home front, my husband shakes his head, rolls his eyes, and laughs whenever I walk into the house with a few new finds from the local bookstore. I know what he is thinking and too smart to say aloud. Every so often, I present myself with a challenge: *I will visit my beloved library even more often. I will continue to read, but only borrowed books. No buying books for one month. It's good for your wallet and good for the earth. Pam, you can do this!* And . . . I fail. I bargain, justify, and placate myself with the idea that this passion is not a problem and, instead, is actually an asset. (Because you picked up this text, I have a feeling you may relate to my affection for all-things books, and I am comforted by knowing we are in this together.)

*Confession 2:* With the exception of professional texts, I rarely read books intended for adults. My sister, Michele, hands me one "grown-up book" a year, insisting I read it so I can participate in some book talk with friends who are not educators. She is persistent in this endeavor. I usually play along, despite the fact that I find complete and utter fulfillment in books written for and marketed to humans from birth through age 16. Wordless texts, alphabet books, picture books, nonfiction texts, graphic novels, poetry, plays, early chapter books, series, novellas, middle-grade fiction, and young adult everything: sign me up for *all* of it.

*Confession 3:* I have always prioritized reading aloud to students. In fact, for me, daily read-aloud is a non-negotiable. Even if it was a poem on a field trip day or one page of a text as we packed up—there has *always* been a read-aloud experience. Since we are in full confession mode, I should add that there have been many occasions where read-aloud extended beyond its earmarked minutes. For me, there is no greater teaching joy than introducing or revisiting a beloved text with students. This daily commitment is centered on a primary purpose: building and sustaining community as we share in the pleasure of reading.

## ALIGNED PERSONAL TRUTH

I deeply believe and trust in the value of grounding classroom instruction and learning in authentic texts. I used to think I needed a different text for each lesson. I spent hours and hours searching for the "perfect" book with a certain feature or the "best" text to teach this lesson or that lesson. The older I get and the more experience I gain, the more I question this practice. *Although I continue to share old and new favorites with students, when it comes to instruction, I have come to believe less is more.* Teachers don't need a different mentor text for each different strategy they teach. Curating and using a small set of texts prepares them for almost infinite teaching opportunities.

*Mentor Texts That Multitask* aims to be a user-friendly teaching resource that shares the beauty and benefits of simplifying our complicated and multifaceted work. It explores the limitless possibilities that lie within one text. Throughout these chapters, I provide explicit examples for *how* to use teaching texts time and time again for a range of purposes and with a range of students. By grounding instruction in a smaller collection of strategically layered, multidimensional texts, teachers are better prepared for integrated, student-centered teaching—in time-efficient ways.

## GROUNDING THIS WORK IN PURPOSE

I enjoy the unique privilege of working with students and educators in a wide variety of communities, settings, and grade levels. As a traveling teacher (or what others sometimes label an *educational consultant*), I am provided with the opportunity to visit with, study alongside, and learn from so many amazing people. Unsurprisingly, these partnerships and ongoing collaborations help me to continuously grow. It's through these daily interactions that I also see bigger patterns emerge. There are two challenges teachers across communities share most often: insufficient time and lack of quality resources. The ever-evolving nature of education frequently requires teachers to do as much as possible with what they've got on hand as priorities shift and funding for new initiatives falls short.

I also consider the perspective of students. The fast pace set for learning a broad range of skills can result in students feeling as if they are always being taught something brand new. Each time a bell rings, the concepts presented may appear to be separate and disjointed. As the practices, goals, and resources shift and change, it can be difficult for students to see a connection between learning happening from period to period, day to day, subject to subject. Learning may feel compartmentalized, and it may not even occur to students that the overarching goal is to integrate, synthesize, and apply. Without the creative and flexible use of a few prioritized resources and deliberately designed instruction to integrate literacy, opportunities to dig in, practice, apply, and transfer learning are inconsistent.

In other words, for both teachers and students, the school day can feel like the plastic bin I try to fit my "winter wardrobe" back into every spring: As I fill it up, a capacity challenge presents itself. I persevere, folding each piece of clothing in different ways and even changing up the order I put items into the bin, but alas, the pile of clothes is always a smidge too high. I sit on the bin, hoping to hear the sweet celebratory sound of plastic clicking together, but once my weight momentarily shifts to one side, the lid pops up on the other. In recent years, this strategy has even resulted in a substantially sized crack. I know I am a smart and capable person, but that bin still has me feeling defeated. Sometimes, my efforts and creativity do not win out. Daily schedules and brains may feel just as overfilled as my plastic bin. Despite teacher and student interest, efforts, and knowledge, long-term, lasting success may at times feel unattainable.

These patterns are well substantiated by research. Studies have documented that educators are more likely to suffer job-related stress than other professionals in similar fields (Busby, 2019). Moreover, the 2017 Educator Quality of Work Life Survey, a poll administered to nearly 5,000 teachers and school staff across the United States, revealed that 61% of teachers believed their work was always or often stressful (Mahnken, 2017). Other surveys report that almost half of all new teachers leave the field within the first five years (Ansley et al., 2018). Elementary teachers are at the highest risk for this detrimental stress. A study by the University of Missouri found that 93% of elementary school teachers reported high stress levels (Herman et al., 2017). And this research was all conducted pre-COVID-19! Even the earliest findings substantiate the transformational effect of COVID-19 on teachers' well-being. According to one study, since the global pandemic began, over 60% of educators surveyed reported enjoying their job less, and 77% reported working harder than ever, putting in substantially more time (Horace Mann Educators Corporation, 2020). Change is necessary.

Let's eliminate some of these hurdles and this negative momentum here and now. When it comes to both teaching and learning, often, less is more. Be gone energy-zapping compartmentalization! In *Mentor Texts That Multitask*, I provide explicit examples of *how* to use high-quality texts time and time again, for a range of purposes and with a range of students. By casting aside the myth that mentor texts are only useful as writing tools, it becomes clear that teachers can use a lean selection of multitasking texts to design flexible, integrated, and multifaceted learning. Throughout this book, there is a marked emphasis on authentically and consistently moving beyond reading and writing. All across Part II, selected mentor texts are also used to support the teaching and transfer of the language standards (spelling, vocabulary, and grammar). *Multitasking mentor texts are instructional touchstones.* One text can support and connect a *multitude* of curricular goals and student goals.

Relish the "ahhhh" of knowing you no longer need a different resource for each strategy you teach. By curating and using a small set of mentor texts in multiple ways, you can feel prepared for almost infinite teaching and learning opportunities.

## HOW THIS BOOK CAN HELP

Part I of *Mentor Texts That Multitask* lays the foundation. Chapter 1 outlines the types of texts included throughout the book. A preview of the processes used to select texts and decide what to teach is presented. Chapter 2 provides an overview of the types of teaching structures included in this book. First, I introduce how and why educators would choose to integrate different facets of literacy into multitasking lessons. Then, inquiry-based practices are explored alongside more traditional gradual release methods. Additionally, a brief introduction to modeled, guided, and independent practice is provided. By reading Part I, you will gain an understanding of how the lessons throughout Part II were created and why they are effective.

Part II of this book highlights specific texts and aligned lesson possibilities. Each chapter spotlights a different type of text and showcases how it can be used with a range of students in a variety of grades and settings. Part II presents ways to use different genres and formats of texts in classroom instruction. Collectively, Chapters 3 through 8 include all of the following:

- Numerous suggestions for high-quality mentor texts, including additional "text pairings" that represent engaging print, digital, and multimedia options

- Multiple lessons to accompany each spotlighted mentor text

- Contextualized and connected lesson sets that infuse multiple facets of literacy: *reading, writing, spelling, vocabulary, grammar, speaking, and listening*

- Balanced attention to discovery-driven practices and more explicit modeled, guided, and independent practices

By reading Part II, you will gain a greater understanding of the multitasking possibilities of texts. Additionally, the lesson ideas and examples (which I enthusiastically invite you to modify to your heart's delight based on your students' interests and needs) can help you build a solid understanding of and fluency in using the instructional practices at the core of this professional text.

Part III is perhaps my favorite. This is where it all comes together. After reading about *why* in Part I and trying the *what* in Part II, you'll learn *how* to make this work on your own in Part III. In Chapter 9, a teacher-friendly method of using formal and informal assessment formatively is explained. The DIY responsive teaching (evident in the selection of text, teaching structure, and decisions about what to teach) that follows is laid out in detail. Chapter 10 takes it one step further, encouraging you to step back and prepare to have students take the lead. Different methods of students teaching students (with multitasking mentor texts) are shared. After reading Part III, I hope you feel excited and motivated to continue on, using your own favorite texts, the resources recommended in district curriculum, and new, engaging titles that are released each year.

The lists, templates, forms, suggestions, and materials included on the companion website at resources.corwin.com/mttm encourage ease of implementation. Additionally, *bonus* lesson sets using fantasy fiction titles are prominently featured.

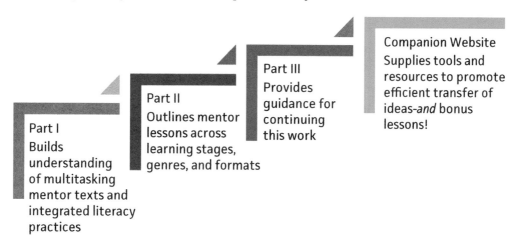

Part I
Builds understanding of multitasking mentor texts and integrated literacy practices

Part II
Outlines mentor lessons across learning stages, genres, and formats

Part III
Provides guidance for continuing this work

Companion Website
Supplies tools and resources to promote efficient transfer of ideas-*and* bonus lessons!

# FANCY A FEATURE WALK?

There are a variety of recurring features embedded throughout this text. Each intends to support turning ideas into teaching! Here is the Rosetta stone of icons you will see throughout the upcoming chapters.

## Recurring Features

| ICON | NAME | WHAT IS IT? |
|------|------|-------------|
| ✔ | Check-Up | This feature is included in every lesson. It provides ideas for how to informally assess student understanding of the concept(s) presented in the lesson. Please note that there are numerous Check-Up-aligned assessment and record-keeping tools available on the companion website. |
| | Content Connections | This feature is included for each featured text. It identifies additional opportunities for using the text and connecting learning to *other* parts of the school day—beyond the literacy block. |
| | Language Levers | These stems appear intermittently in Part II lessons. They help to make language and/or content of a lesson more accessible for a wide range of classroom learners. |
| | Pause and Ponder | To promote interactivity and personalization, reflection questions appear throughout the book. When you see these thinking prompts, take a moment to pause. Ponder your own ideas and next steps. |
| | Stretch Up and Back Suggestions | These suggestions (included at the conclusion of each chapter in Part II) develop your vision of the flexibility of multitasking mentor texts. This recurring element lists other "general" possibilities that can be taught using almost any mentor text! |
| | Text Pairings | This feature is also included for each featured text. These suggestions may be used in lieu of the featured text or in conjunction with the spotlighted choice. These selections represent a range of print, digital, and multimedia options. |
| ? | What Else? | This feature is included with every lesson. It provides a few alternative ideas of *what else* you could teach with the same text. |

# A QUICK WORD ON DEVELOPMENTAL STAGE VS. GRADE LEVEL

In over 20 years of working with students, I have never been in a room full of learners who were all ready for the exact same thing at the exact same time in the exact same way. Because teachers must strive to help all students grow and flourish, in Part II, I provide a range of texts and intentionally sort instructional ideas by developmental readiness instead of using more traditional grade-level labels. Being an educator means having high expectations for all students and believing in everyone's capabilities. Classes are composed of individuals with unique interests, multifaceted identities, and varied learning goals. Teachers need to learn about, welcome, and honor the experiences of each student and then relentlessly strive to shape positive and productive learning experiences that are relevant for the people in the room. It's essential to build a habit of looking for what is in place and prioritizing next steps based on those strengths. This is why I decided to create flexible lesson sets that honor observed areas of readiness. I hope that, in doing so, teachers in all grades and settings feel better prepared to approach their work with district initiatives, state standards, and more personalized student learning goals in mind.

The benefits of asset-based instruction and feedback are well substantiated (Afflerbach, 2016; Briceño & Klein, 2019; Chávez & Longerbeam, 2016; Clay, 2016; Dorn & Soffos, 2011, 2017; Ferlazzo, 2019; Goldberg, 2015; Krutkowski, 2017; Lopez & Louis, 2009; McGee, 2017; Morrell, 2007; Westman, 2018). The importance of working within a student's zone of proximal development or ZPD (Vygotsky, 1978) is usually introduced in the first education class taken in college . . . and repeated on loop thereafter. To further develop this idea, the NYU Steinhardt School of Culture, Education, and Human Development (2018) shared an article eloquently stating, "An asset-based approach to education is key in achieving equity in classrooms across the country. In recent years, while equity and access efforts shined a light on marginalized and underrepresented communities, some efforts treated schools and communities like they needed to be 'saved.' With an asset-based approach, every community is valuable; every community has strengths and potential."

When we get to know students, we become better equipped to choose texts that will fluidly multitask. Celebrating what students already know enables us to thoughtfully select (or co-select) strategies that propel continuous learning. By focusing on and utilizing students' strengths and potential, we are then prepared to connect chosen texts and selected strategies to purposeful teaching. Students are able to access new information and learn to grapple with increasingly complex ideas. Classroom experiences become humanized and compelling, and therefore, students are more successful. The flexibility of tools, processes, and products inherent in *Mentor Texts That Multitask* lessons are the heart of instruction that decentralizes traditional "one size fits all" learning and validates the need for instruction designed *for* and *with* the people in the learning community.

Whether you work with kindergarteners, third graders, eighth graders, or all of the above, please choose the texts and lessons that make the most sense for the learners currently in the room. Also know that the texts and lessons included in *Mentor Texts That Multitask* can be used in any instructional setting and are flexible enough to be shared with students as a whole class, in a small group, or, many times, individually. Be assured that there is a place for each included genre and format. Yes, children of all ages—even older students—greatly benefit from instruction grounded in wordless texts and picture books! Finally, remember that suggestions for inquiry, as well as modeled, guided, and independent practice, are infused throughout Part II. Because of the range of included instructional methods and the inherent lesson flexibility, it is my hope that teachers in all grades and settings will feel equipped and ready to introduce the learners in their care to texts and concepts that *are* prioritized by grade-level standards while also centering on the goals and aspirations of current students.

Check out the chart on pages 19–21 to learn more about the developmental stages validated and celebrated within this text.

Appreciative inquiry celebrates an asset-based approach to instruction.

# CUE THE INSPIRATIONAL MUSIC . . .

*We've named our shared goal:* To feel prepared to implement the included lessons and use the accompanying DIY planning ideas.

*We are clear on our why:* To integrate and connect all aspects of literacy learning.

*We have identified attainable success criteria:* Teachers will have more breathing room in the school day, and students will experience increased transfer—across contexts, subjects, and time.

*We have an action plan:* Read, discuss, tinker, try, reflect, and celebrate.

Here's to smart, streamlined, and succinct teaching that feels like "you" and makes a real difference in the learning lives of students. There's no doubt about it: When teaching is grounded in authentic texts, teachers are better prepared for student-centered, adaptable, time-efficient teaching. Let's get to it! I'm looking forward to partnering with you.

# PART I

# The Essentials of Multitasking Mentor Texts

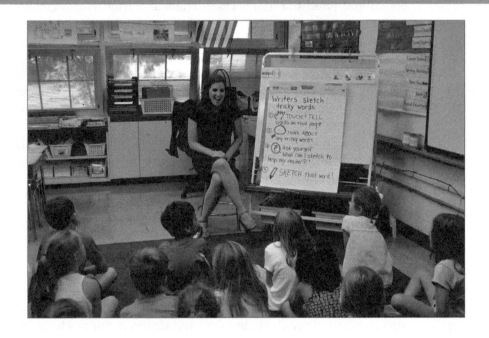

*A mentor text becomes a multitasking mentor text when it provides vision, purpose, and confidence for taking across-the-day learning risks.*

The first few years I spent full-time in the classroom shaped much of my teacher identity. I was a head-down, work-hard, work-long kind of teacher. In retrospect, I was also quite rigid. It pains me to admit this, but because of my well-intentioned hopes of doing everything "right," I always stuck to the book. When I went to a workshop, I implemented the ideas presented exactly as explained. If my mentor shared details of a lesson she led, I carbon copied that idea. When it was evident students were bored or confused, I forged on with what I had planned. Even my small-group lessons came right from a purchased resource! I thought that if I worked hard and prepared enough, all students—and, by extension, I—would be successful. I wasn't yet sure of how to be responsive to what I was seeing and sensing in the moment.

There *were* times my teaching worked. And there were times that, despite careful planning and by-the-book implementation, my teaching missed the mark. These trials and tribulations created a foundation on which I could build my understanding of a *range* of instructional practices. And those students—well, of course, they taught me even more! I found joy and delight in spending my days with middle schoolers. I was only about 10 years older than the students; we listened to a lot of the same music, watched a lot of the same shows, and often had the same sense of humor! These shared interests helped me build respectful relationships. And the resulting connections are what *actually* taught me how to make intentional and responsive teaching decisions. These learners were my guides in how to use book smarts more thoughtfully.

The students I worked with in these formative years were the ones who helped me understand the distinction between planned-and-scripted and prepared-and-agile instruction. Eventually, I learned to merge knowledge of teaching practices with knowledge of students. It was then that I became prepared to mold these understandings into experiences that students were ready for *and* interested in. I've learned how to plan and teach with my eyes and heart open. I am confident in my ability to take what I know about teaching and learning . . . and turn it into something relevant and meaningful for the current community of learners.

In Part I of *Mentor Texts That Multitask*, I aim to do something similar for you and the students you support. Chapters 1 and 2 are the bedrock for all the ideas and lessons that follow. I hope to stretch your thinking beyond what you already know about how and when to use mentor texts, and I intend to show you new ways to use these texts to teach and connect multiple literacy concepts. Let's reaffirm a shared commitment to preparing for intentional and responsive instruction that merges book smarts with teacher hearts. Here in Part I you'll find models for classroom experiences that honor students, appreciate all they *can* do, and nurture next steps that feel enticing and worthy.

# CHAPTER 1

# What Is a Multitasking Mentor Text?

"Teachers should select mentor texts to support students' reading, writing, and thinking skills around the potential to cultivate students' skills, identities, intellect, and criticality." (G. Muhammad, 2020, p. 95)

I have voices in my head. To clarify, these are the voices of my mentors—those who have shown me what this work looks like, found ways to exemplify what's most important, and provide guidance when I am feeling unsure. They remind me that I am always supported. This builds the confidence I need to get focused and take action. For example, when I am tempted to drift away from a central goal in pursuit of something new with strong "curb appeal," I often hear my first principal, Pat, saying, "I would rather see straightforward instruction that works than cute fluff that doesn't make a difference." After every lesson I teach, I again hear her voice, this time reminding me to reflect, "What did you do? How did it go? Why? What else could you do?" When I'm inspired to think totally outside the box, I hear my mentor, Deirdre, saying, "Let's do it!" punctuated by an enthusiastic "Woo-hoo!" In more quiet moments when I am stressing about the small stuff, I again hear Deirdre reminding me, "It's all about the kids. That's why we're here. You know what to do." When I doubt myself, I hear Mike telling me, "I hired you to be you. I trust you to do what you do," and another advisor, Gravity, reminding me, "Don't let perfect get in the way of good."

I could go on and on. There is no doubt: Past and present colleagues, virtual professional connections, and authors I have read and admired from afar have lifted me up time and time again. Just like these mentors have helped shape my own processes, ideas, and practices, mentor texts help students to do the same.

## WHY IS IT NECESSARY TO REDEFINE THE ROLE OF MENTOR TEXTS?

Traditionally, a mentor text is any text (whether formally published, teacher-written, or student-written) that is used in writing instruction to help writers uncover, appreciate, and attempt to replicate the "moves" an author uses. However, have you thought about the ways sounds, letters, words, language, and ideas can also be explored through the use of mentor texts? Children's literature can unearth and demystify the processes used by proficient readers, writers, thinkers, and communicators. Teachers can use a single text to show learners the intricacies of grammar, the mysteries of vocabulary, the nuances of inference— so many possibilities. A text becomes a *multitasking mentor text* when it provides vision, purpose, and confidence for *across-the-day* learning. At the heart of this book is the belief that multitasking mentor texts are one of our most valuable teaching tools!

Early in my career, I thought I needed different mentor texts to teach different skills. For example, I often labeled my reading mentor texts with reading skills such as *envisioning*, *predicting*, or *character change*. Similarly, I would label my writing mentor texts with words like *dialogue*, *setting details*, or *strong introduction*. I used those different texts when I taught those different skills. I would always ask my colleagues questions like "What text do you use to teach [fill-in-the-blank strategy of the week]?" Full disclosure: When I reflect on the rest of my literacy block at that time, I have to admit that most grammar and word study learning (when it even happened) lived *outside* of texts. Workbooks, worksheets, and surface-level center activities filled up those earmarked minutes. It was a lot to manage, and quite honestly, each learning experience felt compartmentalized and disconnected.

Moreover, all of my well-meaning efforts were not yielding successful results. I *hoped* students would intentionally pull from their vast skill set and use taught strategies as needed and when appropriate. But this didn't happen. Instead, reading was more assignment driven. If I used a mentor text to teach predicting, students went back to their seats and all predicted. The same went for writing. If I used a mentor text to highlight dialogue, all of a sudden, student stories were filled with dialogue . . . and almost nothing else! Once I moved on to the next book to teach the next strategy, students stopped using the previously taught one. And who could blame them? There was no connection between the teaching happening across subjects or time. I knew there had to be a better way!

After coming to the important realization that my actions were inhibiting student understanding, transfer, and success, I started to rethink the role of a mentor text. I decided to reevaluate how I used these resources and explore how I could capitalize on the value of each text. I found wonder and possibility in rethinking all the ways a single text could inspire and guide a student through seemingly infinite literacy skills. *My experience led me to realize that a multitasking mentor text is one text that can be used multiple times and for a variety of purposes, weaving together different aspects of literacy.* By using these superstar teacher tools with greater intention and flexibility, teachers can model and foster greater transfer of skills across the literacy block—and across the day.

Reimagining the ways to use mentor texts is simple and fun. I've challenged myself and others to open any book to any page and find as many teaching points as possible. For example, *The Paper Bag Princess* by Robert Munsch (1980) is one of my old-school, go-to favorite mentor texts because I know it, love it, and have enjoyed positive reactions from students while using it. In fact, I have a copy that belonged to my mom back when she taught second grade. I have used this one text while working with students in first through eighth grades. I have used this one text for reading, writing, word study, and grammar. I have used this one text to spark conversation rich with purposeful speaking and active listening. I have used this one text in general education classes, inclusion classes, bilingual classes, and pullout classes. I have even used this one text while tutoring. Countless children and I have together studied the cover, read the pictures, read the words, and thought about characters and takeaways. We've considered different perspectives, alternative lessons, and a multitude of themes. We've delved into perceptions of gender roles and literary tropes. We've found sight words, short and long vowel words, and inflected endings. We've explored parts of speech, sentence structure, word choice, tense, and subject–verb agreement. We've found inspiration, lifted ideas, and tried similar moves in our own writing. We've discussed, questioned, and debated. All with this one, seemingly simple picture book. *This* is the essence of a multitasking mentor text.

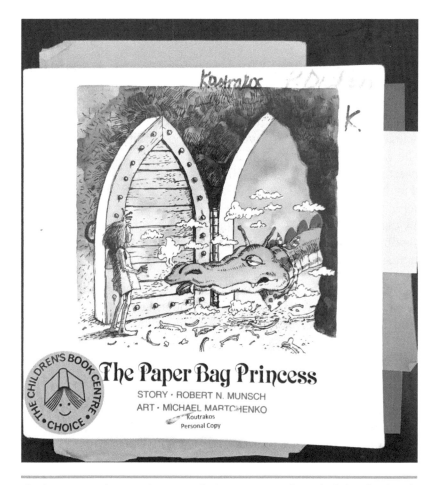

Check out my mom's personalization on the front cover (P. Disken). This beloved multitasking mentor text has been used time and again. Even the cover offers a multitude of teaching opportunities.

 Do you have a favorite text you love to share with students? Why do you love it? Take another look and list the different teaching possibilities that you find. How many opportunities are you able to discover?

## WHAT ARE THE CHARACTERISTICS OF MULTITASKING MENTOR TEXTS?

It is hard to have an "always" list when it comes to text criteria because your instructional goals and students' interests will vary. That said, there are points of consideration when teachers decide which texts to use time and time again with students. Ruth Culham (2016) provides helpful guidance when she writes, "Books can be mentor texts only if we learn something about writing from them. And to make that learning accessible to students, we have to dig into the authors' words and notice their moves" (pp. 6–7). Culham asks us to use mentor texts to teach kids how to read like a writer and focus on the traits of writing to help students draft and revise their writing. This is vital criteria for considering whether a text is worthy for use in writing instruction and can be useful as a jumping-off point. To consider a text for "multitasking" status, we *also* want to cross-reference whether the text will support teaching and learning goals beyond writing.

For example, in *The Ramped-Up Read Aloud*, Maria Walther (2018) shares her criteria for selecting picture books to share with students. She suggests classroom texts have all of the following:

- Engaging characters
- Rich language
- Fascinating illustrations
- Thought-provoking themes
- Kid-appealing content
- An original premise and/or unique perspective
- Horizon-broadening subjects (p. 18)

These features provide a checklist that can build confidence in the choices we make. Walther's work centers on read-alouds to teach important concepts, build community, and spark a joy of reading in children. The attention to rich content, characters, language, and themes enables me to envision an even wider range of possibilities. A text with these features feels worthy of revisiting and invites teaching a variety of goal-aligned lessons. I feel a flutter of thrill contemplating and hypothesizing how texts that check these boxes could also be revisited with a language-themed lens, from a social-emotional perspective, and through the eyes of an active word explorer. These types of texts warrant playful deconstructing, tinkering, and discussion that spotlight current learning goals across the entire literacy block. In other words, they are capable of multitasking!

Moreover, it's essential that educators consistently prioritize inclusivity and critically contemplate representation. I always keep Rudine Sims Bishop's (1990) mirrors, windows, and sliding glass doors analogy in mind as I consider contenders for multitasking mentor texts. We need to prioritize students seeing pieces of themselves and their lives, while also consistently seeing texts centered on the experiences of others. Another foundational aspect of selecting multitasking mentor texts is making sure that, cumulatively, texts feature a variety of topics, perspectives, people, characters, settings, and problems. When we hear, view, or read different kinds of stories, we become more empathetic and compassionate people. We are better prepared to disrupt harmful patterns of thought, problematic practices, and inequitable systems.

I consider *all* of the above when selecting multitasking mentor texts to use with learners. I strive to create a mash-up of dearly beloved old favorites and *plenty* of sparkly new selections. Of course, there is room for a few "oldie and goodie" texts— and I also embrace the unsurpassed excitement of having a (well-prepared) "first" with students. I love featuring new titles, authors, and series. I find delight in expanding multigenre text sets on topics that are notoriously popular with students . . . and also curating new text sets that represent the personal preferences and passions of learners currently in the classroom. The chart that follows shares what I often ponder as I consider the abundant choices available to serve as multitasking mentor texts.

## Reflective Inquiries to Guide Text Choices

### Identity

- Whose voices and experiences does this text reflect, honor, and celebrate?
- How will this choice expand or enhance the set of texts I have already shared with students?

### Community

- Will current students find this text interesting and appealing?
- How could this text be used to nurture the learning goals of current students?

### Curriculum

- How does this text align to *and* integrate current literacy learning goals?
- Could this text extend and support learning beyond the literacy block?

It essentially all boils down to this, though: There is no "perfect" choice. The number of mentor texts that will help us affirm, learn, connect, imagine, celebrate, and laugh is always growing. Audit your library, review the options presented throughout Part II, visit your local library or bookstore to ask for recommendations, and simply ask students. Then look at your top contenders and use the prioritized learning goals of current classroom learners in combination with the guidance provided here. You already have access to everything you need to curate sets of mentor texts that multitask!

How do you usually decide which books you will share with classroom learners? How frequently do you audit and update your classroom library? Where does your classroom book collection need to grow?

## HOW DO TEACHERS CHOOSE TEXTS THAT ARE DEVELOPMENTALLY RESPONSIVE?

Different texts invite different learning opportunities. All the formats and genres spotlighted in Part II are appropriate for learners across grades and settings.

Additionally, this book provides text suggestions for different phases of learning often seen in elementary, intermediate, and middle schools. In this text, the different stages are named *emerging*, *developing*, and *extending*. These *fluid* stages are emphasized because we know that grade-level placement is not always indicative of a student's current strengths and prioritized next steps. The following chart includes more information on each of these stages. It shares a brief overview of each stage and characteristics often aligned with these stages of development. Although many texts feature opportunities for students *across* these stages, it can also be beneficial to "cross check" a text choice and confirm it contains a multitude of possibilities to nurture and develop the current assets of classroom learners.

Common Assets of Learners in Different Stages of Learning

|  | EMERGING | DEVELOPING | EXTENDING |
|---|---|---|---|
| **Hallmark Qualities** | May use drawings, squiggles, letter-like symbols, letter strings, and/or letters to represent ideas<br><br>Letter–sound correspondence developing or newly in place | Consistently writes single-syllable words conventionally, including words with blends, digraphs, long vowel sounds, and "other" vowel sounds<br><br>May use invented spelling for more sophisticated words | Spelling is often conventional<br><br>Employs a wide range of strategies to read and write more complex and/or unfamiliar words<br><br>Developing a stronger understanding of the relationships between |

*(Continued)*

(Continued)

| | EMERGING | DEVELOPING | EXTENDING |
|---|---|---|---|
| **(Hallmark Qualities, continued)** | Listens for sounds and works to write letters to match heard sounds<br><br>Reads and writes some sight words<br><br>Developing knowledge of concepts-of-print<br><br>Reads the pictures in books<br><br>Conventionally reads books with simple patterns and/or controlled language | Usually decodes with accuracy, while maintaining fluency<br><br>Increased sight word vocabulary<br><br>Able to sustain interest and engagement while reading longer texts<br><br>Focuses on both literal and inferential understanding while reading | word parts and spelling (prefixes, suffixes, Greek and Latin roots, etc.)<br><br>Reads longer, in-depth novels<br><br>Comprehends more complex academic texts<br><br>Compares and synthesizes ideas between texts |
| **Often Aligned to This/ These Stages of Reading Development** | Chall (1983)<br>Stage 0: Prereading<br>Stage 1: Initial Reading and Decoding | Chall (1983)<br>Stage 2: Confirmation and Fluency<br>Stage 3: Reading to Learn | Chall (1983)<br>Stage 3: Reading to Learn<br>Stage 4: Multiple Viewpoints |
| **Often Aligned to This/ These Stages of Writing Development** | Gentry (1982)<br>Precommunicative Stage<br>Semiphonetic Stage<br>Phonetic Stage | Gentry (1982)<br>Phonetic Stage<br>Transitional Stage | Gentry (1982)<br>Transitional Stage<br>Correct Stage |
| **Often Aligned to This/ These Stages of Spelling Development** | Bear et al. (2004)<br>Emergent<br>Letter Name (Alphabetic)<br>"Early" Within Words | Bear et al. (2004)<br>Within Words<br>Syllables and Affixes | Bear et al. (2004)<br>Syllables and Affixes<br>Derivational Relations |
| **Commonly Aligned Grade Levels** | *Kindergarten–Grade 2* | *Grades 2–4* | *Grade 4 and Beyond* |

**Example of Student Work in the Emerging Stage**

## Example of Student Work in the Developing Stage

Feb. 7, 2013

Dear Mom and Dad,
You are the best! Thank you for everything I have. I would like a map of the U.S. If I have it I will be very happy. I will also be able to memorize the capitals. I know you might say no but it will make me smarter than ever! I can also be like petar from superfudge. When I do know the states, I can learn countries. I know it will make me smarter and that's what matters. I also would not rip it and I will take VERY good care of it.

From,

...now you know which state borders which in the south. ...world.

## Example of Student Work in the Extending Stage

### The Depths of the Ocean

Below the top of the ocean, past coral reefs and schools of fish, lies an amazing environment called the deep sea. In this pitch-black biome where no human could ever venture unarmored lies a mysterious environment, glowing animals, plants, and amazing creatures. The deep sea is an extraordinary biome.

#### A Mysterious Environment

The deep sea is one of the darkest places on Earth. Its depths delve so deep that the only light is from the adapted animals, who glow with bioluminescence. The sea floor consists of mud and ooze.

Two important characteristics unique to the deep sea are tube worms and hydrothermal vents. Hydrothermal vents can be considered an sea "volcano", but really there is so much more than that. However, they do often "erupt", spewing black smoke and hot magma. Magma below the vent gave of heat and soon, these grew to be large, chimney-like structures.

Tube worms are an **invertebrate**. They can easily be mistaken for plants. When scientists first discovered hydrothermal vents, they were surprised entire ecosystems lived near these incredibly hot areas. Namely, Giant tube worms. The "worms" food is molecules given of by bacteria from hydrothermal vents. This means that they are especially unique because they do not use photosynthesis. Together, these two make the deep sea the way it is.

Fun Fact: 90% of all volcanic activity occurs in the oceans

#### Bioluminescence

In this amazing biome, animals have adapted to its extreme conditions in many ways. The most important way animals have adapted to the deep sea is glowing with bioluminescence. **Bioluminescence** is a process that makes an animal or plant glow. Only a select few insects and plants can do this. The rest of bioluminescence is found in the deep sea.
Bioluminescence occurs when certain **chemicals** mix

together to create a glow. Because blue/green light travels best in water, many fish glow this color.

The Atolla wyvillei (A-tolla WY-vill-EE) jellyfish is a great example of this. Because it lives so deep, it has developed a glow that brightens up the water. There is a picture on the left of this.

A very famous example is the Angler fish. As shown in the movie *Finding Nemo*, the Angler fish has a draping bell on its head that glows. It uses this to lure prey so it can devour them in an instant. The most important way animals have adapted to the deep sea is glowing with bioluminescence.

#### Amazing Creatures

Hidden away at the depths of the sea lie an amazing array of sea creatures. Many are scary-looking or hideous, but all are special and amazing. Let's highlight a few important ones.

The Oarfish is a recently discovered eel-like creature. It is the longest bony fish in the sea. Long ago, the Oarfish inspired tales of sea monsters and serpents. It has a very long and pinkish-white body. Along its body is a bright red **plume**. It can reach a length of over 50 feet! That is about a quarter of a football field.

The Hatchetfish is an extremely scary-looking fish. Named for its ax-shaped body, it shouldn't be confused with the **freshwater** Hatchetfish, a common pet. Its seemingly pupil-less eyes look up to search for prey above. Hatchetfish are bioluminescent due to the darkness where it lives.

The Lanternfish is a small, purple, bioluminescent fish. It is actually specifically bioluminescent in certain spots to attract fish that it eats. It lives **worldwide** and is an extremely deep-dwelling fish, living from 1,200 to 3,000 feet below sea level!

Finally, we will talk about the Sperm whale. This giant can reach up to 65 feet and is found around 10,000 feet below sea level. One of the deepest fish and definitely the deepest diving whale, the Sperm whale is a toothed whale and uses echolocation to locate prey.

#### Conclusion

As you can see, miles below the surface of the sea, a entire new kingdom awaits. One filled with amazing plants and caves, bioluminescence, and amazing animals. Sadly, many of these animals are hunted and/or endangered. Please try to preserve this beautiful biome. Remember all of its amazing qualities.

*The Firefly squid is a particularly pretty bioluminescent mollusk.*

#### Credits

**Environment of Deep Sea:** Marinebio.org
**Types of animals + Bioluminescence:** Sea&Sky.org
**Bioluminescent animals:** LiveScience.org

#### Glossary

bioluminescence: A process that makes plants and animals glow
chemical: An ingredient in chemistry
freshwater: A biome in which water does not contain salt
invertebrate: An animal without a backbone
ooze: A type of mud with more organic remains
plume: A part that sticks up, usually hair-related objects
worldwide: Around the globe

---

Across Part II you will find lesson sets specifically designed for learners working on skills aligned with the emerging, developing, and extending stages of development.

It is important to note that children do not move through these stages in lockstep. In other words, it is likely that you will work with students who exhibit characteristics aligned with more than one stage of development. "Typical" is an enigma. When embracing an asset-based approach to instruction, teachers celebrate what's currently in place and become genuinely curious about what could come next. The flexibility of multitasking mentor texts supports this exciting, student-centric work.

## HOW DO MULTITASKING MENTOR TEXTS BECOME TOOLS FOR STUDENT-CENTERED (NOT TEXT-CENTERED) LEARNING?

When I start with students (their identities, interests, strengths, and aligned next steps) and work from this vantage point, I can mine a prospective text and uncover a multitude of *responsive* teaching opportunities that transcend any one subject area. It's the students who guide my decision making. In this way, I strategically use vetted texts to center what students are ready for, not "everything" the text offers.

I make decisions about how to best utilize selected mentor texts by thinking formatively. In *Word Study That Sticks*, I wrote, "Most everything we hear and see in our classroom can be used formatively if we alter or modify instruction because of these observations" (Koutrakos, 2018, p. 92). While I realize it is very likely that you are required to collect formal and measurable data, I also want to remind you that not all assessment needs to be formal and measurable. There are many ways to gather intel on students' assets, interests, and challenges. Yes, formal assessment provides insights, but so do conversations, eavesdropping, and good old "kidwatching" (Goodman & Owocki, 2002). Assessment is authentically interwoven into all you already do, living in "little" moments that happen each day.

The more consistent and varied a teacher's assessment methods, the clearer the picture gleaned. It is the cumulative impact of casual observations, brief interactions, and mining more formal assessment that helps us identify priorities and plan aligned instruction. Perhaps it all boils down to what Dylan Wiliam (2011) writes in *Embedded Formative Assessment*: "The big idea is that evidence about learning is used to adjust instruction to better meet student needs—in other words, teaching is *adaptive* to the learner's needs" (p. 46). It's through this process that multitasking mentor texts find their purpose, supporting teachers in facilitating student-centric and goal-aligned instruction.

As *you* think through what you see, hear, and notice each day, you may (or may not) feel that the lessons throughout Part II are "just right" for the learners you are currently working with. I hope that you will use what you know about students to amplify the included instructional ideas. If necessary, each lesson can (and should) be tweaked and adjusted to spotlight the present priorities of the students currently in the room. And in Part III, I will walk you through how to use formative assessment to plan from the "ground up" with other favorite classroom mentor texts.

 In *We Got This*, Cornelius Minor (2019) wrote, "My job as the teacher is not to teach the curriculum or even just to teach the students; it is to seek to understand my kids as completely as possible so that I can purposefully bend curriculum to meet them" (pp. 104–105). How do you learn about students? How do you gauge student understanding? How do you hope to grow in your use of formative assessment practices?

# CHAPTER 2

# Instructional Practices That Support Mentor Text Multitasking

"At the end of the day, programs and pedagogies don't teach, teachers do" (McGee, 2017, p. xi).

Oh, how I love and appreciate these words from Patty McGee! Educators have a critically important job, and it is not something a manual, program, or district curriculum can do. Teaching is something *people* do—with expertise, love, and grace. Responsive instruction is centered on students and crafted by teachers with careful attention to developmental readiness, standards, and professional expertise.

Chapter 1 discussed what a *multitasking* mentor text is and does. In discerning why one might choose a particular text and what could be taught with these texts, the emphasis was clearly on *mentor texts*. But mentor texts—even *fabulous* mentor texts—are not enough. Let's examine how the noun *mentor text* metamorphoses into a verb. Spoiler alert: It is the teaching and learning in a classroom that bring a multitasking mentor text to life. Here, in this chapter, the processes that transform mentor texts into *multitasking* mentor texts are investigated and explained:

- The lessons in this book *first* begin to multitask by integrating different aspects of literacy: reading, writing, word study, vocabulary, grammar, and conversation.
- The multitasking factor is *further amplified* by employing a combination of instructional methods.

- Together, these multitasking methods spark student interest, model prioritized skills, guide students through supported approximations, and foster independent practice.

Each lesson set in Part II aims to "verb-ify" mentor texts by using these kinds of instructional practices. In order to prepare to implement these lessons, let's first take some time to scrutinize integrated literacy, then focus on inquiry and gradual release as instructional frameworks.

## WHAT IS INTEGRATED LITERACY, AND HOW DOES THIS RELATE TO MULTITASKING MENTOR TEXTS?

The need to effectively communicate and comprehend permeates each facet of the day. As school districts rise to the challenge of meeting state standards and exceeding community goals, there is an increased understanding of the essential role literacy plays within *all* content areas. When educators look beyond standards and mandates, the true importance of integrated literacy is crystalized. Integrated literacy helps students feel better supported in *all* they do, all across the day—from 8 to 3 and well beyond!

I personally consider integrated literacy to be twofold. First, each aspect of literacy does not live in isolation. We can't separate the work of readers and writers. Language (vocabulary, spelling, and grammar) is interwoven into all we hear, say, read, and write. Rather than thinking of reading, writing, vocabulary, spelling, and grammar as separate entities, we achieve much more when we take on a more holistic view of literacy. These elements of literacy are not only complementary, but inseparable.

Second, integrated literacy extends beyond the literacy block. Mathematicians, social scientists, historians, scientists, musicians, and computer coders all speak, listen, read, and write. In *Culturally Responsive Teaching and the Brain*, Zaretta Hammond (2015) writes about building intellective capacity as we teach learners how to learn. Virtually all the cognitive routines suggested to support the input, elaboration, and application of information processing are deeply rooted in, you guessed it, literacy. As we ignite learning and get the brain's attention, chunk information to make it more digestible, synthesize information through active processing, and review information through opportunities for application, we are often speaking, listening, reading, and/or writing. This second part of integrated literacy—embedding literacy throughout the day using cognitively and culturally responsive methods—is at the heart of learning anything, not only how to read, spell, or write.

This book aims to provide vision for a more streamlined, more practical, more doable approach to teaching. Part II features lessons that integrate different aspects of literacy (reading, writing, speaking, listening, vocabulary, spelling, and grammar). Often, suggestions are made to also integrate a bit of math, social studies, or science. Critical aspects of personal and community wellness are embedded throughout. Teachers *can* use a short stack of multitasking mentor texts to design contextualized, flexible, and multifaceted learning. These mentor texts become essential aspects of integrated literacy instruction, weaving together not only reading and writing, but also language standards (spelling, vocabulary, and grammar) and even content areas. In the chapters that follow, the work described will move beyond creating connections between mentor texts and student work; it also forges ties between different areas of literacy.

But first, let's look at the instructional frameworks—inquiry and gradual release—that guide these lessons and make integrated literacy instruction possible.

## WHY IS INFUSING INQUIRY IMPORTANT?

Near and far, teachers share that truly engaging students in content can be challenging. Inquiry is a natural solution because discovery-based methods pique student interest and garner engagement. This is fuel for critical thinking and deep learning that transfers, as many researchers, educators, and authors have corroborated (see, for example, Cooper & Murphy, 2016; Daniels, 2017; Harvey & Daniels, 2015; Keene, 2018; MacKenzie, 2019; Mitchell, 2018; Ritchhart, 2011, 2015; Wilhelm et al., 2019). Keene (2018) writes, "Engagement is not just 'caught': it can be taught. If we take the long view—what we want children to be able to think, feel, believe, and act upon . . . it will become clear that engagement is one of the most critical learning tools we can help children develop . . . engagement is a significant part of what makes us feel truly alive" (p. 17).

And while some may have the impression that inquiry-infused learning is "loosey-goosey," surface, or extraneous, in practice, nothing could be further from the truth. Meaningful and worthwhile classroom inquiry is prepared and thoughtful. It embeds ongoing assessment and aligned, explicit teaching. Classroom inquiry nurtures ongoing collaboration, problem solving, persistence, flexibility, and "real world" transfer. Inquiry, when used effectively, is deeply rooted in the values, beliefs, and practices that research tells us make a difference.

The merits of classroom inquiry also extend far beyond the classroom. I particularly appreciate the message shared by Harvey "Smokey" Daniels and Sara Ahmed (2015), which asserts that inquiry helps teachers meet the imperative that students "learn to read, write, think, investigate, and collaborate" (p. 4). In *Collaboration and Conversation*, Stephanie Harvey and Daniels (2015) describe inquiry-rich learning as "highly engaging, experiential, deeply supported pedagogy" and then share the intent of classroom inquiry as not only preparing students for high-stakes testing, but *also* "growing curious, lifelong learners who could not just hold a job but change the world for the better" (p. xi). Inquiry is far from a free-for-all!

Lessons throughout this book spotlight an inquiry approach because there is so much to be discovered about words, language, ideas, and writing techniques in multitasking mentor texts. The following chart tackles some common misconceptions. Across the rest of this book, I hope to provide a clear vision of what classroom inquiry (grounded in multitasking mentor texts) looks like in action.

## Classroom Inquiry Truths and Misunderstandings

| WHAT CLASSROOM INQUIRY IS ✔ | WHAT CLASSROOM INQUIRY ISN'T ✘ |
|---|---|
| Purposefully incorporated | Spur-of-the-moment |
| Scaffolded and supported | Disconnected from classroom learning, an "add on" |
| Student-centered, relevant to students' lives and experiences | Unstructured, free-time exploration |
| Celebrates curiosity | Rigid completion of predesigned projects |
| Ignites interest, engagement, and motivation | Assigned research |
| Invites collaboration | Surface fact-finding or fact-curating |
| Closely and deliberately tied to prioritized learning outcomes, designed to exceed set expectations of state standards | One-size-fits-all |
| | Narrow in range |
| A tool to build conceptual understanding | Disconnected from assessment |
| Actively utilizes authentic, high quality texts | Completely teacher-driven |
| | Completely student-driven |
| Fosters perseverance | Lacking an authentic audience and clear purpose |
| Flexible: Can be used as a protocol to spark learning, a vehicle to practice and deepen learning, and/or a means to reflect on and celebrate learning | Devoid of modeling or differentiated, responsive support |
| | One way, always the same |
| Necessitates action and application | Passive |
| Inherently playful and exciting | Boring |

# WHAT ROLE DOES GRADUAL RELEASE PLAY IN MULTITASKING MENTOR TEXT LESSONS?

In *Every Child Can Write*, Melanie Meehan (2019) shares, "The goal of learning should always be transfer. If what we are teaching today has no chance of being integrated or approximated in tomorrow's writing, then we're not teaching the right thing" (p. 179). The hallmark of gradual release is moving thoughtfully from the "I go" phase (explicit modeling) to the "we go" phase (guided and supported practice) to the "you go" phase (independent practice). When used responsively, gradual release helps students transfer learning to a variety of contexts and settings.

In other words, by thoughtfully preparing connected learning experiences and strategically stepping back, teachers can ensure that students become more confident, competent, and independent. Ideally, the gradual release of support does not end with "you go" but instead moves past even that—getting to the "you go because you choose to and feel ready to do so" phase. That is when students have transferred the learning and made it their own. Multitasking mentor texts bring increased efficiency and success to this work across the entire literacy block. Because children are unique and learning is multifaceted, throughout this book, lessons that support a gradual release approach complement the inquiry-based lessons. This helps us see that when it comes to "how" we teach, it is never an either–or situation. There is space for both discovery *and* explicit teaching in our day, and it is quite possible for these methods to overlap. In the pages that follow, let's walk through the "why" and "what" of the phases of gradual release.

> Do you believe that it is important to utilize a variety of types of instructional methods? If so, what do you see as the benefits of balancing inquiry learning with more explicit strategy instruction? If not, what type of instruction do you feel best supports classroom learners—and why?

## "I GO" AND "WE GO": TEACHER-DIRECTED PRACTICES (MODELED AND GUIDED)

Modeled and guided practice is the hallmark of teaching within the model of gradual release. However, it is important to note that when inquiry is new for classroom learners or when the goal is to lift the level of inquiry processes, modeling makes sense! Moreover, teachers often strategically guide students as they begin inquiry investigations and again as they prepare to deepen the level of this critical work. We can flexibly feature selected mentor texts in each of these (often connected) methods of instruction. The chart in this section gives an overview of a few of the most common structures used to model and guide.

## Instructional Structures at a Glance

| | WHY | WHAT | HOW | WHEN |
|---|---|---|---|---|
| **Interactive Read-Aloud (IRA)** | IRA models what readers do as they work to comprehend and think about texts. | IRA is a planned read-aloud with an instructional purpose. The teacher chooses 2–3 instructional focus areas. The teacher reads aloud, modeling this work. The students listen, watch the teacher, and dip in for a low-stakes try. | The teacher reads a text aloud to students. The teacher stops at intentional, preplanned points to model thinking related to instructional focus. The teacher may also prompt students to give this work a try. | IRA is used when comprehension work is new or tricky for classroom learners.<br><br>Although traditionally implemented whole-class, IRA can also be used in small groups. |
| **Shared Reading (SR)** | SR models what readers do as they read texts. Because students have their eyes on the text, concepts of print, spelling, vocabulary, grammar, and fluency work can also be infused. | SR happens in a cycle. The teacher selects a short text (poem, song, chant, 2-page spread from a previously read text, short article, etc.). Each day in the cycle, the teacher spends approximately 5–10 minutes modeling and guiding students while using this text. Each session has a different instructional focus. | The teacher selects a short text and plans a cycle of about 3–5 sessions. Each session uses that same text, but has a different focus. The teacher can model the work of readers, word explorers, language learners, thinkers, and conversationalists. Students are highly supported as they participate. | SR is used when a teacher believes students will benefit from seeing *all kinds* of authentic literacy-rich work in action.<br><br>Although most traditionally implemented whole-class, SR can also be used in small groups. |
| **Shared Writing (SW)** | SW models what writers do as they work on writing projects. | SW happens in a cycle. Each day in the cycle, teachers spend approximately 5–15 minutes leading work connected to the processes inherent in writing. Each session has a different instructional focus—for example, generating ideas, planning, drafting, developing, and polishing writing. | The teacher leads students in the work that commonly happens as writers plan, draft, and revisit their writing. In each session, the students participate by orally sharing ideas and suggestions. The teacher does the "heavy lifting" and does all of the physical writing. Students see how writing processes look in action. | SW is used when a teacher believes students will benefit from seeing writing processes in action. Although always beneficial, it is most often used as a heavily scaffolded introduction to a new genre or format for writing.<br><br>Although most traditionally implemented whole-class, SW can also be used in small groups. |

| | WHY | WHAT | HOW | WHEN |
|---|---|---|---|---|
| **Interactive Writing (IW)** | IW models and guides students as they see how ideas get from their heads onto paper or onto a computer conventionally. | IW is often "one and done." In this structure, the students see how ideas make their way onto the page, conventionally and efficiently. Students are guided as they share ideas and dip in for small pieces of the writing. | The teacher leads students in planning and sharing ideas for writing—any purpose or subject. The students share ideas, and the teacher does *most* of the writing. However, at intentionally planned spots—tied to current learning goals—the teacher passes the pen, marker, or keyboard, and student volunteers dip in to do small pieces of the actual writing. Dip-in points usually reflect how to think about, remember, and apply what students know about spelling, grammar, and word choice. | IW is used when a teacher feels it is important to model how to get ideas down in a conventional way.<br><br>Although most traditionally implemented whole-class, IW can also be used in small groups. |
| **Whole-Class Strategy Modeling, or** *Minilessons* **(MLs)** | MLs provide teachers a time-efficient way to prepare students to try prioritized work with more independence. | MLs allow for implementing brief, direct instruction to the class. Here, the teacher models (showing and telling) the process of a strategy and then guides students as they try it out themselves. | The teacher reminds students of prior knowledge (what has been taught and is in place). The teacher then shows and tells the process of a connected and prioritized next step. Next, the teacher guides students through a try of the next step that was just modeled. Finally, the teacher reminds learners of what was just done, why they would try this out, and when they would use this strategy. One ML takes approximately 5–15 minutes total. | MLs are used when the teacher feels that a strategy is essential for unit learning and matches the current priorities of classroom learners. |

*(Continued)*

(Continued)

| | WHY | WHAT | HOW | WHEN |
|---|---|---|---|---|
| **Small-Group Strategy Modeling, or** *Strategy Groups* **(SGs)** | SGs are more personalized than MLs and enable a teacher to support small groups of students who are all ready to work on the same next step. | SGs allow for implementing brief, direct instruction to a small group of classroom learners. Here, the teacher models (showing and telling) the process of a strategy a few members of the class are ready to work on, and then guides students as they try it out themselves. | The structure of SGs is exactly the same as that of MLs, except for the fact that the teacher is modeling and guiding a small group of students instead of the entire class. Often 3–6 students are a part of the strategy group, and the lesson takes about 5–10 minutes. | SGs are used when the teacher feels that a few students will benefit from modeled and guided practice of a particular strategy. The teacher pulls small groups while other students are busy working. |
| **One-to-One Conversations, or** *Conferring Conversations* **(CCs)** | CCs are the most personalized form of instruction. The teacher supports students with prioritized next steps that are truly "just right" for them. | CCs allow for implementing brief, direct instruction to individual classroom learners. Here, the teacher models (showing and telling) the process of a strategy and then guides the student through trying it out. | The structure of CCs is exactly the same as that of MLs, except the teacher is modeling and guiding an individual student instead of the entire class. The whole experience takes about 3–8 minutes, with about 5 minutes being average. | CCs are used when the teacher wants to provide truly personalized, responsive instruction—modeling and guiding a student through a strategy aligned to a current goal. A teacher engages in these conversations while other students are busy working. |

## "YOU GO": STUDENT-DIRECTED PRACTICES (PEER AND INDEPENDENT)

The goal is for students to choose which strategies to use and feel comfortable trying this work on their own—because they see personal value and need, not because a teacher has told them to do so. The explicit modeling and responsive guided practices detailed in the chart play a big part in preparing students to rise to this challenge. However, it is the ongoing, more independent practice that leads to students becoming competent! Modeling, guiding, and coaching are temporary scaffolds.

As we step back, touchstone mentor texts step up. These texts continue to be instructional resources; students lean on these tools as they build understanding and independence. They increase the likelihood that students will make the choice to dive in on their own and use strategies as needed. If instruction models, supports, and encourages developmentally appropriate learning, you can trust that students will progress. Of course, deeply ingrained in this work is the ongoing flexible and contextualized use of multitasking mentor texts.

Douglas Fisher and colleagues (2016) describe a three-phase model for literacy instruction: surface learning, deep learning (which integrates thinking, consolidating ideas, and taking action), and transfer. By revisiting multitasking mentor texts and spiraling literacy concepts, learning deepens. Furthermore, by using a carefully constructed combination of inquiry, modeled, guided, and independent practices (that feature these texts), teachers support students in their endeavors to not only replicate what was taught but also choose when and how to apply gained knowledge. Essentially, when we repeatedly revisit quality texts and turn them into multitasking mentor texts, students are better prepared to practice, transfer, and apply what they have learned—from every corner of the literacy block!

The ongoing transfer and application that happens through independent practice makes learning stick. Students become more proficient, and their success yields excitement. Perhaps no one says it better than Katie Egan Cunningham (2019) in her gem of a book, *Start With Joy*: "If we take certain steps, we can support students to be successful readers, writers, and communicators while also greatly increasing the chances that they will find joy in learning, and more importantly, that they will be laying the foundation for sustained happiness that they can learn to keep creating for themselves their entire lives" (p. 4).

 How do you decide what to teach whole-class, small-group, and individually? How do you find the time and space to teach into these priorities?

# PART II

# Teaching With Multitasking Mentor Texts

*The heart and soul of this book is using authentic texts to meaningfully and naturally integrate learning across the period, block, day, week, and unit.*

$N$ ow, the fun begins.

Each chapter in Part II features three sets of lessons. These lesson sets have been specifically designed to support the goals of students across the three stages of learning: emerging, developing, and extending. For instance, the "emerging" lesson sets center on concepts that are commonly taught to students in this stage of learning. The same goes for each chapter's "developing" lesson set and "extending" lesson set. Because of this, teachers working with students in kindergarten through eighth grade are bound to find many appealing and appropriate lessons! As you peruse Part II, I encourage you to also remember that the grade levels commonly aligned to the emerging, developing, and extending stages are guidelines and not absolutes. For example, a middle school teacher might first be drawn to the extending lessons. Yes, these extending lessons are closely tied to state standards at those grades and common learning goals of students in those grades. However, many middle school teachers may *also* find developing lessons that match the goals of certain classroom learners. So, no matter what grade or type of setting you currently teach in, I recommend you check out the lesson sets *across* developmental stages. As you responsively support the continuous academic growth of each student, it is likely that you will appreciate the variety of suggestions provided.

Each of the lesson sets across Part II provides a vision of what it looks like to revisit the same text multiple times, for different purposes. Moreover, in each lesson set, you will always find a lesson that invites inquiry, a collaborative lesson with lots of modeling and guidance, and a lesson to support independent practice. The included ideas intend to show a *small sampling* of the many ways that each recommended mentor text can multitask. These lessons are not discrete, nor are they designed to stand on their own. Integrate and infuse lesson ideas where they make sense. Cast aside the suggestions that make you feel as though you are working too hard for limited results. (You know the analogy about trying to fit a square peg into a circle hole.) The heart and soul of this book is using authentic texts to meaningfully and naturally integrate learning across the period, block, day, week, and unit. This less-is-more approach is about streamlining, not handing you one more thing to add into your day. I encourage you to peruse the pages ahead, considering the identities, interests, and areas of readiness of current students. Remember that the concepts and ideas shared are not bound to any one text and can live within the pages of virtually any mentor text that will spark the interest and attention of current classroom learners.

At the end of each chapter in Part II, you will find a new set of *Stretch Up and Back Suggestions*. This recurring feature offers a vision of *additional* teaching opportunities. These suggestions provide insight into how you can use the same multitasking texts to teach an even wider range of strategies, specifically those that make sense for students across the stages of development. Teachers may choose to utilize these *Stretch Up and Back Suggestions* during small-group and one-to-one instruction. By doing so, they preserve whole-class community experiences while also efficiently facilitating more personalized instruction. When teachers welcome a known mentor text into these more customized instructional moments, classroom time is used adeptly. In the hands of a thoughtful teacher, the multitasking capabilities of a mentor text come alive!

Across Part II, you will see curated sets of mentor texts doing what they do best: multitasking. Beginning in Chapter 5, the featured texts celebrate specific genres. Chapters 3 and 4 are a bit different in that they celebrate a *format* (wordless texts and graphic texts). Skim through the lesson sets and suggestions throughout Part II with a flexible mindset. Slow down when and where the lessons fit with current classroom priorities and goals. Above all, have fun! This is meant to feel and be playful.

> **NOTE:** During the time this book was written, COVID-19 was deeply impacting our communities. Teachers were trying their best to figure out how engaging, student-centered learning looked in remote and hybrid contexts. Unsurprisingly, educators everywhere displayed superhuman strength, courage, imagination, and creativity while navigating this seemingly insurmountable challenge. Throughout Part II, you will notice photos of lessons and work done in traditional brick-and-mortar classrooms, hybrid scenarios, and fully remote settings. These lessons were originally designed to be flexible and adaptable. As they continued to be field-tested during the global pandemic, I discovered that the included lessons could be implemented in a wider variety of learning settings than originally imagined.

In some ways, the experience of teaching and learning during COVID-19 exemplifies the primary purposes of this book: forging connections between student learning experiences, efficiently integrating different aspects of literacy, igniting interest through inquiry, supporting independence through gradual release, and yes, of course, doing more . . . with less!

# CHAPTER 3

# Wordless Texts and Images

"Viewing illustrations and other visual images is an excellent way for students to practice identifying specific details that aid comprehension" (Bryan, 2019, p. 10).

Images tell stories. They give us a glimpse into a scene or world that we want to know more about. Sometimes an image relays an entire story. As noted by Trevor Bryan in the quote that opens this chapter, artwork and photographs can be a starting place for students to notice details and build comprehension skills. The multiple entry points offered up by visual images promote independence as students construct meaning, grow thinking, and extend ideas. This is why I reserve a special part of my heart (and bookshelf!) for wordless texts—of all genres. The chart that follows lists the many benefits of using wordless texts in the classroom.

In this chapter, the proposed inquiry work is steeped in vocabulary. The meaningful context of wordless texts and images offers a foundation and springboard for vast vocabulary-rich learning experiences. Interactive writing is another highlighted teaching structure used throughout Chapter 3. In fact, interactive writing is my "secret ingredient" for modeling the transfer of language learning. It is highly scaffolded magic! Finally, the highlighted wordless texts are prominently featured in the included comprehension and conversation suggestions for independent practice. Remember, the text recommendations are just that. You can easily switch out titles or substitute images. Use favorite wordless books, photographs, pieces of art, and dialogue-free video clips to promote similar types of learning experiences. Without words to define limits, these mentor texts can multitask in every imaginable way!

Wordless Texts Offer Many Benefits!

| GENERAL BENEFITS | TEACHER BENEFITS | STUDENT BENEFITS |
|---|---|---|
| Wordless texts:<br><br>* Are suitable and appropriate for students of all ages.<br><br>* Even the playing field and play to the strengths of a wider range of students.<br><br>* Ignite imaginations and invite new possibilities each time they are revisited. | Wordless texts:<br><br>* Jump-start dynamic literacy practices and provide support when teaching complex concepts.<br><br>* Act as a bridge to sophisticated skills (e.g., perspective, inferencing, theme, mood, tone, bias, symbols, use of repetition); without words present, the offering and consideration of multiple interpretations often feels safer.<br><br>* Are great resources for teaching into planning techniques, structure, elaboration and development, craft moves, and evoking feelings and reactions in an audience. | Wordless texts:<br><br>* Build the confidence of students acquiring English as an additional language, often increasing the likelihood of more confident sharing of knowledge, thoughts, and opinions.<br><br>* Provide greater access to practicing inferential and analytic thinking skills for students who have difficulty with decoding.<br><br>* Transform some reticent readers into engaged learners. |

 How and when do you already use wordless texts and images in the classroom? What goals do you have around widening these purposes?

**NOTE:** Remember to always first enjoy featured texts as a community of readers. Then, *revisit* the text, repurposing it as a mentor text for any number of instructional priorities and goals.

# Lesson Set Aligned to the Emerging Stage

## Featured Text: *Another* by Christian Robinson (2019)

 **Text Pairings**

- *Anno's Journey* by Mitsumasa Anno (1997)
- *Journey* and *Quest* by Aaron Becker (2013, 2014)
- *Harold and the Purple Crayon* by Crockett Johnson (1955)
- *The Red Book* and *The Secret Box* by Barbara Lehman (2004, 2011)
- *Chalk* and *Fossil* by Bill Thomson (2010, 2013)

### WHAT?

In this book, the main character and her cat enter another world where they encounter different perspectives and even their own doppelgangers.

### WHY?

In this imaginative book, Robinson plays with perspective, colors, shapes, and ideas. Different readers have slightly different interpretations of the main character's journey. This book inspires joyful engagement, wonder, and rich discussion. The vibe is playful and fun. Students will beg to revisit this book again and again!

### WHEN?

*Another* fits well with any narrative reading or writing unit.

 **Content Connections**

Art: colors, shapes, positive and negative space, paint, collage

Math: numbers, patterns, geometry

Personal and Community Wellness: exploring different aspects of personal identities, the power of imagination, nourishing creativity, considering different perspectives

# INVESTIGATING IDEAS THROUGH INQUIRY

*ANOTHER* BY CHRISTIAN ROBINSON (2019)

In this inquiry-rich lesson, students play around with the vocabulary of predicting. They use what they see to wonder about what may happen next.

**Guiding Inquiry:** *How can exploring the outside of a book help you discover what may be on the inside?*

- **Study** the front cover of the text, closely examining the details.

- **Use** explicit language to name what you see, wonder, and predict. Infuse words like *character*, *setting*, and **problem**. Repeat for the back cover.

- **Encourage** students to share if they agree or disagree with your initial musings—and why!

- **Scrutinize** the inside cover (remove the book jacket). Ask students to share what they see, wonder, and predict with a partner.

- **Invite** a few volunteers to share their predictions. Record predictions.

- **Investigate** the end pages and title page. Use this exploration to spark additional wondering and predicting.

- **Storytell** as you share each page with students.

- **Review** the guiding inquiry of the day. Revisit initial predictions and decide if they "came true" or not.

- **Summarize** the experience. Share that taking the time to explore the outside of a book is always worthwhile because readers can use these wonder-inciting peeks to prepare for what they may see, read, and learn on the inside.

---

 **Language Levers**

You may want to use some of the following thinking stems. You can encourage students to use this language or similar language as they participate in this inquiry experience.

*I think . . .*      *I predict . . . I wonder if . . .*

*I'm thinking . . . Perhaps . . . Maybe . . .*

---

✓ **Check-Up**

Listen in as students share their ideas. As you do, informally note the readiness you observe:

- Are students able to specifically name what they see?

- Do students create logical predictions that are connected to their observations?

This lesson artifact displays student predictions. Clearly, students enjoyed using the lingo of predictors.

- Are students able to use "prediction lingo" as they name and explain their ideas?

Use this informal assessment to guide follow-up instruction.

## ? What Else?

Instead of engaging in a prediction-themed inquiry, you might choose to partake in an illustration-focused inquiry.

- Ask students to use the details on the page to say *more* about what they see and think. Model using vocabulary like *character, setting, problem, solution, color, shape,* and *background* to support more precise and nuanced conversation.

- Investigate different books with similar styles (classics like books by Ezra Jack Keats, Leo Lionni, Faith Ringgold, and Eric Carle would work well). Ask students to compare the images they see. By using illustrations to spark conversations around comparing texts, you are naturally scaffolding this often complex and challenging thinking work.

# BUILDING VISION VIA MODELED AND GUIDED PRACTICE

## ANOTHER BY CHRISTIAN ROBINSON (2019)

Telling a story and retelling a story are quite complex! Here, interactive writing is used to guide students through a well-sequenced retelling (of one version of *Another*). Use recent class observations to plan an interactive writing experience that guides students in a process that is a notch above what they are currently doing independently. For example, you might decide to simplify the retell by focusing on the beginning, middle, and end or, on the flip side, create a more nuanced retell by stretching the number of events and details or by featuring story elements in this collaborative writing experience.

- **Recall** prior experience(s) of reading *Another*. Reexamine the cover. Flip through the pages, orally retelling the story.

- **Rehearse** for writing by asking the students to "copycat" this retell with a partner.

- **Elicit** student input as you compose the written retell.

- **Invite** student volunteers to contribute by adding small, targeted parts of the writing. (See *What Else?* for suggestions on how students might participate in the actual writing.)

- **Reread** and polish the interactive writing piece.

- **Summarize** the process of retelling and share that whenever readers finish reading a book, they can think about, talk about, sketch, or jot what they remember.

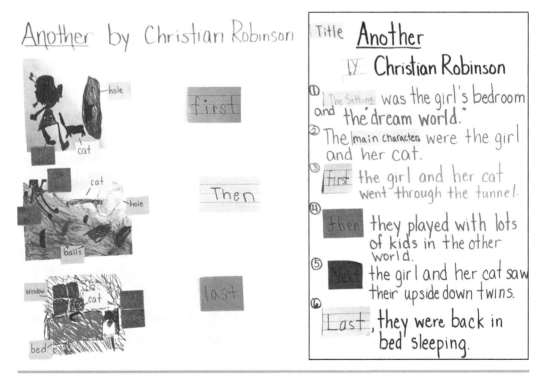

The example on the left shows how a kindergarten class used this experience to co-create a picture retell with labels and transition words. The example on the right shows how a second-grade class co-created a sequenced list of events.

## ✓ Check-Up

In modeled and guided experiences, informal observing is enough. You might:

* Listen in as students talk with each other.
* Watch as students "dip in" to practice transferring taught concepts and conventions.

Use this high-support experience formatively, and follow up with more explicit instruction in areas that feel the most relevant for current learners. You may find the informal assessment resources available on the companion website (resources.corwin.com/mttm) useful.

## ? What Else?

Your choices about where and how students "dip in" to the writing will likely align to the goals of current classroom learners.

* IF you choose to nurture students' use of "order words," THEN you might have students dip in to add in sequence words like *in the beginning, first, then, after that, at the end, finally,* and/or *last.*

* IF you choose to nurture students' use of "story words," THEN you might have volunteers interact to add words like *title, author, illustrator, character, setting, problem, solution, lesson, learned,* and/or *think.*

* IF you choose to nurture students' use of words with specific phonics sounds or spelling patterns, THEN you could have students come up to add in the words that contain those sounds or letters.

* IF you choose to nurture students' use of a grammar concept, THEN you might encourage class members to write in the words that align with that concept. For example, if you have been learning about prepositions, you may ask students to add in common prepositions like *in, into, near, of, off, on, to, under, before, beside,* and/or *below.*

# NURTURING AND SUPPORTING INDEPENDENT PRACTICE

*ANOTHER* BY CHRISTIAN ROBINSON (2019)

In this lesson, the teacher supports students as they practice using the pictures to read and retell stories.

- **Recall** previous readings of *Another*.
- **State** that readers can read the illustrations in a text. They can also remember and share stories by examining the pictures on each page.
- **Model** the following process as you storytell the first few pages of *Another*:
  - Look at the page.
  - Ask yourself, "What do I see? Who do I see? What is happening?"
  - Use those details as you storytell (and/or retell).
- **Encourage** students to try this same process. Flip through the next few pages and ask students to use the details in the illustration to tell the story. Listen in as students practice with a partner.
- **Remind** students that they can always use the pictures to read, think, or talk about a text.
- **Invite** students to go off to read their own books. Provide time for them to practice storytelling and retelling texts.
- **Observe** students as they read and meet with partners.
- **Celebrate** what you see classroom readers trying and doing.

## ✔ Check-Up

Circulate, observe, and listen in as students read, retell, and work with a partner. Notice and name what you see. For instance, you might notice students:

- *Pointing* to objects they see on each page and *naming* those objects or concisely sharing what is happening.
- *Summarizing* the story with more detail (like what was done in the interactive writing experience).
- Truly *storytelling*, using colorful and descriptive language to tell (or retell) the story.

Jot your observations. Record-keeping templates are available online (resources.corwin.com/mttm). Use what you see and hear students doing to provide in-the-moment feedback and guide next steps for instruction.

## ? What Else?

Instead of teaching this lesson whole-class and sending everyone off to practice, you might instead:

- Encourage follow-up practice with "conver-stations." This is a conversation-focused center. As students visit this learning station, they use the images and pictures within texts to storytell and retell.
- Focus on students examining books and deciding if the books could be mirrors, windows, and/or sliding glass doors (Bishop, 1990). In *Another*, the main character definitely has a "mirror" experience! You might teach a lesson or set up a conver-station where students analyze books and contemplate if they are mirror books, window books, or sliding glass door books . . . and why!
- Encourage students to use this book for inspiration as they create their own (wordless) text in which they go on an adventure.

# Lesson Set Aligned to the Developing Stage

## Featured Text: *Brave Molly* by Brooke Boynton-Hughes (2019)

 **Text Pairings**

- *Wemberly Worried* by Kevin Henkes (2000)
- *The Girl Who Never Made Mistakes* by Mark Pett and Gary Rubenstein (2011)
- *Guts* by Raina Telgemeier (2019)
- *What Do You Do With a Problem?* and *What Do You Do With a Chance?* by Kobi Yamada (2016, 2018)
- *Piper*, a wordless animated short by Pixar, directed by Alan Barillaro (2016) (online resource)

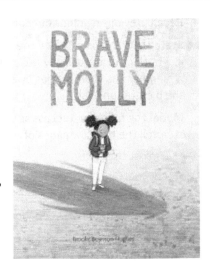

### WHAT?

*Brave Molly* tells the story of Molly, a heroine who appears to be experiencing some anxiety. She faces her fear and the "monsters" that keep getting in her way.

### WHY?

Many of our favorite book characters are larger than life. Their charisma pulls us in and keeps us hooked from cover to cover. But, in real life, student dispositions vary. Moreover, we *all* occasionally experience feelings of uncertainty. Many readers will relate in some way to Molly, and those who don't will gain a better understanding into the experiences of others.

### WHEN?

*Brave Molly* is a great first-day-of-school story. It also works well with social issues reading units. This text can be utilized in personal narrative, memoir, or fiction writing units. Furthermore, it can easily be woven into *any* narrative reading or writing unit.

 **Content Connections**

Personal and Community Wellness: developing appreciation for *all* aspects of personal identities and the identities of others, recognizing and understanding emotions, mindfulness, breathing techniques and other calming strategies, navigating and overcoming challenges, empathy

# INVESTIGATING IDEAS THROUGH INQUIRY

*BRAVE MOLLY* BY BROOKE BOYNTON-HUGHES (2019)

This book provides a wonderful opportunity to explore the use of precise and nuanced vocabulary to describe character feelings. The teacher will do more facilitating than modeling during this inquiry experience. The idea is for students to ponder, investigate, and hypothesize ideas about the main character. More formal teaching will follow.

> **NOTE:** During this inquiry experience, you may want students to jot their discoveries and ideas in a reading notebook.

**Guiding Inquiry:** *How can a reader uncover big ideas about a character?*

- **Examine** the cover of *Brave Molly*. Recall prior reading experience and briefly summarize the story.

- **Remind** students of the importance of moving beyond using simple words (*good, bad, happy, sad*) to describe a character and challenging oneself to ponder more precise lingo. Offer that by doing so, readers are able to develop more nuanced theories about characters.

- **Explore** the book for a second time, starting with the cover. Collaboratively consider words that describe how Molly may be feeling. Use details on the cover to guide these playful musings.

- **Contemplate** a *precise* word to describe Molly while investigating the title page. For example: "I'm wondering if Molly is feeling *content* because she is sitting in her room and surrounded by some of her favorite things. She is in that cozy nook sitting on comfortable pillows. She seems lost in the book she is reading."

- **Investigate** the images on the page where Molly is crumpling up the paper. Ask students to consider a "just right" word that describes how they believe Molly now feels, along with a brief explanation that supports that idea.

- **Repeat** two to three more times asking students to investigate a page, generate a precise word, and briefly explain their opinion. Suggested pages to choose from:
  - The page with the zigzag lines
  - The page where Molly is climbing in the trees
  - The page where Molly is shouting at the monsters
  - The page where we see the only words in the book: "Hi"

- **Revisit** shared ideas (or notebook jots). Can students discover any patterns? Are there any words they used repeatedly? Are there any words that are quite similar in meaning?

- **Hypothesize:** After exploring these pages, investigating the details, and reviewing their ideas, what have students discovered about Molly? Invite them to either share ideas orally (with a partner) or do a bit more jotting.

- **Summarize** the experience by reminding students they can always explore images to discover more about characters in the books they read—and then use that thinking to develop precise and nuanced ideas about characters.

## ✓ Check-Up

Look through student jots and/or listen in on their partner conversations. Use these observations to plan follow-up instruction where you model the process for:

- Making inferences about how a character is feeling.

- Using precise vocabulary to describe characters.

- Exploring and investigating the details on a page (images and/or words) to support ideas about characters.

- Exploring and investigating in-the-moment jots to discover bigger and more powerful ideas about characters.

Depending on your informal noticings, this connected instruction could take place whole-class, small-group, and/or one-to-one.

**? What Else?**

You could instead choose to focus this inquiry on:

- Discovering more in each illustration's details and using this knowledge to enhance the "storytelling" of the book.

- Uncovering thinking about how the problem unfolds and evolves across the story.

- Discovering more about nuanced storytelling (versus bland summarizing) and then connecting these reading experiences to independent writing projects.

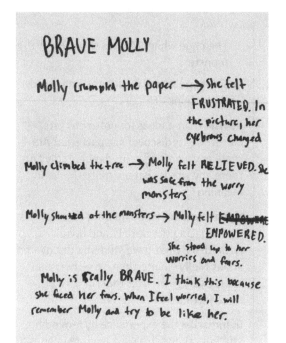

These student work samples show how two classmates each delved into the guiding inquiry.

# BUILDING VISION VIA MODELED AND GUIDED PRACTICE

*BRAVE MOLLY* BY BROOKE BOYNTON-HUGHES (2019)

This interactive writing experience provides a vision for what it looks like to write "long and strong" about characters and use precise vocabulary while doing so. In interactive writing, the teacher does most of the actual writing. Students participate by sharing ideas orally—and doing small, intentional pieces of the writing. Here, the recommendation is for students to dip in to add the precise vocabulary that describes Molly and/or the phrases that help readers refer to the text to support their ideas.

> **NOTE:** Before beginning, you may decide to post the *Language Levers* provided with this lesson.

- **Recall** the inquiry experience. Encourage students to think back to their conversations or look back at the notes they jotted during that session.

- **Share** that today the class will collaborate to create a long and strong entry in which they reflect on what they learned about the main character.

- **Rehearse** for this class writing by asking students to share their ideas about Molly with a partner.

- **Elicit** student input as you begin to compose the text. Encourage students to use precise vocabulary as they describe Molly *and* to share sentence ideas that use the language of readers. (See the *Language Levers* suggestions.)

- **Invite** students to write or type in these specific words and phrases.

- **Reread** and polish the co-composed piece.

- **Summarize** the experience, specifically reflecting on how the class incorporated

precise language as they shared ideas about a character.

 **Language Levers**

Language Levers can be posted in multiple languages. Class members could also contribute stems that reflect the language they feel most comfortable using.

- *Molly is the type of person who . . .*
- *At the beginning . . . but later . . .*
- *At first . . . but then . . .*
- *In the text, it showed . . .*
- *In the illustration, we see . . .*

 **Check-Up**

Informal assessment works best here. Observe students and listen as they share ideas. Use observations to plan follow-up, responsive instruction. You might decide to more explicitly teach about:

- In-the moment character inferences (that use precise vocabulary).
- Investigating a pattern across time.
- How to grow an idea about a character.
- Using the text to support ideas about characters.

Nurture prioritized skills across time, providing feedback as students begin to try this work on their own.

**❓ What Else?**

Instead of inviting students to participate in the writing of nuanced vocabulary and text-support statements, you might ask them to dip in to add:

- Words with pretaught spelling patterns (perhaps words with long vowel patterns, targeted diphthongs, consonant clusters, or inflected endings).

- Commonly confused words and high-frequency words (*to, too, two; there, their, they're*; etc.).

- Words that are a particular part of speech (adjectives, adverbs, verbs, etc.).

- The sentence parts that feature recently taught grammar concepts (perhaps collective nouns, proper nouns, irregular verbs, or commas and conjunctions).

We read <u>Brave</u> <u>Molly</u> by Brooke Boyton-Hughes. At the beginning, Molly was lonely. For example, Molly sat in her room while other kids were together outside. Also, she walked to school By herself. Later, the author chose to have Molly fight back. Molly stood up to her worry. In one illustration, Molly yelled at the monsters. At another point, Molly ignored the worry monsters and talked to a friend. We find Molly inspiring!

Here is a lesson artifact from a third-grade class. Students "dipped in" to write words with recently taught spelling patterns.

# NURTURING AND SUPPORTING INDEPENDENT PRACTICE

## BRAVE MOLLY BY BROOKE BOYNTON-HUGHES (2019)

In the inquiry lesson and modeled/guided lesson, students were supported in uncovering and explaining ideas about characters. Moving from in-the-moment jots to more reflective thinking is a critical yet challenging skill. This lesson intends to support students in doing this work with greater independence.

- **Review** what the students remember about *Brave Molly*. Use the cover to spur recollections about recent work.

- **State** that readers often think about characters and try to uncover bigger ideas. Specifically, one way readers grow more in-depth theories about characters is by studying patterns.

- **Model** a process for doing this work using *Brave Molly*.

  ○ Reflect on recent reading and/or look back at your jots.

  ○ Think, *Do I see a pattern? Does this character often act or feel a certain way?*

  ○ Say or jot that discovery! HINT: This could sound a little like "[Name of character] often [pattern noticed]" or "[Name of character] is the kind of person who [new, big idea]."

- **Encourage** students to try the same with another recently read text.

- **Remind** students that in-the-moment jots can *always* be used to identify patterns and develop theories and claims. Doing so helps students grow more sophisticated ideas. It also helps them better understand the texts they read.

- **Invite** students to try similar work as they read narrative texts.

- **Observe** students and provide feedback as they try this work in the coming days and weeks.

- **Celebrate** when you see students practicing this important work.

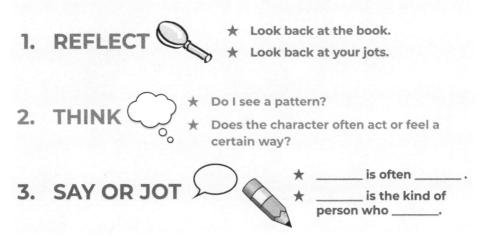

## Readers uncover ideas by studying patterns.

**1. REFLECT**
- ★ Look back at the book.
- ★ Look back at your jots.

**2. THINK**
- ★ Do I see a pattern?
- ★ Does the character often act or feel a certain way?

**3. SAY OR JOT**
- ★ _____ is often _____ .
- ★ _____ is the kind of person who _____ .

This chart was co-created by a fourth-grade class during a virtually facilitated lesson.

## ✔ Check-Up

This work is easily replicated in all kinds of texts—whether they are wordless texts, picture books, early chapter books, or novels. While students work, briefly meet with learners and:

- Ask them to orally share their ideas about the characters in the books they are reading.

- Encourage them to locate parts of the book that support this thinking or share previous jots that do the same.

- Mentor them, wherever they are along this continuum, to develop thinking that is just a bit more nuanced, precise, and supported than what they originally shared.

You could also flip through recent student notebook entries and use any noticing discovered though this quick, informal assessment to help inform decisions about next steps that are instructionally sound and personally relevant. You are welcome to use the provided record-keeping templates found on the companion website (resources.corwin.com/mttm) to keep track of your teaching and students' progress.

## ? What Else?

Other lesson ideas include:

- Developing and revising ideas around lesson or theme.

- Proving ideas—grounding theories in what the text says and shows.

- Pondering real-world significance of texts.

- Considering "text takeaways" that feel personally relevant and meaningful.

 In *Disrupting Thinking*, Beers and Probst (2017) talk about "BHH thinking": book, head, and heart comprehension. Very often in school, there is an overemphasis on book and head thinking, and less focus on heart thinking. It is critically important for learners to also consider the personal impact of texts read. How do you move beyond text-centric thinking? What impact has this had? What else could you try?

# NOTES

_____

_____

_____

_____

_____

_____

_____

_____

_____

_____

_____

_____

_____

_____

_____

_____

_____

_____

_____

_____

_____

_____

_____

_____

_____

_____

_____

# Lesson Set Aligned to the Extending Stage

## Featured Text: *Sanjay's Super Team* by Sanjay Patel (2015)

### 📖 Text Pairings

- *A Movie in My Pillow / Una pelicula en mi almohada* by Jorge Argueta (2001), with art by Elizabeth Gómez
- *Inside Out and Back Again* by Thanhhà Lại (2011)
- *The Year of the Dog* by Grace Lin (2005)
- *The Art of Sanjay's Super Team* by Sanjay Patel (2015)
- *Other Words for Home* by Jasmine Warga (2019)
- *Sanjay's Super Team*: The Backstory, interview by Christopher J. Farley (2015) and video created by *The Wall Street Journal* (online resource)
- Select clips from *Never Have I Ever* created and directed by Mindy Kaling and Lang Fisher (2020) (online resource)

### WHAT?

This animated short film shares the daydream of a young boy. At the beginning, Sanjay is home sketching in his notebook while his dad is meditating. The dad wants Sanjay to join him. An initially reluctant Sanjay joins his dad and begins imagining Hindu gods as superheroes.

### WHY?

This beautifully animated short, loosely based on director Sanjay Patel's own life experiences, is quite moving. In just a few minutes, it touches on family, culture, and identity. The story focuses on the main character's feelings about his heritage and culture. The colorful imagery is stunning. Even without explicit narration or dialogue, the execution of the story is clear, captivating, and poignant.

### WHEN?

This visual storytelling is easily infused into any fiction, comprehension, or theme-centered reading unit. It also fits with storytelling, filmmaking, or narrative writing units. Of course, this text also aligns with memoir units.

**Content Connections**

- Art and STEM (Science, Technology, Engineering, and Mathematics): animation studies

- Social Studies: ancient civilizations, world history, immigration, culture and heritage studies

- Personal and Community Wellness: exploring and celebrating aspects of personal identities, sharing and celebrating family and cultural traditions, connecting with family and loved ones, nurturing personal interests, exploring the importance of imagination and the benefits of cultivating creativity, developing strategies for problem solving and compromising (in a way that feels comfortable for all involved parties)

# INVESTIGATING IDEAS THROUGH INQUIRY

*SANJAY'S SUPER TEAM* BY SANJAY PATEL (2015)

In this lesson, students explore how stories are told and understood, even without words. While students may have already spent time studying photographs, artwork, architecture, primary documents, wordless books, and other images, here the class delves into exploring a wordless video.

**Guiding Inquiries:** *How do creators tell stories without using words? How do creators make their audience understand and feel—without using words?*

- **View** the video. Afterward, briefly discuss the plot and characters. Then, pose the guiding inquiries.

- **Divide** into small groups: a "sound" study group, an "image" study group, and a "character" study group. Each group will focus on that *one* element during the next viewing. For instance, the sound group will focus specifically on the music, naming what they hear and contemplating the mood. The image group will focus on what they see and how those images make them feel. The character group will study the two characters, watching what they do, noticing how they interact, and then growing larger ideas about each character and their relationship.

- **Scrutinize** the video during a second viewing. Students are welcome to jot quick notes about what they see, hear, notice, and discover.

- **Investigate** these initial observations further, with groups meeting to discuss their discoveries and ideas. Encourage students to use precise vocabulary to describe what they saw, heard, noticed, understood, and felt as they viewed the film. What words would they use to describe the sounds? Images? Characters? And how would they describe their reactions as viewers?

- **Summarize** small-group conversations in a whole-class discussion. Invite volunteers from each group to share their observations and subsequent discoveries. Use these questions to focus student reflections:

  ○ In what ways does sound help tell a story (and contribute to a viewer's understanding and response)?

  ○ How do specific images help tell a story (and enable an audience to understand and respond)?

  ○ How does an audience learn about and understand the characters—even without words?

Discuss how creators combine these elements to tell a story without words and to make the audience react and feel.

## ✔ Check-Up

Observe and listen in as students collaborate and share ideas with their peers. Jot anecdotal notes on participation and content understanding. Nurture observed areas of readiness during future instruction. You may decide to use one of the informal assessment tools found on the companion website (resources.corwin.com/mttm).

## ❓ What Else?

You might instead have students focus on lessons learned and themes portrayed. For example, the inquiry posed could be:

- How do viewers grow ideas about themes when viewing multimedia texts?

- What lessons and takeaways were uncovered for you as you watched *Sanjay's Super Team*? How did you come to these understandings?

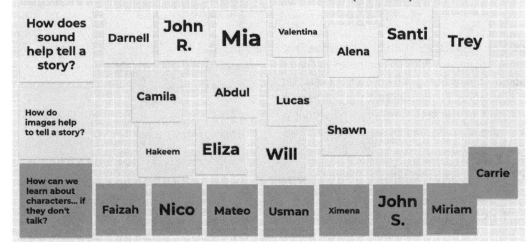

# How do creators tell stories without using words?

## How do creators make their audience understand (and feel) without words?

| How does sound help tell a story? | Darnell | John R. | Mia | Valentina | | Santi | Trey |
| | | | | Alena | | |
| How do images help to tell a story? | Camila | Abdul | Lucas | | | |
| | Hakeem | Eliza | Will | Shawn | | |
| How can we learn about characters... if they don't talk? | Faizah | Nico | Mateo | Usman | Ximena | John S. | Miriam | Carrie |

During this inquiry, students investigated ideas through focused, small-group exploration.

# BUILDING VISION VIA MODELED AND GUIDED PRACTICE

### *SANJAY'S SUPER TEAM* BY SANJAY PATEL (2015)

In this interactive writing experience, the class zooms in and co-composes a piece about character conflicts and character relationships. Remember that the teacher will do most of the actual writing, and students will "dip in" to do specifically targeted pieces of the writing.

- **Recall** previous experience(s) with *Sanjay's Super Team*.

- **View** the film again. This time, ask the class to zoom in on the relationship between Sanjay and his father, noticing first impressions, how the relationship is portrayed, and if/when/how the relationship changes. Remind students that they are welcome to take notes if they feel it will be helpful.

- **Rehearse** for class composing by inviting students to turn and talk with a partner, sharing their ideas and, wherever possible, referencing specific parts of the video. (*Language Levers* may support this thinking and conversation.)

- **Elicit** students' ideas. Orally plan the entry you will compose together. For example, the first sentence could be *Sanjay and his father have a _____ relationship.* Begin transcribing student ideas.

- **Invite** select students to "dip in" and do specific, targeted parts of the class writing. You might choose to have the students add "reader analysis" lingo (see *Language Levers*).

- **Reread** the class-composed piece, reiterating the process used to synthesize and formulate these ideas.

- **Remind** students that they can do this same work whenever they choose to write about character relationships, no matter what medium or format the text is in.

 **Language Levers**

*In the beginning . . .*

*At first . . .*

*This was shown when . . .*

*. . . because . . .*

*The film portrayed . . .*

*I noticed that . . .*

*The filmmakers made the decision to . . .*

*At one point in the film, . . .*

*Later . . .*

*By the end . . .*

*Their relationship . . .*

**NOTE:** Where and when appropriate, post stems in more than one language. You may also decide to co-create stems with students during the lesson.

 **Check-Up**

Informally assess student participation and understanding. Jot anecdotal notes. You may find it helpful to reference the informal assessment tools provided on the companion website (resources.corwin.com/mttm). Then, in future sessions, provide explicit instruction aligned to these observations.

**?** **What Else?**

Here are other ideas for where students could "dip in" and do portions of the writing:

- Students could write words with recently taught spelling patterns, perhaps related to inflected endings, recently studied prefixes, recently studied word parts and roots, or commonly confused words.

- Students could add in words and punctuation related to recently taught grammar concepts, such as pronouns in different cases (subjective, objective, and possessive), relative pronouns and relative adverbs, or coordinating and subordinating conjunctions (and related commas).

Instead of focusing this experience on character relationships, you could choose to compose a class piece related to mood and tone, conflict, theme, or imagery.

# NURTURING AND SUPPORTING
# INDEPENDENT PRACTICE

*SANJAY'S SUPER TEAM* BY SANJAY PATEL (2015)

A common goal of partner and book club conversations is to chat at length about one topic instead of repeatedly moving on and "grazing" across topics. This lesson supports students in becoming literate conversationalists. Here, students prepare for rich discussion by identifying moments of significance.

- **Recall** previous experience(s) with *Sanjay's Super Team*. Celebrate prior conversational successes and also normalize the common conundrum of text-aligned conversations stalling out.

- **State** that classroom conversationalists can prepare for discussion by noticing moments of significance when they read/view a text and then talking about these parts.

- **Model** viewing the featured text through the lens of significant moments. You might use this process:
  - View or read a text. Stop when you find yourself having a strong feeling or reaction.
  - Reflect: Why is this moment significant?
  - Jot a few thoughts about this moment. TIP: Prioritize time to discuss these moments with partners and clubs.

- **Encourage** students to try. Before restarting the film, ask the students to signal (e.g., with a snap or clap) when they feel there is a significant moment. Start viewing the film. Whenever students signal, pause the video and provide a few moments for students to efficiently jot a few notes.

- **Invite** a volunteer to "nominate" a significant moment. Then, provide time for students to chat in partnerships or small

groups to share their interpretations of, reactions to, and wonders about this same moment.

- **Observe** these conversations and informally jot notes about what you see students doing and trying.

- **Celebrate** what you observed. Ask students to share how it felt to discuss these moments with peers. Co-create a chart listing the processes used.

- **Extend** the experience by regularly practicing using significant moments as entry points for literate conversation, no matter *what* text has recently been viewed or read.

## ✓ Check-Up

Building (student-driven) literate conversation is a meaningful goal, so it makes sense to remind yourself to hold back when you see a bit of productive struggle. Instead, watch as students navigate awkward lulls or conversational missteps. Over the next few days:

- Jot what you see and hear during student conversations.

- Use observations to drive follow-up instruction and coaching.

## ❓ What Else?

Instead of (or in addition to) facilitating a whole-class learning experience, you might:

- Decide to teach this lesson to a small group of learners who you feel are ready to learn a new conversational move to enrich their partner and book club conversations.

- Highlight and celebrate student efforts and progress by periodically "fishbowling" peer conversations: A few students model conversation while other peers observe and share what they notice.

No matter how or when you choose to support this conversational work, remember to focus on student practice. "Teacher talk time" should be minimal.

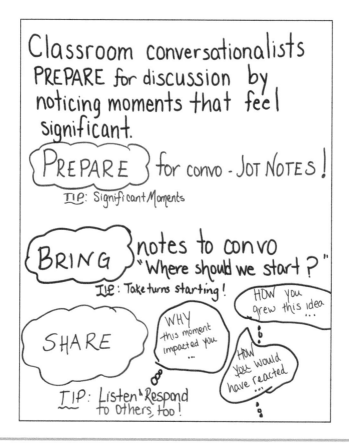

This chart was created with a sixth-grade class as they worked on building conversational repertoires.

# STRETCH UP AND BACK SUGGESTIONS: CONVERSATIONAL SKILLS

This chapter spotlights suggestions for how teachers can cultivate strong classroom conversation using almost any book. In *Read, Talk, Write*, Laura Robb (2016) shares that language-rich conversation needs to be explicitly taught and modeled. I especially appreciate Robb's advice to avoid asking narrow questions and editorializing questions. She sagely offers the following: "When students compose their own questions, they are motivated to talk about them, leading to greater independence with reading and discussion" (p. 12). The end goal of teaching *conversational skills* is that students learn to trust one another and develop the skills necessary to orchestrate conversation without teachers present.

The following concepts and skills can be taught in *any* subject. When instruction is grounded in the rich context of a text (wordless or not), learning about conversation feels authentic and natural instead of forced.

- Attentive and respectful body language of speakers and listeners
- Sharing complete thoughts
- Drawing on full linguistic repertoires while speaking
- Using language that fits the type of conversation (casual or more formal language)
- Ways to start a conversation
- Listening and saying back what someone shared
- Listening and showing if you agree or disagree (without interrupting or using your voice)
- Listening and sharing why you agree with what someone just shared
- Listening and respectfully sharing why you disagree with what someone just shared
- Listening and asking a follow-up question related to what someone said
- Listening and adding on to what someone just said
- Methods for encouraging others to add their ideas to a conversation

- What to try when a conversation stalls out

- What to try when a conversation gets off track

- What to do when the conversation is spiraling instead of deepening

- What to do when only one perspective is being considered

 Which of these conversational skills make the most sense for current classroom learners? Do different class members have different conversational goals? How and when could you responsively work toward personalized goals?

# CHAPTER 4

· · · · · · · · · · · · · · · · · · · · · · · · · · · · · · · · · · · · · · · · · · · · · · · ·

# Graphic Texts

"The reading of the comic book is an act of both aesthetic perception and intellectual pursuit" (Eisner, 2008, p. 2).

Graphic texts, like wordless texts, are a *format* that spans all genres. Because of this, graphically formatted texts can be infused into any unit of study. This medium also represents a format that students almost universally find incredibly intriguing and engaging!

Graphic *novels* are narrative texts written in a style *similar to* a comic book. Although there are marked differences, in both formats the pictures and words work together synergistically. Some of these novels spotlight adventure or high fantasy. While there are numerous laugh-out-loud-funny options, others are realistic, touching, and thought-provoking. Some previously reticent readers enjoy both contemporary stories and retellings of classics in a graphic format. In addition, there are a growing number of informational graphic texts. These share captivating accounts of historical events and time periods and the fascinating life stories of noteworthy individuals. Complex nonfiction topics garner greater interest when translated into a graphic format. This multitasking medium offers amplified comprehension of a wide range of topics. Moreover, many popular graphic novels and texts are now available in multiple languages.

Graphic texts present teachers with a wide range of opportunities. Despite what some may believe, graphic novels are not "dessert" books. These misconceptions are wholly unwarranted. The number of high-quality graphic texts has ballooned in recent years! The benefits are clear: There's no doubt that visual literacy (which is a fundamental component of graphic texts) is becoming increasingly essential in modern-day society. Additionally, the visual support within graphic texts makes this medium accessible *and* enticing. This structure frequently serves as a conduit between weighty topics and far-reaching relatability. Without question, graphic texts are a means to not only engage students, but also challenge them!

Throughout this chapter, you will find a variety of lessons to spark classroom learning. For instance, inquiry opportunities center on investigating structural elements. Modeled and guided learning experiences are implemented using interactive writing. This is an ideal structure to foster application of word knowledge and conventions. Finally, the suggestions for supporting and nurturing independent practice center on peer conversation and collegial support. Don't be turned off by the perceived length of a graphic text. Although they often have more pages than a typical picture book, the reading of graphic texts is quite quick. I am confident that as you delve into this fascinating medium, you will discover the multitasking capabilities of graphically formatted texts.

**NOTE:** Remember to always first enjoy featured texts as a community of readers. Then, *revisit* the text, repurposing it as a mentor text for any number of instructional priorities and goals.

# Lesson Set Aligned to the Emerging Stage

## Featured Text: *Little Robot* by Ben Hatke (2015)

 **Text Pairings**

- *Peter and Ernesto: The Lost Sloths* by Graham Annable (2019)
- *The Flying Beaver Brothers* (series) by Maxwell Eaton III (2012)
- *The Great Pet Escape* by Victoria Jamieson (2016)
- *The Shark King* by R. Kikuo Johnson (2012)
- *Owly* (series) by Andy Runton (2004)
- *Binky the Space Cat* (series) by Ashley Spires (2009)
- *Sleepless Knight* by James Sturm, Andrew Arnold, and Alexis Frederick-Frost (2015)
- *Hamster and Cheese* by Colleen A. F. Venable and Stephanie Yu (2010)

### WHAT?

A young girl with an adventurous spirit finds a box with a robot inside. Together, they explore, and unsurprisingly, a friendship forms. When a factory sends another robot to retrieve her new friend, the young girl devises a plan so they can stay together. The little guys win!

### WHY?

This sweet tale of tinkering and friendship is a crowd-pleaser. It is told with few words, making it an ideal graphic text choice for emerging readers. The female protagonist has plenty of courage and know-how. She is creative, brave, tech-savvy, and a true friend. Ben Hatke is an amazing author, and this text, geared for a younger audience, includes all of the adventure and spirit of his other books while extending accessibility.

### WHEN?

This text fits easily into a launch unit or any narrative reading or writing unit, including character study. Although it is a lovable fantasy story at heart, the story elements inherent in *all* narrative tales are clearly outlined. Even with so few words, the characters and plot are quite well developed. Many primary writers use a combination of sketches, labels, and words to tell their stories, so even if you are not in a graphic text writing unit, the format still makes this a fabulous mentor text.

 **Content Connections**

Technology: tools, making, design cycle

Personal and Community Wellness: friendship, compassion, creativity, imagination, independence, problem solving, perseverance

# INVESTIGATING IDEAS THROUGH INQUIRY

*LITTLE ROBOT* BY BEN HATKE (2015)

In this inquiry, learners discover more about the structure of graphic texts and how readers access these texts.

**Guiding Inquiry:** *How do we read a graphic novel?*

- **Engage** learners by sharing the covers of a few graphic texts you have in the classroom, including the cover of *Little Robot*.

- **Encourage** the class to "spy" on you as you reread a bit of *Little Robot*, and then report back what they saw you do. Remind students to watch what your hands do and what your eyes do as you read. Model reading . . . playfully exaggerating how you use your finger to track the sequence of the frames and how you use your eyes to "read" the images and any words.

- **Invite** the students to turn and talk with a partner, sharing what they saw you do. (*Language Levers* may support students as they speak and listen.)

- **Ask** the "spies" to submit their report, sharing what they observed. Make a quick chart to list out those reading behaviors.

- **Summarize** findings and remind students that your mind was also working as you read. Share what your mind was doing to make sense of the text and add this to the class list.

---

 **Language Levers**

As always, you may choose to post pre-created stems or eavesdrop on students as they speak, listening to what words they use and posting student-generated stems.

- *I noticed . . .*
- *I saw you . . .*
- *Your eyes . . .*
- *Your hands/finger . . .*

---

After investigating and discovering how to access a graphically formatted text, first-grade "spies" enjoyed trying it out for themselves.

## ✔ Check-Up

During this inquiry experience, no formal assessment is needed. Observe students, gauge readiness, and then prepare follow-up instruction:

- Consider building on this inquiry by explicitly teaching these "reader behaviors" during whole-class lessons.

- Once you have explicitly taught these processes, informally check for transfer when you meet one-to-one with classroom readers. Begin by asking them to "act out" (demonstrate) how they are reading the text. Then, either narrate what you see or ask the students the follow-up question, "What did you just do?" Name the impact of their actions so students see a connection between their actions, engagement, and comprehension. (Jot observational notes using the Anecdotal Record-Keeping Template available at resources.corwin.com/mttm.)

## ? What Else?

You might choose to:

- Extend the inquiry by inviting small groups of students to "test the theories" you listed when you modeled reading the graphic text. Provide each group with a graphic text. Ask students to take turns reading a small part of the book aloud to their group. Did they do what you modeled? Did they do anything else (with their hands, eyes, or minds)? End by returning to a whole-group setting and having students share out *what else* they did while reading a graphic text.

- Invite students to delve further into this inquiry, asking, "How is reading a graphic text the same as and different from reading a traditional text?" Volunteers can "act out" reading graphic texts *and* traditional texts. Class spies can continue to observe readers and report their findings. A side-by-side chart (e.g., T-chart or Venn diagram) could be created to summarize similarities and differences.

# BUILDING VISION VIA MODELED AND GUIDED PRACTICE

*LITTLE ROBOT* BY BEN HATKE (2015)

One purpose of jotting is to support students in becoming active readers. Often, teachers introduce jotting by providing students with sticky notes and asking them to put a blank one on a page where they had a strong reaction. Later, students use simple sketches, coding marks, or one to two words to represent their thinking on the sticky note. Eventually, they learn to use a "because" statement to say more. In this lesson, you will use interactive writing to provide a vision of how to lift the level of reading jots.

- **Recall** prior experience(s) with *Little Robot*. Model looking at the cover and sharing thoughts about the main character. This may sound something like "I think the main character likes to build and make things because she always carries a wrench" *or* "I think the main character is kind because she has her arm around her friend." Make a big deal about using the lingo of a reader and quickly jotting the idea you just said aloud on a sticky note.

- **Rehearse** for class writing by turning to another part of *Little Robot* (suggestion: pages 20–21) and reviewing the pages together. Ask students to consider what they are learning about the character on these pages. Students may signal preparedness to share with a thumbs-up.

- **Elicit** student ideas. If necessary, prompt volunteers to add on a "because" statement to explain their thoughts. Record student statements, ideally on large sticky notes.

- **Invite** class volunteers to add in specific letters, sounds, or words. For example, students may dip in to add consonant–vowel–consonant words like *sad* and *mad* or "reader lingo" words like *character*, *think*, and *because*.

- **Repeat** this process, creating two or three more sticky notes together.

Suggestions for *possible* pages to revisit include pages 34–35, 44–45, 74–75, and 114–115.

- **Reread** co-created sticky notes, polishing as necessary.

- **Summarize** the experience, reminding students that readers pause to think and jot as they read.

## ✔ Check-Up

Use informal observations from this lesson to plan follow-up instruction.

- After this skill is explicitly taught, you could use a progression chart (like the one shown) to guide assessment.

- Students could also use a progression chart to reflect on the type of jotting they often do in reading, celebrate, and then set a "next step" goal as part of the progression. Over time, support students as they work toward this self-initiated goal.

## ? What Else?

You could choose to have students share the marker or keyboard for something other than reader lingo. Other "dip in" options include:

- The capital letter at the beginning of the sentence and the punctuation at the end of the sentence.

- Any high-frequency words that are included in the sentence being jotted.

- Any included words with taught letters, sounds, or spelling patterns.

- Any emphasized part of speech (for example, if the class is delving into adjectives, the students can come up to write in the adjective they are using to describe the main character).

The second graders who co-created this sticky note progression chart used it for self-assessment and goal setting.

# NURTURING AND SUPPORTING INDEPENDENT PRACTICE

*LITTLE ROBOT* BY BEN HATKE (2015)

The shared inquiry experience is a springboard for this lesson. Here, partners learn a new way to read together. They do this by using an image–word reading protocol.

- **Recall** prior experience(s) with *Little Robot*.

- **State** that partners support one another as they read. One way they do this is by playing the image–word game, in which partners read together, using images *and* words to build understanding of a text. (Essentially, Partner A "reads" the images on a page. Partner B then reads the words on the page.)

- **Model** this partner reading protocol using *Little Robot*. If there are not any other adults in the room, a student can act as your partner. (Offer to briefly rehearse with the student ahead of time.) As you model this "game" for the class, be sure to explicitly show how you take turns looking at the images on the page, naming what you see, *and then* reading the words.

- **Encourage** observing students to share what they noticed. Affirm observations.

- **Remind** students that they can play this game with a partner whenever they are reading a book with pictures and words. When they do so, their comprehension and enjoyment increases.

- **Invite** student partnerships to try the protocol with one of the books they are reading (it can be a graphic text or any text with both pictures and words). Coach them as students work together.

- **Celebrate** partner reading success.

 **Check-Up**

The informal coaching you do as students practice this protocol will provide you with

Students enjoy playing partner games as they read together.

the information you need to assess students' ability to use this method of partner reading.

- You might need to mentor students as they learn to figure out who will start as Partner A and who will start as Partner B or how to remember to switch roles.

- If necessary, pull a small group of students to provide more scaffolded and explicit support.

- You may find the informal assessment tools available online (at resources. corwin.com/mttm) helpful as you observe students and track progress.

## ? What Else?

Many students enjoy reading with peers. I like to teach different partner reading protocols *s-l-o-w-l-y* across the year. There are many ways partners can read together. Just a few other partner protocols ("games") include these:

- Choral Reading (partners read together, in unison)

- Echo Reading (Partner A reads a page; Partner B echoes the page)

- Seesaw Reading (Partner A reads the left side; Partner B reads the right side)

- Read–Retell Reading (Partner A reads the page; Partner B reflects on and explains what just happened)

There are also fun partner reading protocols that highlight acting out the story, predicting, making connections, wondering while reading, talking about character feelings, and so on. If *readers* do it, it can be turned into a partner reading protocol.

You might also choose to share these partner games with caregivers. The games can be played outside of school as well.

# Lesson Set Aligned to the Developing Stage

## Featured Text: *Red Panda and Moon Bear* by Jarod Roselló (2019)

 **Text Pairings**

- *Giants Beware!* by Jorge Aguirre (2012), with art by Rafael Rosado

- *Dinosaurs in Space: Out of this World!* by Pranas T. Naujokaitis (2017)

- *Hilda and the Troll* by Luke Pearson (2015)

- *Sidekicks* by Dan Santat (2011)

- *The Cardboard Kingdom* by Chad Sell (2018)

- *Stargazing* by Jen Wang (2019)

### WHAT?

These sibling crime-fighters wear magical hoodies that help them defend their community. As surprising new mysteries pop up, this brother–sister duo need to use their imaginations to save the world.

### WHY?

This graphic text is so fun! The fantastical storyline draws readers in and keeps them captivated. Red Panda is passionate and brave. Her hoodie gives her the power of 12 fully grown red pandas. Moon Bear is a bit more reserved, but equally committed to fighting villains. Together, they make quite the team. The artwork on each page is just as bright and engaging as the characters. Spanish is interwoven throughout the text, and a full Spanish translation of this book is also available (*Panda roja y oso lunar* by Jarod Roselló, 2020).

### WHEN?

This text fits easily into any narrative reading or writing unit, including character study. It works *particularly* well with fantasy units. Partners and book clubs will enjoy discussing the characters and fantastical plot.

Writers of fantasy fiction and graphic authors will find plentiful points of inspiration in this text.

 **Content Connections**

Personal and Community Wellness: facing fears, creative problem solving, teamwork, collaboration, being an ally, advocating for others, contributing to building and/or sustaining a safe and healthy community

# INVESTIGATING IDEAS THROUGH INQUIRY

*RED PANDA AND MOON BEAR* BY JAROD ROSELLÓ (2019)

Many students are fans of graphic texts. They may not immediately realize that the term *graphic text* refers to a *format* and not a *genre*. Here, students work to uncover more about one type of graphic text—the graphic novel. To prepare, curate a small collection of texts. Ideally, this stack will include informational texts, graphic novels, comic books, picture books, and traditional chapter books.

**Guiding Inquiry:** *What makes a graphic novel a graphic novel?*

- **Invite** partners, triads, or small groups to quickly caucus, responding to the guiding question.

- **Discuss** and list some initial ideas. Keep this brief.

- **View** a short video—like the Barnes & Noble (2018)–sponsored video *Graphic*

*Novels vs. Comic Books* with Aaron Reynolds, which can be found on YouTube—to clarify the difference between a comic book and a graphic novel. Add gained insights to the class chart. (This step is *optional*).

- **Investigate.** Provide a few minutes for small groups of students to explore the texts you curated with the goal of clarifying and deepening their understanding of what makes a graphic novel a graphic novel. As students collaborate, listen in on their conversations. Challenge and nudge student thinking so it becomes even more nuanced and precise.

- **Discuss** newly gained understandings as a class.

- **Synthesize** learning by collaboratively crafting a class definition for the term *graphic novel*.

Instead of composing a traditional definition, a second-grade class created this chart to show off what they discovered during this inquiry.

## ✓ Check-Up

Observe and listen in as students work collaboratively. Coach students. Use strategic questioning to get student investigators to think more, say more, and develop their thinking further. You might look to see:

- Are students able to correctly identify genres and formats?
- Can students explain why a text is (or is not) a graphic novel?
- Do students know common features of graphic novels?

## ? What Else?

You could choose to have small groups of students each create their own definition of a graphic novel. In the closing, students could share and compare their definitions and then collaborate to co-create a class definition of the term *graphic novel*.

You could also choose to end by revisiting the curated stack of texts and having students identify each as an example or a non-example of a graphic novel—justifying their thinking by using gained knowledge to explain their answer.

# BUILDING VISION VIA MODELED AND GUIDED PRACTICE

*RED PANDA AND MOON BEAR* BY JAROD ROSELLÓ (2019)

In this interactive writing experience, the teacher uses student input to compose a reflection about *Red Panda and Moon Bear*. The class contemplates which character they prefer and then explains this opinion. Students dip in to do small, targeted pieces of the writing.

- **Recall** precious reading experience(s) with *Red Panda and Moon Bear*. Use the cover to activate thinking about the book's plot *and* the two main characters. Ask the class which character they prefer.

- **Rehearse** for writing by encouraging students to turn and talk, sharing and supporting their ideas. Perhaps Partner A shares which character they prefer and why, and then Partner B shares if they agree or disagree and why. Come back together and take a class vote.

- **Elicit** student ideas as you use interactive writing to craft a "long and strong" entry. The first sentence could be something like this: *We read* Red Panda and Moon Bear *by Jarod Roselló and decided that we prefer [character's name]*. Write what students share.

- **Invite** students to dip in for *some* of the actual writing. For example, if you want to emphasize how readers include evidence in their entries, you might have students come up to add in the "push prompts" (like those listed in *Language Levers*) that help them say more about their ideas from a text.

- **Reread** the co-created piece, polishing where needed.

- **Summarize** the work done and invite students to use this same process whenever they write their own long and strong reflective entries about what they have recently read.

 **Language Levers**

Depending on class composition, you may decide to post stems in more than one language.

- *I prefer Red Panda/Moon Bear because . . .*
- *What I really liked about Red Panda/Moon Bear was . . .*
- *Another example of this was when . . .*
- *Also, I remember when . . .*
- *This shows . . .*
- *This is why . . .*

## ✔ Check-Up

Interactive writing is a great way to informally determine what students are ready to do on their own and where they may need more support. Use observations from this lesson to decide on the next steps for the class and/or small groups of learners.

- You may choose to follow up (in future reading or writing sessions) by teaching a lesson on how to gather and craft ideas for a long and strong reflective entry on recent reading.

- Over time, continue to coach students as they work on reflective entries, nurturing next steps in lifting the level of thinking in these entries.

## ❔ What Else?

Interactive writing is inherently flexible. You could choose to invite students to share the marker or keyboard for something other than push prompts. Use this opportunity to model and scaffold transfer of any current classroom priority. For example:

- IF students are not yet applying what they learned about a taught sound, spelling pattern, or word part, THEN you could invite them to come up and write the words with those target word features.

- IF students could use support in spelling high-frequency words correctly in their writing, THEN you might call them up for these words.

- IF students mix up commonly confused words, THEN they can come up and correctly spell those target words.

- IF the class is learning about a specific grammar concept (comma usage, subject–verb agreement, conjunctions, possessive pronouns, etc.), THEN invite students to write those specific words.

You might decide to use interactive writing to focus on writing a different kind of reflective entry, perhaps one that focuses on sharing and supporting an opinion about the book (like a mini-review), reflecting on a favorite part, identifying and explaining a lesson, or comparing characters across texts.

This reading notebook entry was created by a third-grade student after participating in the class interactive writing experience. It shares the student's ideas on another graphic text.

# NURTURING AND SUPPORTING INDEPENDENT PRACTICE

*RED PANDA AND MOON BEAR* BY JAROD ROSELLÓ (2019)

Talking is great rehearsal for writing—including writing about reading. Partners can support each other in developing ideas about what they read. The focus of this lesson is teaching peer "coaches" phrases they can use when they meet with a reading partner. These questions and prompts encourage partners to say more about their ideas.

> **NOTE:** *If you co-teach or there is another adult in the room, you can model this work with a colleague. If not (or even better!), you can model this kind of conversation with a student. You may want to quickly rehearse with this student before modeling in front of the class.*

- **Recall** prior learning experience(s) with *Red Panda and Moon Bear*.

- **State** that peers can lean on one another. For instance, readers can support their partners by nudging them to say more.

- **Model** a partner conversation where the partner's job is to be a coach. Focus the discussion on a previously shared portion of *Red Panda and Moon Bear*. Ask observing students to watch and listen for the "moves" used by the coaching partner that got the reader to think more, say more, and return to the text to support their ideas. (TIP: As you model, use some of the questions listed in the *Language Levers* chart.)

- **Encourage** the student observers to share what they saw and heard that helped the reader reflect and think. List those conversational moves on a chart.

- **Remind** students that they can always support one another—no teacher necessary! One way to do this is to use questions and prompts (like those modeled) to support a partner as they think through ideas.

- **Invite** students to meet with their reading partners and engage in literary conversations. Move around the room, listening in and supporting partnerships. Expect to model strategies related to staying on track and ways of saying more.

- **Reflect** on the experience as a class. Ask students to share what it felt like to be in the role of reader—and what it felt like to be in the role of coach.

- **Celebrate** ongoing partner work.

 **Check-Up**

Informal observing and anecdotal notes make perfect sense here. Utilize the Conversation and Collaboration Observational Checklist and/or Anecdotal Record-Keeping Template (available online at resources.corwin.com/mttm) to bring efficiency to this work.

**?** **What Else?**

There are so many different ways partners can coach one another. The provided questions may be used to jump-start conversation or delve deeper into initially shared ideas. They are purposefully broad (so that they fit into a wide range of conversations). Begin by introducing a *few* conversational moves. Then, work to slowly expand students' conversational repertoires. Remember that the goal is not to have students use *this* exact lingo, but instead for students to sound like themselves.

**Language Levers for Partner Conversation**

| IDENTIFICATION QUESTIONS | ANALYZING QUESTIONS | BRAINSTORMING QUESTIONS |
|---|---|---|
| • What have you been thinking about?<br><br>• What jots did you want to talk about today?<br><br>• Is there an idea you want to start with?<br><br>• At what point did you notice . . . ?<br><br>• Where in the book did you realize . . . ? | • How did you get that idea?<br><br>• Can you tell me more about . . . ?<br><br>• Is there anywhere else where . . . ?<br><br>• Is this also shown in another part?<br><br>• Why do you think this is important?<br><br>• Is this always true?<br><br>• Why do you think the author . . . ?<br><br>• Why do you think the character . . . ?<br><br>• Are there any other possibilities? | • How do you plan to explain . . . ?<br><br>• What are some ways you could show that/prove that?<br><br>• How would that sound if you were writing this down?<br><br>• Which pages might you refer back to in order to prove this idea? |

# Lesson Set Aligned to the Extending Stage

## Featured Text: *New Kid* by Jerry Craft (2019)

### 📖 Text Pairings

- *Be Prepared* by Vera Brosgol (2018)
- *Class Act* by Jerry Craft (2020) (sequel to *New Kid*)
- *Real Friends* and *Best Friends* by Shannon Hale (2017, 2019)
- *Sunny Rolls the Dice* by Jennifer L. Holm (2019), with art by Matthew Holm
- *When Stars Are Scattered* by Victoria Jamieson and Omar Mohamed (2020)
- *Hey, Kiddo* by Jarrett Krosoczka (2018)
- *New Kid With Jerry Craft* created and uploaded by #HarperKids (HarperCollins Publishers, 2021) (online resource)
- *The Writer's Block: An Interview With Jerry Craft* by Kevin Springer (2019) (online resource)
- *Jerry Craft Breaks Barriers With Historic 2020 Newbery Win* by Kara Yorio (2020) (online resource)

### WHAT?

This award-winning graphic novel follows seventh grader Jordan Banks as he transitions to life at a private, mostly white middle school. As a student who is biracial and travels to school from a different community, Jordan regularly encounters microaggressions. Throughout the book, Jordan tries to adjust to being the new kid at a new school and stay connected to his home community.

### WHY?

Jordan's story is both unique and relatable. Readers empathize with the awkwardness and turbulence of middle school. Throughout the text, Jerry Craft brilliantly balances and weaves together heavier moments with lighter moments. Readers learn and grow alongside Jordan as he encounters family, peer, and personal conflicts. This read-again-and-again text is not only thought- and discussion-provoking; it's also heartwarming and funny! This graphic text is sure to have wide appeal with middle-grade readers.

**WHEN?**

*New Kid* fits into narrative units, fiction units, character units, social justice units, and graphic text units focused on both reading and writing. It begs to become a multitasking mentor text for all aspects of literacy teaching and learning.

 ## Content Connections

Art: graphic text processes and craft—including, but not limited to, penciling, inking, coloring, and lettering

Personal and Community Wellness: exploring different aspects of one's identity, nurturing creative passions, family relationships, fitting in, navigating peer relationships, dealing with bullies, recognizing and disrupting existing power dynamics, identifying and responding to microaggressions

> **NOTE:** I encourage students and classes to enjoy this whole book. However, because this is a longer text, the forthcoming lessons do not require that students have read the whole book. All of these lessons can be carried out after providing a short introduction to the book and reading the first few pages together.

# INVESTIGATING IDEAS THROUGH INQUIRY

## *NEW KID* BY JERRY CRAFT (2019)

If students are going to be reading graphic texts and/or writing using a graphic format, they need to know how to talk the talk. By now, students likely know the basics of this medium, so this inquiry is purposefully designed to build a more comprehensive understanding of graphic texts. Specifically, it explores the features (and aligned vocabulary) associated with graphically formatted texts. To prepare for this inquiry, curate a small set of graphic texts from any genre.

**Guiding Inquiry:** *What else can we discover about the format and lingo of graphic texts?*

- **Discuss** graphic texts: general opinions, favorite titles, and basic information about the format. Share that today the class will broaden their existing expertise.

- **Organize** inquiry groups. Set out a few graphic texts (like *New Kid*). Ask students to explore features and use sticky notes to mark up a text—annotating the selected text with the names of the different features and structural elements they see.

- **Investigate** unknowns. If students are unsure of how to label what they see, they can look it up!

- **Invite** groups to share highlights of their inquiry work, using the annotated text to heighten peers' understandings.

- **Summarize** takeaways. Remind students to use learned lingo as frequently as possible—so that it begins to become part of their vocabulary.

> **NOTE:** Do your own research before beginning. A few foundational terms include *panel*, *frame*, *tier*, *splash*, *spread*, *gutter*, *bleed*, *foreground*, *midground*, *background*, *speech balloon*, *thought bubbles*, *captions*, *emanate*, and *lettering*.

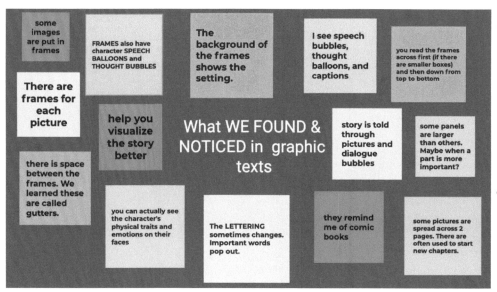

Image credit: Katie McGrath

Students in this middle school class practiced using newly discovered lingo as they identified and described features of graphic texts.

## ✔ Check-Up

- Observe students as they collaborate. Jot anecdotal notes. The online companion contains several different informal assessment tools you may find useful (resources.corwin.com/mttm).

- You could also gauge student use of discovered terms (in conversation and jotting) in the days and weeks following this mini-inquiry.

## ? What Else?

If this book has previously been read aloud or shared with students, you might instead decide to do an inquiry around the various microaggressions in this text and then extend the idea of microaggressions beyond *New Kid*. Amplify learning by also investigating microaggressions that exist in other texts and/or in the surrounding world. Sara Ahmed (2018) includes a poem analysis lesson around microaggressions in her book, *Being the Change: Lessons and Strategies to Teach Social Comprehension*. This lesson may be helpful as either an introduction to or a follow-up to this social comprehension inquiry.

# BUILDING VISION VIA MODELED AND GUIDED PRACTICE

## *NEW KID* BY JERRY CRAFT (2019)

Examining the "moves" of a writer is beneficial on many levels. In this interactive writing experience, the class reads with their writer's eyes, identifying craft moves and contemplating their impact. Format-specific vocabulary continues to be prominently featured.

TIP: Before beginning, post the lingo students discovered during the class inquiry. Encourage use of this lingo throughout the lesson.

- **Recall** previous inquiry work with *New Kid* and use the cover to spark conversation about the text. Then, read aloud the first two pages of the text (pages 2–3). If possible, project these pages using a document camera.

- **Rehearse** for writing by asking the students to consider the creator's decisions. For example, ask them, "What did Jerry Craft do on these first two pages? What did you learn, even from just two pages? How did his decisions impact and/or support you as a reader?" Provide a few moments for students to mull this over (or a few minutes for them to quickly and informally jot in their notebooks). Ask volunteers to share ideas.

- **Elicit** student input, using shared ideas to compose a class piece that begins with a sentence that's something like "The first two pages of *New Kid* say so much" or "Jerry Craft made thoughtful and important decisions about how to start *New Kid*." As students share input, encourage them to use the lingo of graphic novels as they explain their noticings and understandings.

- **Invite** students to share the writing responsibility and dip in for small pieces of the actual writing. Specifically, student volunteers could add in graphic format terms.

- **Reread** the class piece, improving and polishing as needed.

- **Summarize** this experience, reminding students to think about the decisions an author makes from the perspectives of both a reader and a writer. Also, remind students to do their best to "talk the talk" of those who read and write graphic texts.

> ### The first few pages of *New Kid* by Jerry Craft piqued our interest.
>
> From the first **caption**, we were hooked! We wondered, *Why does Jordan want to be Batman? Why does he need a jet? What is he trying to get away from?* Right away, in the first few **panels**, we were introduced to three of the main characters, Jordan and his parents. In each **frame**, the included **speech bubbles** helped us get to not only know the characters, but also begin to understand the relationships between Jordan, Mom, and Dad. We liked that Jordan talks like a normal kid. The dialogue sounds real. His mom reminded many of us of people in our lives- when she ran to go get the camera, it was hysterical! In this first **spread**, we also were introduced to two of the main problems in the book. One problem is around Jordan and which school he will go to and the other is around Jordan and his art. It is AMAZING to us that Jerry Craft was able to share so much on these first few pages. We can't wait to read more!

Digital interactive writing works just as well! Here, student volunteers in a sixth-grade class added the highlighted and bolded words to the class writing.

**Our reactions to pages 1-3 of *New Kid***     ***Breakout Room 2***

What did you learn—even from just two pages?
How did his decisions impact and/or support you as a reader?

Jerry Craft made some interesting decisions of how to start *New Kid*. On the first spread to introduce Chapter 1 he drew a picture of Jordan falling. He is falling away from his sketches or drawings. That's probably important to the story.

On pages 2 and 3 we see many frames and panels. The speech bubbles of Jordan's mom and dad show that they have different views on where he should go to school. His mom thinks a fancy school is better, but his dad isn't so sure. The drawings of Jordan (in the foreground) show he is sad about the idea of going to that school (panel 2) and frustrated that his parents are talking about this (frame 2). When Jerry Craft includes the drawings and speech bubbles, it lets us know the beliefs and thoughts of some of the important characters.

---

The teacher in this seventh-grade class felt the students were prepared to do this work with greater independence. She asked students to respond to the prompt in small groups, infusing graphic text lingo as they wrote collaboratively.

### ✔ Check-Up

You may decide to observe and informally note student participation during this lesson. You may also gauge transfer by:

- Listening in on student conversations and informally assessing their dialogue (around author craft and/or inclusion of graphic text lingo).

- Mining student reading notebooks and informally assessing their entries (thinking around author craft and/or inclusion of graphic text lingo).

- Checking out any writing students are doing using a graphic format (or any genre/format) and discussing their process and the "why" behind the decisions they made as an author.

### ? What Else?

Remember that each text offers limitless options. To provide vision for writing in a graphic format, retell a recent class happening—and then write it using a graphic format. After brainstorming together, students can share ideas that you can quickly sketch and jot. Enhance interaction by inviting students to add specific details to the text. For instance, you may ask volunteers to add the words within the speech balloons and thought bubbles or ask them to add specific details to the visual part of the text. Encourage use of discovered graphic text lingo as you work to co-create the piece.

# NURTURING AND SUPPORTING INDEPENDENT PRACTICE

### *NEW KID* BY JERRY CRAFT (2019)

Partners can be great coaches for one another! Teacher feedback and coaching will always be integral, but *peer feedback* and coaching is also tremendously valuable. Here, students begin to learn how to provide specific feedback to peers. In this lesson, writing partners practice providing writing feedback.

> **NOTE:** Select a partnership to highlight before this lesson begins. Prepare the demo with these students ahead of time so that they feel comfortable.

- **Recall** work previously done with *New Kid*, reminding students of when they carefully examined the first couple of pages. Share that Jerry Craft worked hard to craft these pages—and that it is unlikely his initial draft was identical to his final submission.

- **State** that all authors, even professionals like Craft, get feedback from others; in fact, they have editors and copy editors who essentially act as writing partners. Briefly discuss why feedback is important and how it feels to receive feedback. Then, explain that peers can also provide meaningful feedback to one another—no teacher needed!

- **Introduce** a slightly modified version of Gravity Goldberg's (2015) 4M model to students. Here, partners learn how to be "mirrors" for one another, noticing and appreciating specific aspects of each other's work. Explain the first two steps:
  - **Notice:** Students look for and notice what their partner has done well.
  - **Name:** Students share what they see their partner *has* done—as specifically as possible. They then share the impact/result of this effort.

- **Invite** the selected writing partnership to demonstrate noticing and naming.

- **Debrief** what students saw, heard, and felt.

- **Observe** students as they go off and practice this feedback protocol with a writing partner. Coach partnerships as they try this work.

- **Reflect** on the entire experience, discussing why and how students provide peer feedback by noticing and naming. Brainstorm other times and places students can use this feedback protocol beyond writing!

 This lesson uses a slightly modified version of the 4M model of feedback made popular by Gravity Goldberg (2015) in *Mindsets and Moves*. What benefits do you see in peer feedback? How do you already incorporate peer feedback? When else might you try this particular protocol?

## ✔ Check-Up

When coaching a partnership, remember that less is more. You might decide to:

- Silently motion to a tool or anchor chart (like the one pictured) to remind students to use what they know to get themselves unstuck.

- Pass a sticky note to the coaching partner, providing some language to use to get unstuck (a question or prompt).

- Quietly share a question or prompt the coaching partner can then use to jump-start the conversation.

- Only when absolutely needed—jump in and model what it looks like and sounds like to be a proficient partner, and then debrief what you did with those students so they are prepared to try it on their own next time.

## ? What Else?

- You may decide to teach students to provide feedback to themselves so they are ready to celebrate their efforts and take next steps, even when they work independently.

- You may next decide to introduce a third step for peer feedback: *coaching*. In this step, partners use noticings to provide specific tips, advice, or hints on what their partner could do next to take this work to the next level. At that point, remind students that coaches never do the work *for* their partner. They consider ways of going about the prioritized work—and support partners as they do so.

- You may instead decide students will enjoy hearing from a professional! Beloved author Jarrett Lerner created a video that helps students build an "I can" mindset when it comes to drawing their images for graphic texts. (His insights can be extended to any scenario.) In this video, Lerner helps students see what they have done and find small ways to improve what is already on the page (Authors Everywhere!, 2020).

This class-created chart provides a visual reminder of the notice and name feedback protocol.

**Language Levers for Partner Feedback**

| NOTICE | NAME | COACH |
|---|---|---|
| • *What have you been working on lately?*<br><br>• *Is there a part you are especially proud of—or a part that has been a little tricky for you?* | • *I see that you . . .*<br><br>• *Here you . . .*<br><br>• *Because of this, as a reader I was able to . . .*<br><br>• *Because of this, I now understand . . .*<br><br>• *Because of this, I felt . . .* | • *Since you already . . . then maybe together we can build on that by . . .*<br><br>• *If you want, we can work together to . . .*<br><br>• *I have a related idea of something else you can try. Would you like to hear about it?* |

 **Language Levers for Self-Feedback**

| NOTICE | NAME | COACH |
|---|---|---|
| • *What have I tried lately?*<br><br>• *Is there a part I'm especially proud of?*<br><br>• *Is there something that has been a little tricky for me?*<br><br>• *What strategies have I actually tried out? Where did I do that work?* | • *Here I was able to . . . and this works well because . . .*<br><br>• *Here I tried out . . . and because of this, my reader will understand, feel, or learn . . .* | • *Since I already . . . I can build on this by . . .*<br><br>• *Something I can do to take this to the next level is . . .*<br><br>• *Since this is solid, I can use a mentor text to help me next try . . .* |

# STRETCH UP AND BACK SUGGESTIONS: VOCABULARY

The *vocabulary* suggestions spotlighted in this section can be used with almost any book. These ideas can support next steps of a wide range of learners across the developmental continuum. As you skim through the options that follow, you will quickly notice that these strategies are not word-specific. They can be used with virtually any word, thereby increasing wide application and consistent transfer.

**Word explorers clarify the meaning of a new and interesting word by:**

- Reading around the page
  - Mining the details within the illustration(s)
  - Examining text features
  - Looking for word boxes
- Using their prior knowledge and imagining what could make sense here
- Considering the punctuation used in the sentence and the clues this provides
- Examining the grammar or syntactical structure of the sentence to learn more about what kind of word this is
- Reading around the word, specifically looking for:
  - Context clues
  - Definition sentences
  - A definition within parentheses
  - A definition included within an appositive
  - A comparison to something more universally well known
- Exploring and contemplating known word parts

**Word explorers extend their understanding of new and interesting words by:**

- Stating a definition in their own words
- Providing an example (or multiple examples)
- Talking with the word
- Considering nuances of the word (shades of meaning)
- Thinking about antonyms of the word and creating word continuums

- Considering other words they often see and hear "with" this word

- Contemplating different times, places, and situations where this word may be seen, heard, or used (contextualizing the word)

- Exploring why the author chose this word and what impact it had on the reader

- Challenging themselves to use this word while speaking

- Trying out using this word in their own writing

As you select the strategies that make sense for the hardworking learners you spend time with each day, remember the idea of "Goldilocks" teaching: explicit modeling that is specific enough to show how the strategy can be used here and now (e.g., on this one page of this one book), but also general enough to be employed again and again (e.g., on virtually any page of any book). This promotes consistent transfer and application.

 Which of these word-exploring options can you imagine teaching? Where, when, and how will you introduce and support students in this work? Can you find places to highlight or try this work in the books featured in this chapter?

# CHAPTER 5

# Realistic Fiction

"The greatest bond that a human being can create can be done through the exchange of narratives" (Jason Reynolds, quoted in Scholastic, 2019).

The genre of realistic fiction offers rich opportunities for social connection. Stories are wonderful vehicles for discovering more about ourselves, others, and society. Realistic fiction picture books, especially when acting as multitasking mentor texts, help students feel deep purpose in their learning. This chapter outlines lessons that use realistic fiction to support inquiring, collaborating, and learning across the literacy block.

The inquiry practices in these lessons center on students discovering more about conventions. Grammar becomes fun and engaging when student discovery is at the heart of learning. Students contemplate and investigate the language choices made by respected authors. As Mary Ehrenworth and Vicki Vinton (2005) write, "we value students' perceptions and their need to learn. We try to always ground our grammar lessons in the notion that *writers make choices*" (p. 21). When teachers feature grammar in discovery-themed lessons, students move beyond naming and identifying grammatical concepts. These contextualized mentor text lessons set the stage for classroom writers to use gained knowledge as they make choices in their own writing.

Additionally, throughout this chapter, cycles of shared reading are used to model processes and guide students. Reading, vocabulary, word work, grammar, fluency, and speaking and listening are all brought together by revisiting the same two-page spread of a book. The concepts presented within each cycle of shared reading are priming learners for the more explicit teaching and practice ahead. What teachers focus on, model, and discuss during shared reading becomes fuel for future conversation, reading, and writing. Furthermore, for emerging, developing, and extending learners, important inferential comprehension skills are nurtured through lessons designed to transfer to independent practice. There is so much that can be done with a small set of multitasking, realistic fiction picture books!

And if you are looking for *more* fiction lesson sets, be sure to check out the bonus chapter available online (resources.corwin.com/mttm), which features emerging, developing, and extending lesson sets for *fantasy fiction* texts.

> **NOTE:** Remember to always first enjoy featured texts as a community of readers. Then, *revisit* the text, repurposing it as a mentor text for any number of instructional priorities and goals.

# NOTES

# Lesson Set Aligned to the Emerging Stage

## Featured Text: *The Invisible Boy* by Trudy Ludwig (2013)

### 📖 Text Pairings

- *The Sandwich Swap* by Queen Rania Al Abdullah (2010) with Kelly DiPuccio and art by Tricia Tusa
- *The Big Umbrella* by Amy June Bates (2018)
- *Will I Have a Friend?* by Miriam Cohen (1967) with art by Lillian Hoban
- *The Day You Begin* by Jacqueline Woodson (2018) with art by Rafael López
- *Be a Friend* by Salina Yoon (2016)
- *Be Kind* by Pat Zietlow Miller (2018) with art by Jen Hill

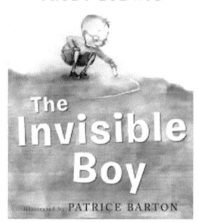

### WHAT?

In this sweet story, the main character, Brian, feels invisible. He is a quiet child and often feels left out. When a new student joins the class, Brian works hard to make him feel welcome. The two boys connect. Brian's kindness and sensitivity are appreciated, and a new friendship blossoms.

### WHY?

This book tells the story of those who are more introverted. Many readers will relate to not feeling fully seen, heard, or appreciated for who they are. This vulnerability is portrayed respectfully and eloquently through the words and illustrations. Additionally, the illustrations brilliantly show the main character's feelings. Brian starts out being drawn in black and white, but as he feels seen, included, and accepted, he transforms into color.

## WHEN?

This book easily and naturally fits into launch units and any reading or writing unit featuring narrative texts.

 **Content Connections**

- Social Studies: community, citizenship

- Personal and Community Wellness: celebration of personal identities, friendship, belonging, inclusive communities, self-confidence, becoming an upstander

# INVESTIGATING IDEAS THROUGH INQUIRY

## THE INVISIBLE BOY BY TRUDY LUDWIG (2013)

In this inquiry, students explore adjectives.

Optional Prep: Find the adjective–noun pairs on the page (listed later in this section). Use one color of highlighting tape to highlight the nouns and another color of highlighting tape to highlight the adjectives.

**Guiding Inquiry:** *What do we notice about adjectives?*

- **Reread** the two pages that begin with "At Choosing Time" and end with "wherever they go." Review previous learning around nouns and ask the students to ponder the following question: *What do you notice about the word right before each listed noun? What is its purpose or "job" in the sentence?*

- **Explore** the adjective–noun pairs on the page. If you are not using highlighting tape, other ways to model finding and listing out the pairs include using chart paper, a whiteboard, or a SMART Board.

  ○ *choosing* time, *board* games, *fire-breathing* dragons, *tall* buildings, *space* aliens, *intergalactic* battles, *greedy* pirates

- **Invite** students to hypothesize and explain their initial ideas.

- **Explore** ideas, collaboratively proving or disproving each presented theory.

- **Summarize** discoveries. For example: *Adjectives describe nouns. Adjectives tell what kind or how many.*

- **Celebrate** knowledge of adjectives, perhaps using call and response questions and answers. For example: *What kind of dragon? Fire-breathing dragons! What kind of battles? Intergalactic battles!*

- **Discuss** why the authors chose to include these describing words, and encourage learners to add adjectives to their own writing.

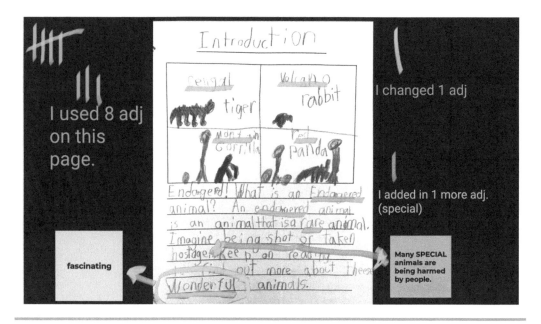

This second-grade student quickly transferred the class inquiry experience to their own writing.

## ✔ Check-Up

You might consider one or some of the following:

- Use a checklist or anecdotal records to note informal observations during the inquiry experience.

- Meet with students. Discuss the adjectives they found while reading and the impact it had on them as readers.

- Meet with students to discuss the adjectives they used while writing and discuss the processes they used for applying inquiry learning to their own writing.

- Flip through student work and note the adjectives they used in their writing.

No matter which check-up you decide to use, turn your observations into next-step lessons that make sense for current classroom learners. Use the assessment templates and planning guides in the online companion to help bring efficiency to this work (see resources.corwin.com/mttm).

## ? What Else?

Using the same two-page spread, you might instead try a language-focused inquiry on any of the following:

- Ellipses
- "Action" verbs (*play, read, sits, draws, scaling, locked, digging, toasting*)
- Simple prepositions (*at, in, to, for*)
- "Kind" words (*thank you, hi, friend*)
- Nouns (*kids, games, dragons, buildings, marshmallow, pirates, treasure, aliens, battles, crackers, friend, cookie, superheroes*)
- Sorting found nouns by category (person, place, thing, other)

# BUILDING VISION VIA MODELED AND GUIDED PRACTICE

### *THE INVISIBLE BOY* BY TRUDY LUDWIG (2013)

Facilitate a cycle of shared reading using the two-page spread from the previous lesson (beginning with "At Choosing Time" and ending with "wherever they go"). Return to these same two pages for each shared reading session.

## Session 1: Literal Comprehension (retell)

- **Reread** the two side-by-side pages.
- **Model** thinking about what came *before* this part of the story. Name a couple of events, and then flip through the first few pages of the book to add more detail to these statements.
- **Support** retelling and sequencing by asking partners to recall what happened *after* this part of the story. Listen as students share ideas. Flip through the last part of the book so those who need extra support can reference the illustrations and refresh their memory.
- **Use** student input to retell the story—from start to finish—across your fingers.

## Session 2: Word Work (high-frequency words)

- **Reread** the two pages.
- **Remind** students that there are certain words they always want to recognize and read in a snap.
- **Model** how to look at the left-hand page and find the high-frequency words that you have already studied. Show enthusiasm!
- **Invite** learners to hunt the right-hand page (text and illustrations/speech bubbles) to find previously studied high-frequency words.
- **Play** a quick game of point and say, where someone points to a word and everyone else says the word (perhaps in different

designated voices: whisper, yell, etc.). Student volunteers may act as pointers.

> **NOTE:** Early high-frequency words found on this two-page spread include (in the narrative text) *and, at, do, for, he, his, in, the, they, to, what,* and *with* and (in the speech bubbles) *you, for, my, I, have,* and *a.*

## Session 3: Inferential Comprehension (character feelings)

- **Reread** the two pages.
- **Model** looking carefully at the illustration, specifically at Brian's face. Name and describe what you see, and then use these observations to make an inference about how you think he is feeling and why.
- **Examine and analyze** the different characters in Brian's illustrations (e.g., focus on the man holding the marshmallow).
- **Invite** students to try doing this work for the pirate, the superhero, and the boy offering the cookie. Each time, start by saying what is seen, describing the character's facial expression. Then name an emotion that aligns with that expression.

## Session 4: Fluency (reading with expression)

- **Reread** the two pages.
- **Remind** students that readers always try their best to sound like they are talking. One way to do this is to change your voice and read with expression.
- **Model** reading the speech bubbles on both pages. As you model, warm up by naming what you know about how the character is

feeling (remember the last session?). Then, try reading the words.

- **Reread**, showing how the speaking character is feeling. Use echo reading or choral reading to include students.

## ✔ Check-Up

Observe students throughout each session. Listen as they discuss ideas with partners.

If shared reading sessions spiral and target previously taught skills, informally assess students' abilities to do similar work during small-group instruction and one-to-one conferring conversations.

## ❓ What Else?

Using the same two pages, you might decide to highlight the following in a cycle of shared reading:

- Literal Comprehension: Which parts of the illustration are really happening, and which are Brian's imagination?

- Word Work—Syllable Sort: Find and classify words with one, two, three, and four syllables.

- Grammar: Identify words that are a particular part of speech (see the inquiry lesson's *What Else?* feature). Discuss and generate additional examples.

- Social Comprehension: Invite students to think about and share how they can relate to Brian's feelings, and actions they might take if Brian were a member of the class community.

- Writing: Celebrate Brian's imagination and interest in writing. Encourage class members to write their own imaginative stories.

# NURTURING AND SUPPORTING INDEPENDENT PRACTICE

### *THE INVISIBLE BOY* BY TRUDY LUDWIG (2013)

In this lesson, the process of using illustrations to infer is explicitly taught. This closely connects to the work the class did in the cycle of shared reading. There you modeled and guided the work. Here you prepare students to do this work with greater independence. You will model inferring using the same two pages in *The Invisible Boy*.

- **Recall** previous reading of *The Invisible Boy* and prior lessons using this text.

- **State** that readers do more than read the words; they also spend time thinking about characters and the way characters feel. One way readers infer character feelings is by looking carefully at the expression on a character's face.

- **Model** a process for using illustrations to infer character feelings:

  ○ Look carefully at the illustration, the character's face in particular.

  ○ Think aloud: *What do I notice about the character's expression? How does this character feel?*

  ○ Say or jot that inference (idea).

- **Encourage** students to try the same process, perhaps using another part of *The Invisible Boy*.

- **Remind** students that when readers take the time to think about character feelings, it helps them to better understand and enjoy the book they are reading.

- **Invite** students to try this strategy again and again and again—whenever they are reading storybooks that have characters.

- **Observe** students as they read books with illustrations and try this process. Provide opportunities for students to share their inferences with a classmate.

Photo credit: Jonathon Casiano

Caregivers can support in-school efforts by using this strategy while reading with their child at home.

## ✓ Check-Up

Over the next few days, as you meet with small groups and individual students, invite students to show you how they do this work and/or where they have tried out this strategy. You might ask students questions like:

- What are you learning about this character?
- How did the character feel when that happened?
- Have you tried using the illustration to help you figure out the character's feelings? Can you show me where?

Try using the record-keeping templates shared online (resources.corwin.com/mttm) to jot what you notice students doing. Use these experiences as you prepare follow-up instruction.

## ? What Else?

You may also choose to support more sophisticated methods for inferring by teaching select classroom readers to:

- Connect! Think of how they would feel if what happened to a character happened to them.
- Pay attention to what the character is doing.
- Reread a part of the text, using plenty of expression, and then name the feeling.
- Look at the dialogue tag (if there is dialogue). Remember: It's not only *what* characters say but *how* they say it that gives us a clue about how they are feeling.

# Lesson Set Aligned to the Developing Stage

## Featured Text: *The Proudest Blue: A Story of Hijab and Family* by Ibtihaj Muhammad (2019), With S. K. Ali

### 📖 Text Pairings

- *The Name Jar* by Yangsook Choi (2001)
- *Sheila Rae, The Brave* by Kevin Henkes (1987)
- *Ling and Ting* (series) by Grace Lin (2010)
- *Ish* by Peter H. Reynolds (2004)
- *Exclamation Mark* by Amy Krouse Rosenthal (2013)
- *Hair Love*, an animated short film written by Matthew A. Cherry (Cherry et al., 2019) (online resource)

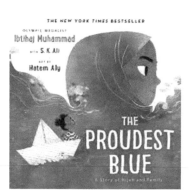

### WHAT?

This beautiful and captivating first-day-of-school story follows Faizah and her older sister, Asiya. It highlights the excitement of new milestones, including Asiya's first day of hijab. *The Proudest Blue* spotlights the powerful bond of sisterhood as Asiya teaches Faizah what it means to be proud of who you are and how to rise above the misinformed, hurtful words of others.

### WHY?

The storyline is uplifting and inspiring. The writing is poetic and includes a variety of thoughtful choices around language and conventions. The illustrations are colorful and whimsical, and visually storytell alongside the words.

### WHEN?

This text fits well with a fiction genre study, a character study, and social justice units. It can also be a mentor text in a narrative writing unit.

**Content Connections**

- Math: ordinal numbers, number forms (standard, word, and expanded form)

- Personal and Community Wellness: identity affirmation, learning about and celebrating different family and community traditions, friendship, bullying, bystanders, upstanders, advocacy

# INVESTIGATING IDEAS THROUGH INQUIRY

### THE PROUDEST BLUE: A STORY OF HIJAB AND FAMILY
### BY IBTIHAJ MUHAMMAD (2019)

This inquiry lesson focuses on apostrophes.

**Guiding Inquiry:** *What is the job of an apostrophe?*

- **Remind** students of previous reading of the text. Look closely at the cover and use this image to recall information about the characters, basic plot, and so on.

- **Discuss** what students already know about apostrophes. Pose the guiding inquiry.

- **Explore** initial ideas. Then, project the text using a document camera.

- **Examine** each page and locate the apostrophes. Use highlighter tape to mark each word and/or list the found words with an apostrophe. Here are the included words with apostrophes: *there's, it's, we're, I'm, C'mon, she's, what's, don't, Asiya's, isn't, can't, kids', won't,* and *I'll.*

- **Ask** the class, "What can we discover/ confirm about apostrophes from reading *The Proudest Blue*?" Invite students to use prior knowledge *and* these findings to share and support ideas about the job(s) of an apostrophe.

- **Investigate** shared ideas by using partner discussion to build thinking, test theories, and debate discoveries.

- **Summarize** findings. Sort the found words by "function" of the apostrophe. Ask students to label each group.

### ✔ Check-Up

- Listen in on partner conversations. Invite partnerships to talk more about the "label" given to each type of apostrophe and generate additional ideas that fit into that group.

- Over the coming days and weeks, continue to identify apostrophes while reading and try on correct use of apostrophes while writing.

### ? What Else?

- Provide time for students to hunt their independent reading books to find other words with apostrophes. Sort found words according to the purpose of the apostrophe. Add found words to the class list.

- Ask students to hunt their own writing for words with apostrophes. Ask them to check to see if an apostrophe was needed and/or properly used. Provide time and support as students confirm proper use and/or fix up (as needed).

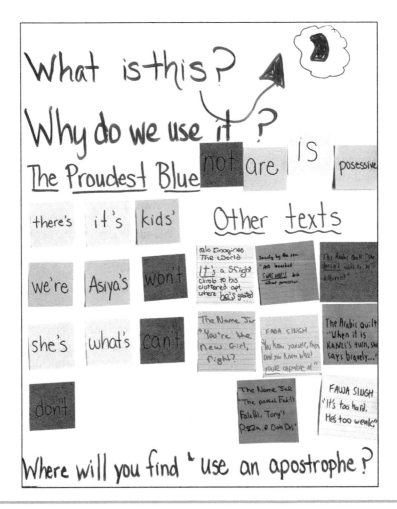

This color-coded chart was created during the inquiry. Third graders then added additional examples in the days that followed this inquiry.

# BUILDING VISION VIA MODELED AND GUIDED PRACTICE

*THE PROUDEST BLUE: A STORY OF HIJAB AND FAMILY*
BY IBTIHAJ MUHAMMAD (2019)

For this entire cycle of shared reading, use the two-page spread from *The Proudest Blue* that starts, "Recess time is for five cartwheels in a row."

## Session 1: Literal Comprehension (plot sequencing)

- **Reread** the two pages.

- **Model** using think-aloud: *What's happened so far?* State one or two events. Invite students to signal (thumbs-up or thumbs-down) if they agree or disagree with you.

- **Prompt** students to talk in partnerships: *What happened* after *this part?*

- **Discuss** a few key events from the story.

## Session 2: Word Study (homophones)

- **Reread** the two pages. Review prior knowledge of homophones.

- **Play** "I Spy" to find examples of homophones on these pages (*blue, to, shoes, not*).

- **Discuss** what these words mean, and then have volunteers share how to spell the homophone partner words (*blew, two* and *too, shoos, knot*). Invite students to share more about the meanings of partner words.

- **Summarize** understanding of these commonly confused words.

## Session 3: Word Study (compound words)

- **Reread** the two pages.
- **Discuss** what a compound word is.
- **Identify** the two compound words (*tablecloth, schoolyard*).
- **Collaboratively brainstorm and generate** a list of other compound words.

- **Practice** using some of these words in casual partner conversation.

## Session 4: Analysis (thinking critically about takeaways)

- **Reread** the same two pages *and* the next two pages, which begin, "Asiya's hijab isn't a tablecloth."

- **Discuss** Mama's words: *What do they mean? How are they significant to the story?*

- **Ponder and share** personal takeaways: *What do Mama's words mean to you?* Welcome and validate student contributions and ideas.

## ✔ Check-Up

Observe students during partner, small-group, and whole-class conversation. Jot quick notes to remember which highlighted skills and concepts require continued explicit instruction. Use the checklist and record-keeping templates available online at resources.corwin.com/mttm.

## ? What Else?

You might consider a session of shared reading focused on any of the following:

- Support the work introduced in the inquiry practice, delving further into contractions (*isn't, don't, they are*).

- Discuss possessives, including possessive pronouns (*Asiya's, her, their, yours*).

- Study verb tenses or subject–verb agreement.

- Practice fluent reading, specifically paying attention to and pausing at punctuation.

- Study the author's craft decision: Why did the author use a fragment (*Only blue*)?

After session 4, students in this third-grade class continued discussing their personal takeaways. They considered words they would like to share with the characters in the book.

# NURTURING AND SUPPORTING INDEPENDENT PRACTICE

## *THE PROUDEST BLUE: A STORY OF HIJAB AND FAMILY*
### BY IBTIHAJ MUHAMMAD (2019)

In this lesson, readers are encouraged to look for lasting takeaways in the books they read.

- **Recall** previous conversation around lessons learned in *The Proudest Blue*.

- **State** that when readers finish reading a book, they don't say "that was nice" and pick up the next one; instead, readers take some time to linger on the lesson(s) learned and/or ponder what they will remember.

- **Model** one process for lingering a bit longer on a recent reading experience.
  - Reflect on a recently read text and name a lesson that felt particularly important.
  - Ask yourself, "How could I carry this book with me after today? How might I use this/these lesson(s) in my own life?"
  - Say or jot different ideas.

- **Encourage** students to consider other lessons and/or takeaways. Introduce some of the *Language Levers* to jump-start thinking and conversation.

- **Remind** students not only how to do this work, but also when they would try it and why it is important. Reiterate that readers are always encouraged to consider how a book impacted them and how they could carry a piece of the book with them.

- **Invite** students to try this out whenever they finish a book.

### ✔ Check-Up

Over the subsequent days and weeks, meet individually with students (or meet with students in small groups). Ask them to share their ideas and/or recent jots about book lessons and takeaways. You might look for the following examples of transfer:

- Students are able to name a lesson or takeaway from a recently read text.

- Students are able to name multiple lessons and takeaways from recently read texts.

- Students share how they were impacted by recent reading.

- Students articulate what they will carry with them as a result of recent reading.

- Students explain *how* they lingered on a text and why this strategy is useful.

Use what you observe during these interactions to provide asset-based feedback.

---

 **Language Levers**

You may decide to provide prompts to help some students try this work with greater confidence. You might also *co-create* conversational stems with students during this lesson. A few possibilities include:

- *I learned that . . .*

- *I learned to . . .*

- *[Character name] taught me to . . .*

- *[Character name] taught me that . . .*

- *After reading this book, I will start . . . because . . .*

- *After reading this book, I will stop . . . because . . .*

- *I think differently about . . . now.*

- *Something I want to remember from this book is . . .*

---

## Writers Linger on Lessons

| What I Took Away | Why It Matters | How I'll use it |
|---|---|---|
| I learned that even when people are unkind, we can ignore them and reject their hurtful words. | Asiya taught me to be strong. One is resilient. We all have hard times, but we can make the choice to face our challenges. | After reading this book, I will remember to think before I speak. I don't want my words to hurt others. I want to always remember that words have more powerful than we realize. I need to be responsible. Also, when my feelings are hurt by other peoples words or actions, I will try not to keep that hurt inside. I will talk to people I trust and share my feelings. This is how I can face this challenge |

This example was created by a fourth-grade student during this lesson.

## ♥ READERS PONDER TAKEAWAYS ♥

I just finished reading Blended by Sharon M. Draper

| I LEARNED... | I REALIZED... | I PLAN TO... |
|---|---|---|
| People often do and say ignorant and hurtful things. | It's confusing! Isabella deals with harsh comments from strangers, classmates, and so-called friends. It's EXHAUSTING! | Be more brave. Step in when someone is RUDE. Be a better friend by speaking up WHEN something happens NOT afterward or in private |
| Families are all different. | My family is only one kind of family. I know this seems silly to realize now but I never thought about this before. I didn't realize what it was like to go back and forth between family members and live in two different places. That's got to be HARD. | Thank my mom for all she does. Also, I want to get to know Kayla's dad better. I only really know her mom and I've only been to her mom's house. |

This artifact was created by a fifth-grade student after this lesson.

### ? What Else?

- Connect to the lessons inherent in the story. Invite students to use those connections to engage in oral storytelling or flashdraft a personal narrative. A possible prompt could be *A Time When You Felt/Learned* ...

- Building social comprehension is an important aspect of school learning. Sara Ahmed's (2018) *Being the Change* offers many lesson ideas that help to build social comprehension. You might decide to collaborate as a class to create the identity webs Ahmed describes for the main character(s) in this book. Students could then follow up by creating or adding to their own personal identity webs. The conversation that results may be as powerful as the experience of making the webs themselves.

# NOTES

# Lesson Set Aligned to the Extending Stage

## Featured Text: *Mango Moon* by Diane de Anda (2019)

📖 **Text Pairings**

- *Two White Rabbits* by Jairo Buitrago (2015)
- *Like the Moon Loves the Sky* by Hena Khan (2020) with art by Saffa Khan
- *La frontera: El viaje con papá / My Journey With Papa* by Deborah Mills (2018)
- *Dreamers* by Yuyi Morales (2018)
- *California Teen Leads Lawsuit to Keep Immigrant TPS Recipients in the U.S.* by Public Radio International, adapted by Newsela staff (2019) (online resource)
- *Children Immigrating From Central America Face Long Road to U.S.* by Washington Post, adapted by Newsela staff (2019) (online resource)

### WHAT?

In this book, Marícela is separated from her Papí. Marícela tries to go on with her daily life, but nothing feels the same. Although they are not reunited, Marícela finds comfort in Papí's letters and understands that even if her Papí is not physically with her, they are still connected.

> **NOTE:** A Spanish-language version of this book, *La luna mango*, is also available.

## WHY?

This poignant story shares the perspective of a child who has a loved one being deported from the United States. Readers get a glimpse into the profound loss and sadness the main character, Marícela, feels. In this text, the author also reminds readers that it's okay to be sad, it's okay to feel lonely, and it's okay to cry. Finding the strength to share difficult feelings with loved ones is important. Even when loved ones can't fix a situation, their support and love can be a source of comfort.

## WHEN?

This mentor text fits with narrative reading and writing units. It aligns with character study and social justice reading. This text can be woven into writing units of any genre. Although the story employs a narrative structure, it tells about a real-life topic that sparks many strong feelings and opinions.

 **Content Connections**

- Social Studies: government, immigration, civics, law, current events, geography
- Personal and Community Wellness: leaning on and supporting family and other loved ones, coping with grief and loss, empathy, courage, compassion

 As defined in Carla España and Luz Yadira Herrera's (2020) *En Comunidad*, translanguaging takes place "when a multilingual person's full linguistic repertoire is used and honored, instead of trying to keep narrowly focused on a single language" (p. 20). Embedding translanguaging throughout a year and across years is a means for social justice. How do you encourage students' translanguaging practices? How might you encourage bilingual and multilingual learners to embrace and utilize their ever-evolving linguistic skills?

# INVESTIGATING IDEAS THROUGH INQUIRY

## *MANGO MOON* BY DIANE DE ANDA (2019)

In this grammar-themed inquiry, students explore commas. Before beginning, briefly (re)introduce the comma to students (name and identify it). Remind students that commas are used for a variety of purposes—and not only when writing dates or to separate items in a series.

**Guiding Inquiry:** *What can we discover or reconfirm about the jobs commas do?*

- **Study** a few pages of *Mango Moon*, locating the commas. Highlight or record each found example.

- **Hypothesize** and share ideas about the purpose of found commas. Continue to collaboratively investigate initial ideas, deepening theories about the different purposes of the commas found across the text.

A few *repeated* examples in this book include the following:

- *After a subordinate clause in a complex sentence*
- *Within dialogue and between split dialogue*
- *Before a coordinating conjunction in a compound sentence*
- *In the middle of a sentence to offset nonessential information*
- *After an introductory clause or phrase*

- **Explore** other books in partnerships, seeking confirmation and refinement of shared discoveries.

- **Summarize** findings. Invite students to share additional examples that support discoveries.

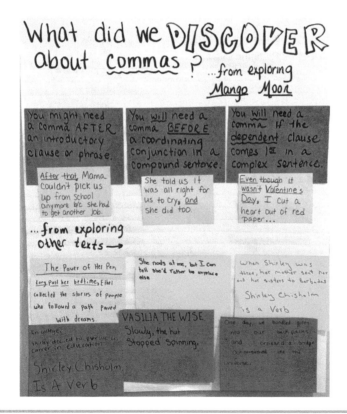

This sixth-grade inquiry artifact shows different "found" examples of commas.

### ✔ Check-Up

- As students work with partners, informally assess understanding by asking students about the examples they found. Encourage students to explain the processes they used to categorize and understand the purpose of found commas.

- After this initial inquiry experience, explicitly model and teach students how to transfer these understandings to their writing.

- In the days and weeks that follow, when working with small groups, ask students to show you an example of where they applied new knowledge about using commas. Celebrate efforts to transfer learning. Coach writers (as needed) to provide additional support.

### ? What Else?

You may choose to focus the class inquiry on one or two specific purposes of comma usage. Afterward, you could revisit this text to introduce other reasons to use commas. For example, if *this* inquiry spotlighted using commas before a coordinating conjunction in compound sentences, *at another time* you may pull other sentences to help students discover more about subordinating conjunctions and complex sentences, or to teach students to correctly punctuate dialogue, no matter where the dialogue tag is positioned.

# BUILDING VISION VIA MODELED AND GUIDED PRACTICE

## *MANGO MOON* BY DIANE DE ANDA (2019)

After reading this text from start to finish, return to a small part for shared reading. In this proposed cycle of shared reading, the class repeatedly revisits the same two-page spread that begins, "The chill catches my shoulder . . ."

### Session 1: Literal Comprehension (understanding figurative language)

- **Read** these two pages. Then focus on the first sentence. Explain that this is an example of figurative language, in this instance personification.

- **Ponder** and discuss: Why did the author choose to craft the sentence this way?

- **Consider** other ways the author could have expressed this idea. Ask students to share different examples. Jot these sentences.

- **Discuss** and decide which sentence has the greatest impact.

### Session 2: Word Work (open vs. closed first syllables)

- **Reread** these two pages.

- **Review** the concept of open and closed syllables. Explain that when a syllable ends in a single vowel and that vowel sound is long (says its name), it is considered "open." When a syllable has a single vowel that is followed by one or more consonants and the vowel sound is short, it is considered "closed."

- **Explain** the benefits of understanding open and closed syllables. This knowledge helps readers confidently decode multisyllabic words as they read and spell more sophisticated words as they write.

- **Locate** words where the first syllable is open (e.g., *because*). Identify words where the first syllable is closed (e.g., *without*). Discuss found examples.

- **Generate** other examples of multisyllabic words. List and sort provided examples based on whether the first syllable is open or closed.

- **Summarize** learning and remind students to use what they know about this spelling concept as they read and write.

### Session 3: Grammar (auxiliary verbs, also known as *helping verbs*)

- **Reread** these two pages.

- **Ponder:** What tense is this story written in?

- **Introduce** helping verbs and discuss their role. (TIP: For now, keep things simple. Explain that auxiliary verbs help express the main verb's tense, mood, or voice.)

- **Identify** examples on this page (*will be*, *will welcome*). Generate and list other common examples.

- **Encourage** partnerships to chat and storytell, practicing using helping verbs in different contexts.

### Session 4: Analytic Thinking (considering perspective)

- **Reread** these two pages.

- **Ponder:** Who is telling the story? How do we know?

- **Ask** students what they know about this narrator. Discuss *why* the author likely chose to tell the story from Marícela's perspective. Consider how that choice impacts the reader's reactions.

- **Connect** students' ideas to the decisions *they* make as writers. Keep the idea of the author's *purpose* for choosing first-person narration central to the conversation.

- **Remind** students that whenever they read (and write!), they will want to carefully consider whose perspectives are being shared and whose are missing—and why!

### ✔ Check-Up

- Follow up on this scaffolded experience by preparing connected whole-class, small-group, and/or one-to-one instruction, delving into one chosen area that was introduced and modeled in this cycle of shared reading.

- In the days and weeks that follow, meet with students (or mine student work) to see if/how they are applying targeted skills and concepts.

### ? What Else?

To more closely align with current goals, this cycle of shared reading could highlight any of the following:

- Literal Comprehension: Determine what can be learned about the main character, the setting, and the problem from this one page.

- Word Work: Introduce or review the different sounds of /oo/ and /ou/ or *r*-controlled vowels.

- Grammar: Learn more about verb tenses, possessives, possessive pronouns, or lengthening sentences without turning them into run-ons.

- Analytic Thinking: Provide vision for thinking about mood/tone, synthesizing ideas from illustrations and words, or comparing ideas across texts (see *Text Pairings* for suggestions).

You could also do an interactive read-aloud that focuses on considering *the author's* perspective and purpose for writing this book.

# NURTURING AND SUPPORTING INDEPENDENT PRACTICE

## *MANGO MOON* BY DIANE DE ANDA (2019)

In this lesson, you will explicitly model one of the many ways to be an active reader. The focus of this lesson centers on how readers could consider both the author's perspective and their own perspective while reading.

- **Recall** previous reading and learning experiences with *Mango Moon*.

- **State** that readers flexibly think about an author's perspective—and their own perspective—by revisiting possibilities throughout reading. One way to do this is to pause, ponder, and process when having a strong reaction to something from the text.

- **Model** this work as you begin to reread the first part of *Mango Moon*.

  - Read a bit. Pause when you notice a strong reaction or feeling.

  - Ponder: *Why am I feeling this? What is the author choosing to show me here? What intention could be behind this decision?*

  - Process ideas by asking yourself, *Do I feel the same? Why or why not?*

- **Encourage** students to provide their input at another stopping point.

- **Remind** students that whenever they read, it is a good idea to consider the author's perspective and to notice what in the book leads them to this conclusion. Share that readers are always welcome to "talk back" to text and share *their* thoughts and opinions, too.

- **Invite** students to try out this kind of thinking and jotting whenever they read.

My choice: Think about the author's perspective

I'm reading: <u>The Teachers March! How Selma's Teachers Changed History.</u>

| Standout Words | What the Author Might be Saying | What I Think/Feel |
|---|---|---|
| "With fire in his eyes, Reverend Reese led marchers to the courthouse to register to vote. | R.R. was angry and frustrated. But, he was also determined- because this was such an important issue. | This was a really tense time in history and there were a lot of big, understandable emotions. |
| Leaders. That's what people called the teachers. The teachers were the somebody somebodies of the community. | The teachers were looked at like pillars of the community. They were educated and well-regarded. Teachers were important! | Is the author reminding us that teachers are important? This reminds me of how teachers are so brave during COVID, too. |
| The teachers fidgeted, as if they hadn't heard. Some sat still like statues. | R.R. was asking a lot of the teachers. It was scary to think about taking this kind of action. | Sometimes, even when we know the right thing to do, it is still hard to do it. It CAN be scary. |
| "We were like giants," Reverend Reese said with a smile. | The teachers were brave and their action was BIG! | The teachers of Selma changed history! |

I'm realizing that the author likely believes that the teachers in Selma were heroes. They took a stand against injustice and it is really important that we learn about these heroes.

Personally, I agree because these teachers really were so brave. I'm glad the author took the time to recognize their action - it is important that we know what they did. Teachers are still taking action and trying to make the world better.

Explicit instruction prepares students for independent practice. This student notebook entry was created by an eighth grader during independent reading time.

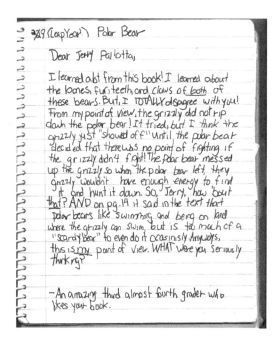

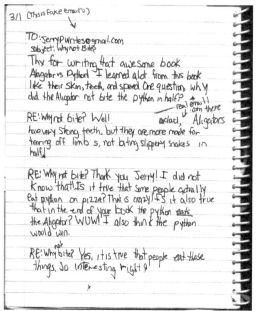

After using this text and lesson with a small group of third graders, one student made it her own. She playfully "talked back" to an author in her reading notebook work.

## ✔ Check-Up

Informally check in with students to see how this work is going. You might skim through students' recent reading notebook entries. You could also chat with students, perhaps asking them questions like these:

- What point of view is used in this text? Do you have any thoughts about why the author/creator made this decision?

- Are there any places in the text that hint at what the author/creator might feel about the topic presented?

- What does the author/creator believe? How do you know?

- What lesson does the author/creator want you to learn? Do you agree or disagree?

- Were there any parts that stood out to you or made you react strongly?

- What's staying with you? What are you thinking, feeling, or believing after reading/viewing this text?

- If you could have a conversation with the author/creator, what would you say?

Use observations and interactions to guide personalized feedback and follow-up coaching. Nurture and nudge different subsets of classroom readers. You could use the record-keeping templates to keep track of observations and progress (templates available online at resources.corwin.com/mttm).

## ? What Else?

Depending on the prioritized learning goals of current students:

- In reading, *Mango Moon* can be used again and again while supporting self-monitoring, fluency, literal comprehension, and inferential comprehension.

- In writing, this book can be used as a mentor for a range of structure, development, craft, and convention strategies.

# STRETCH UP AND BACK SUGGESTIONS: SPELLING

This chapter spotlights suggestions around *spelling* that transcend text type and genre. These teaching ideas represent the exciting range of next steps you might see in the learners you support. Almost every page of every book offers contextualized opportunities to:

- Explore phonemic and phonological awareness concepts like rhyming, segmenting sounds in words, blending sounds in words, manipulating sounds in words, and identifying the number of syllables in words.
- Listen for, look for, and identify initial sounds, medial sounds, and ending sounds.
- Explore simple word families.
- Notice and discuss blends and digraphs (different positions).
- Study vowels—short vowel sounds, long vowel patterns, *r*-controlled vowel patterns, diphthong patterns.
- Discuss commonly confused words (like homophones and homographs).
- Notice and identify high-frequency words.

Many texts will also offer embedded opportunities to find, study, and discuss:

- Consonant clusters.
- Contractions.
- Silent letters.
- Inflected endings.
- Prefixes and suffixes.
- Syllabification.
- Accented and unaccented syllables.
- Cognates.
- Greek/Latin roots and other word parts.

Try this challenge: Turn to *any* page of *any* book and try to see how many of these phonological and phonemic awareness, phonics, and spelling opportunities you see! Take these opportunities to amplify the excitement and delight that can be found in exploring words.

When educators teach the same thing, the same way, year after year, they are not successful in reaching every student. There will always be students who feel unseen, unheard, and simply left out. How do you actively seek information about this year's students and celebrate what makes these learners so special? How do you use this knowledge to design and facilitate learning experiences that make sense and feel relevant for current learners?

# CHAPTER 6

# Creative Nonfiction: Biographies, Autobiographies, and Memoirs

"There's power in allowing yourself to be known and heard, in knowing your own unique story, in using your own unique voice. And there's grace in being willing to know and hear others. This, for me, is how we become" (Michelle Obama, 2018, p. 421).

This chapter spotlights specific creative nonfiction subgenres that set out to tell the true-life stories of famous—or infamous—people. Hearing about the experiences of others, especially those who have accomplished something remarkable or attained a certain status, often intrigues readers. Biographies, autobiographies, and memoirs are popular picks. Personal essays, narrative journalism, and person-centered documentaries also fit the bill.

Although inherently informational, many of these subgenres feel like a natural accompaniment to fiction. Students can consider subjects of autobiography, for example, as characters in a true-life story. Across grades, readers work to develop theories and use more precise vocabulary to describe the people they read about. More experienced readers grow increasingly sophisticated theories about the subjects featured in creative nonfiction, often comparing situations and themes across texts.

Further, students engage in interpretation as they consider what lessons can be learned by reading these books. Students often carry the spirit of these texts in their own lives.

Teaching creative nonfiction helps students move beyond the objectives listed in reading, writing, and language curriculum. Readers unearth excellence, celebrating the creativity and accomplishments of others. Universal traits of strong work ethic, productive struggle, perseverance, imagination, originality, personal responsibility, and community-mindedness often permeate these texts. Finally, because creative nonfiction is a hybrid genre, teachers can model, guide practice, and support seemingly endless reading, writing, grammar, and conversational skills while layering these mentor texts that multitask.

In this chapter, you will see cohesion between lessons described across the three stages of development. The inquiry experiences explore topics connected to featured mentor texts. Interactive read-aloud guides students in trying out prioritized comprehension skills and conversational strategies. The lessons that encourage independent practice highlight multitasking mentor texts as invaluable resources while writing. Jeff Anderson (2005) teaches that if "what we hear and see will end up in our writing sooner or later . . . the literature we read aloud to our students and the closer in proximity the reading is to the next writing experience, the more likely it is that a spillover of rhetorical techniques will occur in student writing" (p. 18). What a fabulous reminder of the benefits of an integrated approach to literacy. The cohesion we aim for when using mentor texts that multitask results in exactly this: authentic connection from one part of the day to another!

> **NOTE:** Remember to always first enjoy selected books as a community of readers. Then, *revisit* the text, repurposing it as a mentor text for any number of instructional priorities and goals.

# Lesson Set Aligned to the Emerging Stage

Featured Text: *Planting Stories: The Life of Librarian and Storyteller Pura Belpré* by Anika Aldamuy Denise (2019)

## 📖 Text Pairings

- *Mae Among the Stars* by Roda Ahmed (2020), with art by Stasia Burrington
- *Digging for Words: José Alberto Gutiérrez and the Library He Built* by Angela Burke Kunkel (2020) with art by Paola Escobar
- *Queen of Physics: How Wu Chien Shiung Helped Unlock the Secrets of the Atom* by Teresa Robeson (2019), with art by Rebecca Huang
- *Frida* by Jonah Winter (2002), with art by Ana Juan
- *Carmen Agra Deedy: Family Stories From a Master Storyteller* (and other select videos) from the Library of Congress (2020) (online resource)
- *Storytime Video [en Español]: Planting Stories: The Life of Librarian and Storyteller Pura Belpré* by WeAreTeachers (2019) (online resource)

### WHAT?

This picture book biography tells the story of Pura Belpré, who was New York City's first Puerto Rican librarian. Belpré was also a highly skilled storyteller and puppeteer.

### WHY?

There are not nearly enough biographies of librarians and storytellers! This one has an innate folktale quality that aligns well with Belpré's beloved storytelling. The captivating illustrations also share plenty of information about Belpré's life experiences. The bits of Spanish sprinkled throughout the story captivate readers and listeners. I have repeatedly witnessed young students become engrossed in this important true story. It is also important to note that not all students who are practicing "emerging" literacy skills are chronologically young! Older learners (including, but not limited to, bilingual and multilingual students nurturing their emerging literary skills in English) will also be entranced by the lyrical and descriptive storytelling. You may appreciate that a Spanish-language edition, *Sembrando historias: Pura Belpré: bibliotecaria y narradora de cuentos*, is also available.

## WHEN?

This delightful text is easily woven into a variety of reading, writing, and social studies units. Infuse it into comprehension-based fiction and nonfiction units. The enchanting storytelling will raise the level of any narrative writing unit. This book also begs teachers to consider creating narrative nonfiction writing units, rarely found in elementary schools. Finally, this book can be used in storytelling units and classrooms that employ a "playshop" approach to reading and writing.

 **Content Connections**

- Social Studies: communities, community workers, New York City history, New York history, American history, Latinx history, geography, culture studies, heritage studies, immigration studies

- Art: puppet making and visual storytelling

- Personal and Community Wellness: exploring personal identities, the important role of storytelling, preserving family and community traditions, celebrating changemakers, contributing to one's community

# INVESTIGATING IDEAS THROUGH INQUIRY

### *PLANTING STORIES: THE LIFE OF LIBRARIAN AND STORYTELLER PURA BELPRÉ* BY ANIKA ALDAMUY DENISE (2019)

In this inquiry, students explore who and what inspires them.

> **NOTE:** The interactive read-aloud described in the "Building Vision via Modeled and Guided Practice" section serves as an important foundation to this inquiry. Use that experience to spark this topic-inspired inquiry.

**Guiding Inquiry:** *Where do we find inspiration? Who inspires us?*

- **Remind** students of the prior read-aloud experience. Discuss the facts they remember from the book.

- **Explore** perspectives and personal takeaways: *What is your opinion about Pura? What will you remember about Pura?*

- **Consider** others who inspire. Reflect on what they have done that feels important.

- **Imagine** ways to use the inspiration found in others: *How could we contribute? What could we do?*

- **Invite** students to share their ideas: perhaps through some of their own storytelling, sketching, or writing. (Introduce *Language Levers* or co-create conversational scaffolds if/as needed.)

- **Celebrate** student participation, ideas, and reflections. Keep taking action!

 **Language Levers**

Sentence frames can be useful supports in conversational experiences:

- *I remember that Pura . . .*
- *I think Pura was . . .*
- *_____ was/is also really important because . . .*
- *I will remember to/that . . .*
- *I learned why . . .*
- *I learned that I can also . . .*
- *I hope to . . . and will . . .*

 think Pura did important work

| | | | | |
|---|---|---|---|---|
| Pura red lots of books | Pura told storys about Portro Riko | She talkt lots of langwajis. | Pura shared books. | Pura made chanje happen. |
| She teach about Puerto Rico. | Pura was brave. | Pura helped peepel. | Pura made reading fun. | Pura kept memorys alive. |

GOLD COHORT JOT LOT

This cohort of first graders used interactive writing to co-compose a "big idea" statement about Pura. Then, each student wrote something they learned and found inspiring about Pura.

## My Own Pura Belpré
### By: Alexa

Pura Belpré reminds me of Ms. Pascuzzi. Ms. Pascuzzi inspires me. She reads lots of books to us and she likes to read books en ingles y español. Like Pura, ella nos cuenta muchas historias. La Sra. Pascuzzi me hace sentir segura en la escuela. She helps me try my best. Aprendo en ingles y español. This is gret bicas it is importent to spik dos idiomas. I hope I can be lik Sra. Pascuzzi. Quiero sentirme valiente y try new things.

And I think Pura Belpré is a good percen and so is Ms. Pascuzzi.

Students in this fourth-grade bilingual classroom used Flipgrid to record themselves talking about how Pura inspired them. Each class member also contributed to a slide deck to share where else they find inspiration—and why. Unsurprisingly, this student found great inspiration in their teacher!

### ✓ Check-Up

Discussing sources of inspiration is a chance to learn about students and what they value. You can also simultaneously check in on progress toward speaking and listening standards and/or student language goals. Observe, listen in, and celebrate areas of growth.

You may choose to make note of whether students can recall key facts from the text or share an opinion about the "character"/subject of this biography.

Use your in-the-moment observations to plan responsive instruction. You may decide to use the provided assessment templates or planning forms as you do so (available online at resources.corwin.com/mttm).

### ? What Else?

You might decide to try one of these ideas:

- Use inquiry to support a scaffolded text-to-text comparison. Share other texts (see *Text Pairings* options) and then pose these questions: *Who do you think Pura is more like, ___ or ___? Why?*

- Highlight and explore a few of the Spanish words and phrases included in the book. You might decide to ask another question—for example, *How many different ways could we say ___?*—and invite the class to research together or in small groups. Or, engage in an exploration of cognates instead.

- Follow up by inviting students to find out more about the people and pursuits they admire. Encourage learners to think of the questions they have and consider how to find the answers to these questions. This kind of research is playful and appropriate for a wide range of learners. You may decide to focus these efforts on people students know and/or local changemakers.

- Collaboratively ponder the question, *Why is it important to tell stories and hear other people's stories?* Then, be like Pura! Tell your stories, modeling rich storytelling. Teach into storytelling and periodically take time for students to tell stories from their life and/or share family stories and community stories.

# BUILDING VISION VIA MODELED AND GUIDED PRACTICE

**PLANTING STORIES: THE LIFE OF LIBRARIAN AND STORYTELLER PURA BELPRÉ BY ANIKA ALDAMUY DENISE (2019)**

During this interactive read-aloud, the teacher models learning and remembering important facts. Use this read-aloud as a springboard for other work with this multitasking mentor text.

- **Preview** the text by exploring the cover and reading the book jacket. Take a brief picture walk to orient the students to the style of illustrations.

- **State** that readers use the whole text to build their understanding. One way readers do this is by stopping while they read and thinking about what they are learning from both the images and the words. Begin reading.

- **Stop 1: Model.** Stop on the page that ends with "y una vida nueva—for Pura." Use think-aloud to model what you are learning from the illustrations and from the words. For example: *The pictures show me/teach me . . . The words teach me . . .*

- **Stop 2: Model and Prompt.** Stop on the page that ends with "la lengua y los colores of home." Again, use think-aloud to say what you learned from the words. Prompt students: *What is the picture showing/teaching?* Encourage students to signal (perhaps with a thumbs-up) when they have something to say. Choose a few volunteers to share.

- **Stop 3: Prompt.** Stop on the page that ends with "to the children." Invite students to turn and talk with one another. Partner A shares learning from the pictures. Partner B shares learning from the words. To encourage active listening, ask student volunteers to share out what *their partner* said/learned.

- **Retell.** Take a brief post-read picture walk, and as you do, narrate the most important events. Then, use your fingers to count off three to five facts about Pura. Ask students to hold up their fingers as you say those facts again. Finally, encourage student partnerships to take turns telling each other what *they* remember.

> **NOTE:** The author of this book uses translanguaging in her storytelling. In *En Comunidad*, Carla España and Luz Yadira Herrera (2020) share that interactive read-aloud is an ideal teaching structure that supports pedagogical translanguaging, even if the book is written in only one language. For example, teachers may choose to read a book in one language and share their thoughts and prompt students in more than one language. Refer to the co-constructed chart for conversation-inviting suggestions. These can serve as *Language Levers* in your classroom, too.

 Interactive video-aloud is a highly engaging instructional structure and is almost identical to interactive read-aloud. Together as a class, view a short video. At specifically chosen moments, pause the video, then model your thinking and encourage students to share their thoughts. What benefits do you see to including interactive video-aloud in your teaching repertoire? Can you think of any video clips that you could use?

I can share my ideas.
Puedo compartir mis ideas.

The picture shows...    La imagen muestra...
The words tell me...    Las palabras me dicen...
I learned...            He aprendito...
My partner said...      Mi compañera/compañero dijo...

I can tell what I know.
Puedo decir lo que sé.

First...        Primera...
Next...         Siguiente...
Then...         Luego...
Last...         Al final...
(At the end...)

This *Language Levers* chart includes stems that were co-created by students in a second-grade bilingual classroom. By being actively involved in this process, classmates contributed to each other's success.

## ✔ Check-Up

Observe students, noting participation and the processes used to contribute ideas. You may also choose to informally assess whether students can recall key facts from the text and how specific their language is when talking about the text. Be sure to focus on assets, not deficits, and use these observations to guide subsequent teaching.

## ? What Else?

You could plan an illustration-centric read-aloud. Modeling and prompting might center on questions like these: *What do you see? What else do you see? What does this help you to learn about Pura?* This may sound something like this:

- *I see . . . This makes me understand . . .*
- *I see . . . I see . . . I see . . . I learned . . .*

If sequencing while retelling is a prioritized goal, invite students to stop and sketch while you read aloud. By the time the book is done, students will have a "picture timeline" of key events to help chronologically retell.

# NURTURING AND SUPPORTING INDEPENDENT PRACTICE

### *PLANTING STORIES: THE LIFE OF LIBRARIAN AND STORYTELLER PURA BELPRÉ* BY ANIKA ALDAMUY DENISE (2019)

In the interactive read-aloud previously described, students retold key events across their fingers. In this lesson, students learn to do something similar as they prepare to write.

- **Recall** previous experiences with *Planting Stories*.

- **State** that when writers come up with an idea, they can be like Pura and tell their story aloud. Writers often storytell out loud *before* they start to write on paper.

- **Model** an aligned process with your own story idea. You may choose to model the first three steps of this process:

  - Think of a new idea and remind yourself to storytell out loud.

  - Tell the story across your fingers. Use order words like *first*, *then*, and *last*. (TIP: Repeat this three times so you don't forget.)

  - Sketch each part.

  - Go back and add more. (Add details to sketches and/or add letters, words, and/or sentences.)

- **Encourage** students to storytell with a partner. Then, suggest students to try to use order words as they tell their story across their fingers. (OPTIONAL: Provide a short amount of time for students to begin to sketch the first parts.)

- **Remind** classroom writers that they can always use talking and storytelling to plan their work. This rehearsal helps writers remember their ideas and write clearly.

- **Invite** students to continue working on their writing.

- **Observe** students as they work. Note what you see students doing. Celebrate their efforts.

> **NOTE:** Although this lesson outlines planning events of a story, the same process can be used to help students plan information writing or opinion writing.

### ✔ Check-Up

- Meet with students one-to-one or in small groups. Ask them to show you how they plan their stories. Coach as needed.

- Look through student work. Check to see if stories are focused and told in an order that makes sense. Use what you notice students *are* doing to provide next-step, responsive instruction.

### ❓ What Else?

There are many ways to nurture planning before writing. Here are a few options:

- Co-create a tool that supports independence. If you have a writing center or supply station in the classroom, post a mini-chart to remind students that whenever they get writing paper or a new booklet, they need to rehearse before beginning to write.

- Offer a playful invitation to plan aloud. I used to keep a mirror near the supply station, so students could hear *and* see themselves planning their writing. I have also set up a stuffed animal audience that "listens" to students rehearse their ideas.

- Create a student-friendly tool that supports planning before writing. Students can use a wipe-off checklist (think-say-sketch-write-reread-add more) and dry-erase marker so that the process is remembered each time they start a new piece. Or provide a simple "flow chart" and a moveable marker. Students concretely move their marker (such as a paper clip, counting cube, or sticky note) as they complete each phase of their work.

- Remember that there are many apps and extensions where students can storytell and rehearse aloud, recording their ideas. Mote is one of my favorite voice note and feedback extensions to use throughout the writing process. Additionally, many platforms and devices have embedded accessibility features that will turn speech to text.

# Lesson Set Aligned to the Developing Stage

## Featured Text: *All the Way to the Top: How One Girl's Fight for Americans With Disabilities Changed Everything* by Annette Bay Pimentel (2020)

📖 **Text Pairings**

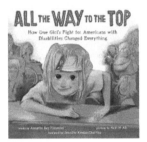

- *Greta's Story: The Schoolgirl Who Went on Strike to Save the Planet* by Valentina Camerini (2019), with art by Veronica "Veci" Carratello

- *The Girl Who Thought in Pictures: The Story of Dr. Temple Grandin* by Julia Finley Mosca (2017), with art by Daniel Rieley

- *All Are Welcome* by Alexandra Penfold (2018), with art by Suzanne Kaufman

- *Just Ask!* by Sonia Sotomayor (2019), with art by Rafael López

- *Emmanuel's Dream: The True Story of Emmanuel Ofosu Yeboah* by Laurie Ann Thompson (2015), with art by Sean Qualls

- Excerpts from *Young Advocate Webinar: Jennifer Keelan* by The Ability Center of Greater Toledo (2020) (online resource)

- *Sprinter Marissa Papaconstantinou on What It Means to Be an Influencer On and Off the Track* by Jonathan Yue (2019) (online resource)

- *You Can't Stop Us* commercial by Nike (Diaz, 2020) (online resource)

- *YouTube Creators Use Platform to Show What Life Is Like With Disabilities* by the Washington Post, adapted by Newsela staff (2019) (online resource)

### WHAT?

This book tells the inspiring story of Jennifer Keelan-Chaffins, who, since she was a young girl, has been a fierce and brave activist for those with differing abilities and para-abilities.

Jennifer shows us how people of any age can make a difference! She has lived her life with bravery and grace—and continues to advocate for needed changes. Jennifer's story reminds us of the importance of speaking up, advocating for ourselves and others.

**WHEN?**

This book can easily find its way into a beginning-of-the-year launch unit, a narrative reading unit, a biography unit, a social justice unit, and, of course, an informational reading unit. It also just as easily serves as a mentor text in almost any writing unit.

 **Content Connections**

- Social Studies: disability rights, civil and human rights, government, law, U.S. history

- Personal and Community Wellness: inclusivity, recognizing and calling out ableist thinking and statements, celebrating changemakers, becoming an upstander, being an ally, advocating for yourself and others, and disrupting the status quo

# INVESTIGATING IDEAS THROUGH INQUIRY

### *ALL THE WAY TO THE TOP: HOW ONE GIRL'S FIGHT FOR AMERICANS WITH DISABILITIES CHANGED EVERYTHING* BY ANNETTE BAY PIMENTEL (2020)

This topic inquiry explores inequity and how each of us can be a changemaker. Engage in this inquiry after reading this book aloud (see the connected interactive read-aloud lesson).

**Guiding Inquiries:** *What inequities do you see or experience in our school and in our community? How could the school/community/each of us work to become more inclusive?*

- **Remind** students about previous experience reading *All the Way to the Top*. Revisit the information and timeline at the back of the book.

- **Pose** the first guiding inquiry question about the inequities students see, feel, or have experienced. Provide time for students to privately ponder their ideas by sketching or jotting.

- **Explore** student thinking while facilitating a class conversation. Volunteers can tell about their experiences or ideas. *Sharing is optional.* List key points from the discussion.

- **Pose** the second inquiry question. Provide additional time for students to consider their own initial thoughts.

- **Provide** an agreed-upon amount of time for small groups to discuss, investigate, and contemplate ideas.

- **Create** time and space for continued discussion, work, and action. This essential work is never "one and done."

### ✔ Check-Up

- Observe students during this inquiry experience. Use the provided conversational checklist to note current assets (checklist available online at resources.corwin.com/mttm). Use collected information to plan more explicit next-step instruction and collaborative experiences that are relevant for current classroom learners.

- Ask students to privately reflect on their own participation, takeaways, and personal goals.

## We Need To Include Individuals With Differing Abilities In Our Classroom Library!

**BOOKS WE ALREADY HAVE**

- All The Way To The Top
- Fish In A Tree
- Blind
- Out of My Mind
- Firegirl
- Insignificant Events in the Life of a Cactus
- Wonder
- Roll With It
- I am Not a Label
- Just Ask
- Rules
- Emmanuel's Dream
- You Don't Know Everything Jilly P
- Al Capone Does My Shirts

**OTHER BOOKS WE WOULD LIKE TO GET**

- El Deafo
- The Chance to Fly
- Born Just Right
- Wink
- Show Me a Sign
- What Stars Are Made Of
- 10,000 Tries
- The World Ends in April
- Mia Lee is Wheeling Through MS
- Anything But Typical
- Paperboy
- Rain Reign
- Joey Pigza Swallowed The Key

- Song for a Whale
- I Funny
- Cyclone
- Soul Surfer
- Mascot
- Braced
- Real
- The Oracle Code
- Disfigured
- Can You See Me?

A small group of students in this multi-grade (3–5) classroom decided to audit the classroom library, looking specifically for books that feature characters or people with differing abilities and para-abilities. They also made a list of new titles that could be purchased for the classroom.

## ? What Else?

- Follow up on this inquiry by co-creating a classroom inclusivity checklist or a class commitment contract around inclusivity.

- Role-play common scenarios students encounter around equity and inclusivity. Discuss different situations and discover more about what can be said and done if/when they find themselves in a similar situation.

- Contemplate personal takeaways from Jennifer's story and then invite students to explore how they can express those feelings through art, music, or movement.

- Ask students to take part in one of the audits described in the *Pause and Ponder* feature.

It is essential to consistently include, center, and celebrate those who have historically been marginalized and underrepresented. It is not enough for this to only happen during a certain unit, when teaching a certain subject, or at a certain time of year. Which of these inquiries will you explore?

*How inclusive is the classroom library? What will you do to feature different topics, people, voices, and perspectives more prominently?*

*Whose voices are actively included in this unit? What changes need to be made?*

*Whose preferences are accentuated in classroom setup, schedules, and displays? What shifts are necessary?*

Remember that audits are step one. Ongoing attention and action are then required to create change.

# BUILDING VISION VIA MODELED AND GUIDED PRACTICE

### *ALL THE WAY TO THE TOP: HOW ONE GIRL'S FIGHT FOR AMERICANS WITH DISABILITIES CHANGED EVERYTHING*
### BY ANNETTE BAY PIMENTEL (2020)

In this interactive read-aloud, the teacher models (and the class practices) moving beyond fact-collecting. While reading *All the Way to the Top*, the class considers how Jennifer may have felt *and* their own reactions to reading about Jennifer's life experiences.

- **Introduce** the text while showing the cover. Read the foreword aloud to gain the background knowledge and context for Jennifer's story.

- **State** that during this read-aloud experience, the class will learn about Jennifer. The class will also take time to consider how Jennifer might have felt—and how *they* feel as they read about her life.

- **Stop 1: Model.** Stop on the page where Jennifer knows that she is a "friend waiting to happen." Model thinking about how Jennifer may have felt on the previous page and what from the text supports this idea. Then, share a personal opinion about Jennifer. For example: *I think that when she first got to kindergarten, Jennifer may have felt lonely and upset. I think this because, in the picture, she is separate from the other students and, in the words, we see that some of the students said, "You'll never be one of us." But, I also think that Jennifer is resilient because these kids didn't make her stop wanting to go to school or make friends.*

- **Stop 2: Model.** Stop on the page where Jennifer is back at school but unable to eat in the cafeteria. Infer Jennifer's feelings and explain what in the text helped you grow that idea. Then, share your personal opinion and explain this viewpoint.

- **Stop 3: Prompt.** Stop on the page where Jennifer's family buys plane tickets for Washington, DC. Prompt students to turn and share their thoughts with a partner.

  ○ Partner A Prompt: *How do you think Jennifer is feeling? What makes you think that?* (Partner A answers; Partner B signals if they agree or disagree.)

  ○ Partner B Prompt: *What is your opinion of Jennifer? What helped you to grow this idea about her?* (Partner B answers; Partner A signals if they agree or disagree.)

- **Stop 4: Prompt.** Stop on the page where Jennifer makes it to the top of the steps. Prompt students to turn and share their thoughts with a partner. This time, ask students to switch roles.

  ○ Partner B Prompt: *How do you think Jennifer is feeling? What makes you think that?* (Partner B answers; Partner A signals if they agree or disagree.)

  ○ Partner A Prompt: *What is your opinion of Jennifer? What helped you to grow this idea about her?* (Partner A answers; Partner B signals if they agree or disagree.)

- **End-of-Book Discussion.** Pose the following question: *What can we learn from Jennifer and her story?* Provide a couple of minutes for students to discuss their thoughts in small groups. Then come together to end the experience with a whole-class conversation.

## ✔ Check-Up

- This supported experience is meant to provide vision, not to explicitly teach students how to do this work. Save more formal assessment for later. Here you may decide to observe and listen to student pairs as they share their inferences and ideas (during turn and talks) or take note of what students stop and jot.

- Promote active listening by asking a few students to share what they heard their *partner* say during the turn and talks.

## ? **What Else?**

While reading this book (or any biography) with students, you might instead decide to focus on any of the following comprehension skills:

- Using story structure to help predict what might next happen in a biography
- Retelling key events (in order)
- Using key events to recognize a pattern and, by the end, grow a big idea about the "character"/subject of the biography
- Thinking about and, as needed, revising ideas about the lesson(s) embedded in a text (For example: *Since ___ just happened, I now think that perhaps the author could be trying to teach us . . .*)

# What can we learn from Jennifer and her story?

**BREAKOUT ROOM 1:** Having CP does not mean you can't learn or play. Everyone should be included.

**BREAKOUT ROOM 2:** It's important to NOT give up. Your words and actions mater.

**BREAKOUT ROOM 3:** Kids can create importent and needed changes.

**BREAKOUT ROOM 4:** Telling your story to others can have a big impact.

**BREAKOUT ROOM 5:** It is important for schools, bisneses, buildings, and playgrownds to be safe and comfortable for everyone.

**BREAKOUT ROOM 6:** It's okay to be scared. That doesn't mean you shouldn't speak your mind.

**BREAKOUT ROOM 7:** The more determined you are, the more you can acomplish!

This Jamboard jot lot shows what students in this third-grade class took away from learning about Jennifer's life story.

# NURTURING AND SUPPORTING INDEPENDENT PRACTICE

### *ALL THE WAY TO THE TOP: HOW ONE GIRL'S FIGHT FOR AMERICANS WITH DISABILITIES CHANGED EVERYTHING*
### BY ANNETTE BAY PIMENTEL (2020)

Teach and encourage students to write about what they know and care about. When students choose personal writing topics that feel relevant, they are more likely to feel engaged and motivated and to persevere through challenges.

- **Recall** prior learning experiences centered on *All the Way to the Top*. Discuss the passion inherent in Jennifer's story. Explain that Jennifer felt inspired to write about something that mattered deeply to her.

- **State** that students can do the same: They can also choose to write about topics they know and care about. When opinion writers deeply care about their topics, they write with passion and conviction.

- **Model** an aligned process for generating writing topics for opinion writing:
  - Generate a list of topics trending in your life. Consider issues you know about and care about, problems you have or see.
  - Think to yourself, *Why is it important for others to know about this? How could this situation be improved?*
  - Jot those ideas!

- **Encourage** students to try this process. Students may talk about their writing ideas with a partner and/or jot a list for themselves. If students feel stuck, they can consult the list created during the class inquiry experience.

- **Invite** students to continue to generate additional writing topics, and then explore one or two of those ideas in their writing notebook.

- **Observe** students as they work. Periodically, reflect on how different students generate ideas and which method(s) they feel work best.

## ✔ Check-Up

You could meet one-to-one or in small groups with students to review their ideas and writing plans. Alternatively, collect student notebooks and review recent work. You might listen for/look to see:

- Are students able to articulate why they chose a topic?

- Does it appear students know about the topic(s) they selected?

- Are students excited to talk about selected topics? Do they write with passion and conviction?

- Is there a relationship between amount of knowledge, level of passion, and volume of writing?

Use observed and identified assets to prepare and implement responsive instruction.

## ? What Else?

You might teach one or some of the following lessons:

- Writers name issues they feel are relevant or problems they see. They gather a small text set, and begin to research the issue/problem. They use findings to decide on an *informed* perspective.

- Writers freewrite about things they know about and/or do often, and then *end* by looking back over their writing and growing or naming a specific opinion about that topic.

- Writers consider what they (or the world) need(s) more or less of and then turn those ideas into more formal claims.

- Writers choose one of their ideas and practice *talking* about their perspective with a partner before writing about that perspective.

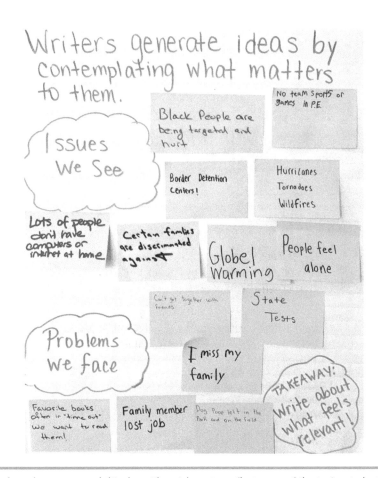

A class of fourth graders co-created this chart. The sticky notes reflect some of the topics students felt were personally relevant.

# Lesson Set Aligned to the Extending Stage

## Featured Text: *Pride: The Story of Harvey Milk and the Rainbow Flag* by Rob Sanders (2018)

### 📖 Text Pairings

- *Queer Icons From Gay to Z: Activists, Artists, and Trailblazers* by Patrick Boyle (2019), with art by Antoine Corbineau

- *Becoming RBG: Ruth Bader Ginsburg's Journey to Justice* by Debbie Levy (2019), with art by Whitney Gardner (graphic format)

- *Queer Heroes: Meet 52 LGBTQ Heroes From Past and Present* by Arabelle Sicardi (2019), with art by Sarah Tanat-Jones

- *Merriam-Webster Declares "They" Its 2019 Word of the Year* by Associated Press (2020), adapted by Newsela staff (online resource)

- *Opinion: By Being Kind, We Can All Become Better People* by Arthur C. Brooks (2019), originally published in *The Washington Post* and adapted by Newsela (online resource)

- *This Is the History of the Rainbow Flag* video created and uploaded by *Time* (2015) (online resource)

### WHAT?

This book tells the story of the Pride flag, which was championed by Harvey Milk, an important gay rights activist who served as the first openly gay elected official in California. The book tells the story of Milk's dream in the 1970s, his collaboration with designer Gilbert Baker, and how this flag has become an important symbol of civil rights and inclusion.

It can be hard for students to truly understand that history is not static, happening only long ago and far away, and that each day becomes a part of our collective history. Harvey Milk was an important part of more recent history. This book, while eloquent and rich in detail, is a simple and direct recount of historical events. It represents the importance of inclusivity, activism, and hope for a better tomorrow.

**WHEN?**

This book fits naturally into almost any launch, narrative, biography, social justice, nonfiction, or content-area research unit. It is tremendously flexible. It can be woven into existing curriculum and used at any point in the year.

 **Content Connections**

- Social Studies: civil and human rights, government, law, politics, U.S. history, U.S. symbols, and more

- Art: units around banners or flag-making, artist studies, art associated with activism, editorial artwork, art in journalism

- Personal and Community Wellness: hope, compassion, empathy, identifying injustice, personal responsibility, activism, contributing to and advocating for change, celebrating changemakers

# INVESTIGATING IDEAS THROUGH INQUIRY

*PRIDE: THE STORY OF HARVEY MILK AND THE RAINBOW FLAG*
BY ROB SANDERS (2018)

This inquiry centers on hope and symbols of hope. You will likely choose to do this inquiry *after* the aligned interactive read-aloud experience.

**Guiding Inquiry:** *How could someone or something symbolize and provide hope to many others?*

**Part 1:** Introduce mini-inquiry and research topics of interest.

- **Remind** students of the initial read-aloud experience by using the book cover to refresh student memories.

- **Revisit** the opening words. Discuss the idea that the Pride flag was designed to be a symbol of hope.

- **Explore** the guided inquiry. Provide time for students to consider topics of interest and break into self-selected groups. (Groups may decide to research a person or symbol aligned to a specific time period, community, social movement, and/or political movement.)

- **Encourage** each small group to collaboratively research their chosen subtopic. This is a wonderful opportunity to practice sharing responsibility, seeking reliable sources, and investigating sources.

**Part 2:** Reconvene small groups and provide time for each group to prepare to share.

- **Discuss** research findings in small groups.

- **Decide** *how* to communicate these discoveries (orally, through a visual display, via approved digital platforms, etc.).

- **Prepare** any needed materials.

**Part 3:** Go public.

- **Publicize** small-group findings.

- **Learn** from peers.

- **Reflect** on the collaborative process and class discoveries. Invite students to decide which symbol(s) they feel are most personally relevant.

> **NOTE:** Although this collaborative mini-inquiry is designed to happen in three class sessions, it can be extended to a full week. It can also be shortened by making Part 3 asynchronous.

## ✓ Check-Up

Observe students as they work, and listen in as they research and discuss their discoveries.

- Are students able to efficiently curate credible sources?

- Do students paraphrase and take accurate notes?

- Are students able to discuss findings, comparing and synthesizing ideas?

- Do students contribute to collaboration? Do they encourage others to also take an active role?

- Are students able to clearly communicate their discoveries?

- Do students manage their time?

Jot your observations (use templates available online at resources.corwin.com/mttm) and follow up, where most pertinent, with responsive instruction.

## ? What Else?

- Tie research to the current social studies unit work: Investigate sources of hope in that specific time or place, perhaps even sorting (and then debating) if particular people or events were providers of hope or opponents of hope . . . and for whom.

- Encourage advocacy. Invite students to share their voice through art, writing, speaking, or otherwise.

- You might also ask students to create a more personal response to this text. For instance, they might create art, music, or movement that reflects the idea of hope. They could also curate images of people and things that personally symbolize hope for them.

## We're researching symbols of hope, inspiration, & solidarity

**Pride Flag**
Mason  Ahmed
Lucia  Abby

**Liberty Bell**
Luis  Ben

**Statue of Liberty**
Dan  Dylan  Martin
Zara  Matt  Fatimah

**Feminist Symbol**
Alison  Alan
Sara  Leo

**BLM**
Juan  Angel
Ella  Ian
Nadia  Omar

**COVID Rainbow**
Paola  Juliana  Jalen
Maryam

**Bald Eagle**
Jack  Horatio
Carlos  Alexa

Image credits: Pride Flag: iStock.com/RobinOlimb; Liberty Bell: iStock.com/Pgiam; Statue of Liberty: iStock.com/Christian Schoenfeld; Feminist Symbol: iStock.com/voinSveta; BLM: iStock.com/Ekaterina Ponomareva; COVID Rainbow: iStock.com/subjug; Bald Eagle: iStock.com/StefanoVenturi

This seventh-grade class brainstormed different symbols of hope, and then signed up to find out more about one symbol.

# BUILDING VISION VIA MODELED AND GUIDED PRACTICE

## *PRIDE: THE STORY OF HARVEY MILK AND THE RAINBOW FLAG*
## BY ROB SANDERS (2018)

This interactive read-aloud provides vision for active reading. Throughout this experience, you will model and guide students in looking beyond the facts to also explore reactions, feelings, and wonders.

- **Preview** the text by showing the cover and providing a bit of background knowledge so that students have context as they prepare to listen to you read *Pride*. This background may come from the quotes and information provided on the book jacket. Alternatively, view the brief video in which the author, Rob Sanders, introduces the text: https://bit.ly/3h2S1RN (Random House Kids, 2018).

- **State** that as you read aloud, the class will focus on how to look beyond facts and also lean into reactions, feelings, and wonderings while reading.

- **Stop 1: Model.** Stop on the page that ends with "Harvey had an idea." Model sharing what you learned and your thoughts about those facts. For example: *Harvey was a hopeful man and had big dreams. He went to protests and rallies and spoke up as an advocate for gay rights. Then, he got elected to office. Hmm . . . first, I'm wondering what Harvey's idea was. I am thinking that perhaps it is connected to the rainbow flag since the book is the story of Harvey and the flag. I am also feeling that Harvey was brave to go up* and speak in front of large crowds and run for office.

- **Stop 2: Prompt.** Stop after reading the page that begins with "Five months later." Prompt students to share their learning and ideas.

  - Partner A Prompt: *What facts have you learned about Harvey Milk's life and/or the history of the rainbow flag?*

  - Partner B Prompt: *What are you thinking about these events? What wonders, reactions, and feelings do you have?*

- **Stop 3: Prompt.** Stop after reading the page that ends with "restaurants, churches, and homes." Prompt students to share their learning and ideas. Partners switch roles.

  - Partner B Prompt: *What facts have you learned about Harvey Milk's life and/or the history of the rainbow flag?*

  - Partner A Prompt: *What are you thinking about these events? What wonders, reactions, and feelings do you have?*

- **End-of-Book Conversation.** Briefly review the biographical notes, timeline, and photos at the back of the book. Ask students what they knew about Harvey Milk and the history of the rainbow flag before today . . . and how their understanding grew.

 In the foreword to *Reading the Rainbow: LGBTQ-Inclusive Literacy Instruction in the Elementary Classroom*, Mariana Souto-Manning (2018) writes that "LGBTQ-inclusive curriculum and teaching are not 'add ons' or 'extras'; they are instead invitations to re-envision well-known curricular structures such as read alouds, book discussions, and writing workshops" (pp. ix–x). How do you currently approach issues of social justice? What possibilities exist for becoming more inclusive of different identities? Who might you talk to or where might you go to find additional resources?

## ✔ Check-Up

Observe students during the interactive read-aloud. Informally assess speaking and listening. You could look to see:

- Are students able to paraphrase true and important facts?
- Do students share their wonders, reactions, and ideas?
- Do students use examples from the text to support their thinking?
- How do students communicate their ideas?

## ? What Else?

Interactive read-aloud is a teaching structure that supports comprehension. You could choose a different focus area to center this scaffolded experience:

- Sorting previously known information from new information
- Keeping the theme of providing hope in mind from the start and looking for/ jotting/discussing places of the book where this theme is highlighted
- Considering (and supporting) other possible themes and takeaways from the book
- Noticing author craft and reacting to word choice while reading

You may also follow up on any of these read-aloud experiences by creating written responses to the text. For instance, you can talk about the importance of feeling seen and hearing different people's stories. Perhaps collaborate as a class to create a six-word response to this text or Harvey Milk. Alternatively, invite students to create six-word memoirs about themselves.

# NURTURING AND SUPPORTING INDEPENDENT PRACTICE

**PRIDE: THE STORY OF HARVEY MILK AND THE RAINBOW FLAG**
**BY ROB SANDERS (2018)**

In this lesson, you will teach students to lean on mentor texts as they craft leads for their own writing.

- **Recall** previous reading of and work with *Pride*. Explain that just as the subjects of creative nonfiction can be inspiring, writers also can glean writing inspiration from the authors who write these books.

- **State** that one way writers can get inspiration for their own "first words" is by studying those in mentor texts. Since there are many strategies for crafting leads, it is worthwhile to examine the first words of a text, think about what the author did, and consider what effect it had. By doing so, writers become better prepared to purposefully try that strategy themselves.

- **Model** doing this work. You may decide to show and tell this process:
  - Reread the opening lines of a mentor text.
  - Name the writing strategy the author used. Think about why it was effective.
  - Try that out yourself. (HINT: Repeat with different mentor texts and then decide which lead works best for the purpose and feel of the current writing piece.)

- **Revisit** the first two pages from the book and reread with your writer's eyes. Notice how the author chose to begin the book with a quote and then follow up with a "larger than life" statement. Ponder the reason why Sanders may have made that decision. Then, craft an opening for your own writing piece where you start with a quote.

- **Encourage** students to provide different suggestions for a "larger than life" statement. Vote on which quote and statement combination works best.

- **Remind** students that mentor texts are extremely valuable writing tools and that writers can always draw inspiration from the work of others.

- **Invite** students to revisit a few mentor texts and choose at least one to emulate in their own writing.

- **Observe** students as they work. Coach and mentor classroom writers.

- **Celebrate** by sharing the leads students composed, where they found that inspiration, and why they feel this lead is effective.

## ✔ Check-Up

When you check in with students over the coming days, ask about their writing choices. This may sound something like:

- *What mentor text(s) did you lean on?*
- *What did you notice in this mentor text?*
- *Where did you try something new?*
- *How do you think this enhances your own writing?*
- *Where else/when else could you use this strategy?*

Coach into this work as needed.

## ❓ What Else?

Instead of focusing specifically on leads, students could zoom out and consider writer's craft across a mentor text. Invite students to get inspired by any part of a mentor text and then playfully try these moves themselves (perhaps as shown on the chart included with this lesson).

# Mentor Text That Inspired Me

## More to the Story by Hena Khan

| Text Example | Craft Move | MY TRY (for my coming of age short story) |
|---|---|---|
| "Do you have your chargers," Mama asks, "And your allergy meds?" | Spot dialogue | "Think about it like this," the conductor offered. "If you come in... You won't be wet and cold from the rain anymore." |
| "We're going to miss you too." I swallow the lump in my throat and try not to think about the things Baba's not going to be here for over the next few months. | Show don't tell using feelings | I sat there, awkwardly, fiddling with my thumbs and bouncing my knee up and down. |
| Lily entering and winning the contest was what made me see for the first time that kids can win awards too. And it showed me that our words can make as much of a difference as adults do— if we can get an audience that's bigger than our teachers and parents. | Foreshadowing for upcoming events | "Sorry, kid. That's not a choice. The train comes to everyone sometime. And the train is here for you now," the conductor explained a little to happily. |

MY LESSON: It's okay to lift things from mentor texts! When I do this, I get inspired to go back and improve my own writing.

This eighth grader discovered different craft moves in a mentor text and then tried found strategies in their own fiction writing. This related work was inspired by the *What Else?* suggestions.

# STRETCH UP AND BACK SUGGESTIONS: READING

Every page of every book offers infinite teaching and learning opportunities. Each page of the books highlighted in this chapter offer numerous possibilities beyond those presented. (Yep, even including the *What Else?* suggestions.) Almost any creative nonfiction text (and many other narrative, informational, and hybrid texts) will provide opportunities to teach and nurture *reading* habits such as the following:

- Activating background knowledge and previewing a text
- Predicting and checking on predictions
- Monitoring understanding while reading
- Summarizing and retelling after reading
- Wondering and asking questions while reading
- Feeling, reacting, and thinking while reading
- Inferring feelings
- Noticing patterns and using patterns to grow ideas
- Noticing moments of change
- Comparing characters, images, facts, ideas, and perspectives within and across texts
- Developing ideas around themes and lessons
- Thinking about mood and tone
- Figuring out possible hidden meanings of symbols
- Supporting ideas with textual evidence
- Determining main ideas and supporting details
- Engaging in conversation about ideas and takeaways
- Sketching or jotting about ideas and takeaways
- Determining an author's purpose, perspective, and/or bias

If students also have their eyes on the text (like in shared reading), you can *also* use almost any book to teach into other *foundational reading* skills:

- Concepts of print, such as one-to-one match, left-to-right reading, and return sweep
- Decoding strategies, such as sliding through the sounds, trying the vowel sound another way, chunking and crashing, and looking for a known part

- Clarifying meaning, such as thinking about what a word might mean by using picture clues, word parts, text features, word boxes/glossaries, or reading around the word

- Fluency, such as scooping words instead of reading them one by one, reading at a "Goldilocks" rate, paying attention to punctuation, or using expression that shows understanding of what is happening

Try this challenge: Flip through a picture book biography and note how many of these reading strategies you see the opportunity to model and teach. Which skills match current unit goals and/or students' learning goals?

# CHAPTER 7

· · · · · · · · · · · · · · · · · · · · · · · · · · · · · · · · · · · ·

# Informational Texts

"Incorporating informational text in the curriculum in the early years of school has the potential to increase student motivation, build important comprehension skills, and lay the groundwork for students to grow into confident, purposeful readers" (Duke, 2004, p. 43).

When you think of informational texts, you likely imagine expository structures. Text features like headings, captions, diagrams, tables, and glossaries may come to mind. But, narrative and literary nonfiction also play an important role in our study of informational texts. Essays, speeches, news articles, primary documents, and other scientific and historic artifacts are part of informational reading and writing as well. By including a wide range of types of informational texts in the curriculum, teachers can pique student interest, spark engagement, and build lasting momentum for learning. One more benefit: Content connections are easy to come by when informational mentor texts are tied to different subjects. As a result, teachers offer integrated literacy *and* weave together an even wider range of subjects. Although this chapter features picture books, the *Text Pairings* include other subgenres and formats of informational texts.

The inquiry practices in this chapter's lessons center on a topic. Students engage in mini-inquiries to hone their research skills and develop informed, well-substantiated ideas. For all three mentor texts spotlighted, shared writing is the structure used to model and guide students. As Dorfman and Dougherty (2014) wrote, "Modeled and shared writing provide a place in the writing classroom for students to play with language, experiment with words, and take risks in a supportive environment with teacher guidance" (p. 25). One of the greatest benefits of shared writing is that it can be revisited after the cycle ends. Students can repurpose the class piece as a mentor text, and teachers can reuse the product as a teaching tool. In this way, the shared writing itself becomes one more classroom mentor text that multitasks! The suggestions for independent practice all have an important feature: They center on classroom learners. Instead of a teacher leading a lesson, here the students drive the learning experiences themselves. The "you go" ideas presented throughout this chapter celebrate that classroom learners are more than ready to do so!

> **NOTE:** Remember to always first enjoy featured texts as a community of readers. Then, *revisit* the text, repurposing it as a mentor text for any number of instructional priorities and goals.

# Lesson Set Aligned to the Emerging Stage

## Featured Text: *Hey, Water!* by Antoinette Portis (2019)

 **Text Pairings**

- *I Wonder* by Tana Hoban (2003)
- *We Are Water Protectors* by Carole Lindstrom (2020), with art by Michaela Goade
- *Over and Under the Pond* by Kate Messner (2017), with art by Christopher Silas Neal
- *Nibi Emosaawdang / The Water Walker* (English and Ojibwa Edition) by Joanne Robertson (2019), translated by Shirley Williams and Isadore Toulouse
- *Water* by Melissa Stewart (2014)

### WHAT?

This jubilant text teaches about water science. The young girl featured in the text finds water in different places and in its three different states (solid, liquid, and gas).

### WHY?

The playful approach to learning about water invites the reader in and holds the reader's interest from the first to the last page. The brush and sumi ink illustrations are incredibly appealing. There is much to explore and appreciate around the whimsical word choice: Lively verbs and adjectives pair well with the personified role of water. The back matter includes information about the states of water, an eye-catching diagram of the water cycle, and information on the importance of conserving water. Cover to cover, there is much to learn.

### WHEN?

This buoyant text easily finds its way as a mentor text in any informational reading or writing unit. It can also serve as part of a text set in a research-based unit or a content-area unit.

**Content Connections**

- Social Studies: geography, water conservation

- Science: water science, water conservation, the human body

- Personal and Community Wellness: caring for our environment, conservationism, clean water activism, evaluating fairness: exploring foundational gender and socioeconomic inequities around water

# INVESTIGATING IDEAS
# THROUGH INQUIRY

### *HEY, WATER!* BY ANTOINETTE PORTIS (2019)

Here, students engage in supported research. They revisit the text, using it as a credible source of information. Students use information from the book, discussion, and their own experience to make sense of ideas and share takeaways.

**Guiding Inquiry:** *Why is water important?*

- **Remind** students of the previous reading of this text by exploring the cover.

- **Encourage** students to share the places (and times) Zoe found water. Pose the questions *Where else?* and *When else?* and take a quick picture

walk through the book to engage and support students.

- **Contemplate** the importance of, need for, and enjoyment of water by offering up the following inquiry: *How do we use water? At home? In school? In other places?*

- **Investigate** and discuss as many ideas as possible for each of these categories. Sketch, label, and/or list ideas on a co-created chart.

- **Hypothesize** reasons why water is so important. Discuss ideas collaboratively. Invite students to use water "lingo" as they share their ideas.

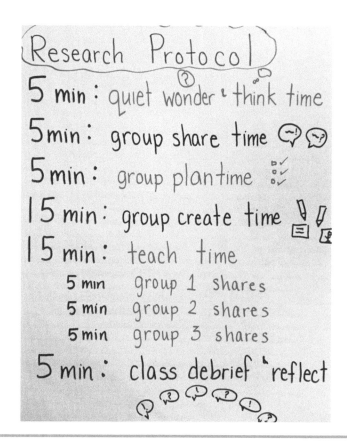

This first-grade class tweaked the inquiry to include a small-group component. This chart shows the research protocol the class used.

**Language Levers**

Visual reminders of vocabulary encourage students to talk the talk of experts. Consider having a content word wall, labeled lingo sketches, or interactive word cards available to encourage the use of domain-specific vocabulary while students engage in conversation. This will promote authentic and ongoing use of new vocabulary.

A few examples include *water*, *forms*, *solid*, *liquid*, *gas*, *freeze*, *melt*, *vapor*, and *because*.

## ✔ Check-Up

Observe and listen in as students engage in conversation with one another. Jot notes to record what you see and hear. Conversation checklists and record-keeping templates are available in the online companion (resources .corwin.com/mttm).

## ? What Else?

Alternative topic inquiries include:

- When/where do we see water as a solid? Liquid? Gas?
- When/where/how do we see and use water in spring? Winter? Summer? Fall?
- How could we encourage school community members/family members/general community members to conserve water?

Other possible inquiries include:

- A language-themed inquiry where students explore the verbs in the text.
- A science-themed inquiry where the class actively investigates the places and ways (states) Zoe found water, seeing and learning more about water for themselves.
- A social studies–themed inquiry around access to water in different places.
- A social action–themed inquiry around water conservation practices.

# BUILDING VISION VIA MODELED AND GUIDED PRACTICE

### *HEY, WATER!* BY ANTOINETTE PORTIS (2019)

In this cycle of shared writing, the class will co-create an informational text about water. Each session in this cycle will likely last 5 to 10 minutes. Remember that students contribute by orally sharing ideas. The teacher will do the actual composing. To prepare for this cycle of shared writing, discuss what *information* students remember from the previous read(s) of this text.

## Session 1: Generate ideas.

- **Share** that the class will be making a "teaching book" to share their knowledge about water.

- **Offer**, seek, and list possible water-related topics (forms of water, the water cycle, inside and outside places where we see water, different uses of water, etc.).

- **Model** stating known facts that support each possible topic.

- **Invite** students to join in.

- **Vote** to decide the topic of the class piece.

## Session 2: Plan and rehearse for writing.

- **Review** the work from Session 1.

- **Invite** students to prepare for writing by thinking about and sharing pertinent information with a partner.

- **Elicit** ideas: *What information should we include in our teaching book on water?*

- **Model** using student input to list the parts of the book. For example, if you chose to write about forms of water, there might be an introduction, a part on the solid form, a part on the liquid form, a part on the gas form, and a conclusion.

- **Summarize** the importance of planning before writing and ask students to join you in chorally stating the plan aloud two or three more times, just so it sticks.

## Session 3: Begin writing.

- **Review** the plan created in the previous session.

- **Model** quickly sketching something that aligns with the goal/purpose of each planned part. For example, if you chose forms of water, you might sketch icicles for the part on the solid form. Narrate what you are doing as you sketch.

- **Invite** students to suggest details that could be added to each of the sketches.

- **Use** student input to label parts of each sketch with key vocabulary, turning sketches into teaching diagrams.

- **Summarize** how yesterday's planning helped the class stay focused while sketching and labeling each part of the book today.

## Session 4: Add to the writing.

- **Review** work from Session 3.

- **Invite** students to contemplate what could be added to each part of the teaching book.

- **Elicit** student ideas as you write. Depending on the readiness of students in the class, model writing a few words, a sentence, or a few sentences for each part of the book.

- **Summarize** the process used to compose the text on each page.

## Session 5: Reread and improve writing.

- **Reread** the class piece.

- **Remind** students of two recently taught language features, perhaps something related to punctuation and something related to phonics.

- **Model** rereading the class book, specifically checking for the first concept.

- **Invite** students to turn and talk with a partner, rereading the piece and checking for the second concept.

- **Use** student suggestions to improve the text.
- **Remind** students of the importance rereading work and looking for opportunities to show off what they have learned in spelling and grammar.

### ✓ Check-Up

Because the goal of shared writing is for students to gain vision of the process of writing, it is not expected that students will be able to do this independently . . . yet. The subsequent transfer will happen once you explicitly teach students how to do the work you modeled during each session of shared writing and they have opportunities to practice. For now, simple observations (and/or anecdotal jotting) focused on student participation suffice.

### ? What Else?

Shared writing products intend to exemplify what most class members will create when writing independently. Depending on the age and readiness of students, you may develop the shared writing piece in different ways. Here are some ideas aligned to the emerging stage:

- Sketches and labels
- A simple "pattern" sentence for each part/subtopic
- Sentences composed for each part, crafted with greater attention to word choice and vocabulary

Instead of engaging in a *cycle* of shared writing, you could do a single *session* of interactive writing. Invite students to "dip in" and do small pieces of the composing. They may add in content-area vocabulary, a recently taught language standard, or words that contain a taught phonics concept.

TIP: Having a content word wall visible can promote greater use of domain-specific vocabulary.

This artifact shows how interactive writing can be used in lieu of a cycle of shared writing. Emerging learners "dipped in" to add content vocabulary.

# NURTURING AND SUPPORTING INDEPENDENT PRACTICE

### *HEY, WATER!* BY ANTOINETTE PORTIS (2019)

There are infinite ways students can support one another in reading, writing, and language study. However, this meaningful partnering needs to be modeled, taught, practiced, and supported. Here, a practice called "Find and Fix Up" (Koutrakos, 2018) is detailed. Partners support one another in rereading work to see if they applied "word knowledge" while writing and, if not, to fix up their work. This is similar to what the class did together in Session 5 of the shared writing experience.

- **Remind** students of a previously introduced phonics concept.

- **Announce** that today, students will play a game called "Find and Fix Up" with their partner. The purpose of this game is to help partners fix up their work and make sure they spelled words with known letters and sounds correctly.

- **Model** playing the game with a partner (see *how* in the mini-chart pictured).

- **Ask** students to take out recent writing and something to write with. Have students sit with a partner.

- **Invite** partnerships to take turns supporting one another, rereading recent work and looking carefully for one specific phonics concept.

  - If partners find an example that is correct, they can celebrate and continue rereading. If students find an example that is not spelled conventionally, the partner will provide peer support as the writer tries again.

  - If partners do not find any examples of words with the focus pattern, they will find a place to add in one or two

aligned words in a way that makes sense and correctly spell the word(s) from the start.

- **Celebrate** all found, fixed, and added words. Share appreciation for a partner's help.

### ✔ Check-Up

You may consider any of the following:

- Invite students to share where they found, fixed, or added words.

- Encourage students to tally the number of times they found, fixed, or added words.

- Ask students to explain the process they used for finding, fixing, and adding words.

- Look through student work to evaluate transfer of specifically targeted sounds, patterns, vocabulary words, or conventions.

### ❓ What Else?

Use this routine frequently. It is flexible enough to work with any phonics sound or spelling pattern (words that start with /p/, words that are a part of the -*an* family, words with a taught digraph, words with a long /ē/ vowel sound, words with a taught diphthong, etc.). It can also be done with any writing in any genre in any subject.

Additionally, partners can support one another using "Find and Fix Up" to:

- Check spelling of high-frequency words.

- Prioritize using new vocabulary.

- Apply a taught grammar concept.

- Enhance word choice, such as active verbs or interesting adjectives.

This primary-grade version of the "Find and Fix Up" mini-chart comes from *The Word Study That Sticks Companion* (Koutrakos, 2019). The full lesson to introduce this partner game can be found in the original *Word Study That Sticks* book (Koutrakos, 2018).

# Lesson Set Aligned to the Developing Stage

## Featured Text: *Gross as a Snot Otter* by Jess Keating (2019)

### 📖 Text Pairings

- *Pink Is for Blobfish*, *What Makes a Monster?*, and *Cute as an Axolotl* by Jess Keating (2016, 2017, 2018) with art by David DeGrand

- *Animals Nobody Loves* by Seymour Simon (2001)

- *The World's Ugliest Animal* video by SciShow Kids (2015) (online resource)

### WHAT?

This book is part of Keating and DeGrand's *World of Weird Animals* series. This text engages readers with jaw-dropping and emotion-inciting photographs. It provides fascinating information about each featured animal (facts, names, habitat, threats, etc.). The cartoon-style illustrations add to the appeal of this informational text.

### WHY?

Animals are a universally popular topic of study. Interesting and lesser-known species are even more fascinating! Truth be told, I also just love anything and everything written by Jess Keating. This author's careful attention to appealing to the intended audience is evident from cover to cover. The design is colorful and eye-catching. The information included often leads to a verbalized "Ewwww," "Wow!," or "No way!" The consistent page-to-page structure helps readers orient themselves to each new page and animal spotlighted. And for word nerds like myself, the inviting glossary at the end of the book seals the deal.

### WHEN?

This expository text easily fits into any informational reading or writing unit. It has appeal as a read-aloud, research source, or independent reading selection. Readers, writers, researchers, science fans, and animal lovers will choose to return to this mentor text time and time again.

**Content Connections**

- Science: animal kingdom, habitats, biomes, food chains and webs, ecology, and so much more!

- Math: measurement

- Social Studies: geography

- Art: photography, cartooning, graphic design

- Personal and Community Wellness: false first impressions, appearance bias, caring for animals and the environment, animal activism

# INVESTIGATING IDEAS THROUGH INQUIRY

### *GROSS AS A SNOT OTTER* BY JESS KEATING (2019)

Here, students collaborate to discover more about one selected animal from Keating's book. Although this research is not intended to be extensive, it does call on students to remember and use what they know about researching. The speed element adds a playful twist.

**Guiding Inquiry:** *What can we find out about notoriously "gross" animals—in just a few minutes?*

- **Examine** the cover as a class, recalling past reading experience(s) with this book.

- **Invite** students to share the facts they remember. Tell students that today, they will have the opportunity to engage in spark research.

- **Choose** and list three to five of the animals featured in the text. Ask students to group themselves based on an animal that they wish to learn more about.

- **Share** the spark research protocol that will be used. Here is one possible example:

  ○ 5 minutes: Group members share why they chose a particular topic, what wonders they have, and what else they hope to learn.

  ○ 10 minutes: Students research.

  ○ 10 minutes: Students share findings with their group, comparing and synthesizing information.

  ○ 15 minutes: Groups prepare to publicize their findings.

  ○ 15 minutes: Groups share their process and found information with other classmates.

- **Observe** students throughout the process.

- **Celebrate** collaboration, contributions, and learning.

## ✔ Check-Up

You might choose to:

- Keep anecdotal notes on what you observe as students research, prepare, and present.

- Use a checklist to evaluate conversation and/or collaboration.

- Evaluate the product and presentation of information.

- Ask students to write up a short reflection sharing what they learned and took away from this spark research inquiry.

- Invite students to complete a self-assessment and/or group assessment.

## ❓ What Else?

To follow up on this inquiry, students may:

- Compare researched topics and decide if the animals are more alike or different.

- Debate whether or not an animal (or the collective group of these animals) is really disgusting—or not.

- Use a similar process to research something related to a current content-area topic.

Additionally, using this book, students might instead engage in:

- Word choice inquiry: Which words lead to the "ewwww" feeling while reading?

- Location inquiry: Plot animal habitats on a map and see which animals live the closest and furthest from one another (or from the class).

- Scientific species inquiry: Learn more about the kingdom, phylum, class, order, or genus that this animal is a part of.

- Language inquiry: Playfully study an included grammar feature or convention.

# THE HAGFISH
## (AKA SLIME EELS)

**Q: What's interesting about their bodies?**
A: They look like eels.
They have no jaw or bones.
They have a skull, but no spine (they are the only animal like this!)

**Q: How does their slime help?**
A: They squirt slime at predators.
The slime travels through the water.
The slime chokes predators- even sharks!

**Q: What's interesting about their habitat?**
A: They often stay on the ocean floor.
They create burrows on the sea floor & live in those burrows.
They eat food found down there and food that drifts down there.

**FUN FACTS!**

Hagfish mate with themselves!
A hagfish will kill- and then eat you!

This inquiry product was created by a small group of fourth graders during remote instruction. The collaboration and connection was as beneficial as the content learning.

# BUILDING VISION VIA MODELED AND GUIDED PRACTICE

### *GROSS AS A SNOT OTTER* BY JESS KEATING (2019)

To prepare for this cycle of shared writing, show and explore the cover of Keating's book, discussing what *information* students learned during previous experiences with this text. Remember that students contribute by orally sharing ideas. The teacher will do all the efficient composing of student ideas. Each session in this cycle of shared writing will likely last 5 to 15 minutes.

## Session 1: Generate ideas.

- **Share** that the class will be collaborating to create a written response to the book. To begin, the class will need to choose a claim they plan to support.
- **Model** sharing one "takeaway" or opinion related to the book.
- **Invite** students to turn and talk to do the same.
- **Elicit** student ideas. List those opinion statements as claims.
- **Test** each claim by identifying and naming text support for each.
- **Choose** the claim that has the most support.

## Session 2: Plan and rehearse for writing.

- **Review** the work from Session 1.
- **Model** using a quick organizational structure (like the one pictured) to plan the written response.
- **Invite** students to review the claim and reasons, orally sharing as much evidence as they can to support each listed reason.
- **Remind** students of the importance of taking a few minutes to think and plan before writing.

## Session 3: Begin writing.

- **Review** work from the previous session.
- **Model** stating a claim and writing a reason. Add in text examples that support that reason.

- **Invite** students to think about and collect as many examples as they can to support another reason.
- **Ask** student volunteers to share examples. Use this input as you continue to compose the piece.
- **Summarize** the process of using planning while drafting.

## Session 4: Add to the writing.

- **Review** work from Session 3.
- **Review** the importance of using transitional words and phrases to connect ideas. Reread the piece and mark spots where transitional words or phrases would enhance connectivity.
- **Invite** students to turn and talk to encourage all students to generate appropriate and varied transitional words and phrases.
- **Use** student ideas as you infuse transitional words and phrases into the piece.
- **Reread** the piece and comment on how using transitional words and phrases to connect ideas created "flow" within the writing.

## Session 5: Reread and edit writing.

- **Review** work from previous sessions.
- **Name** a recently taught spelling pattern or grammar convention.
- **Reread** the class-composed piece, looking specifically for evidence of transfer and application of this featured pattern or convention.
- **Invite** students to find examples, share how to fix up any trouble spots, or direct you to add in more examples.
- **Remind** students of the importance of rereading and checking for one specific spelling or grammar concept at a time.

**Claim**

People are more dangerous to these "gross" creatures than they are to humans.

- loss of habitat
- pollution
- global warming
- human consumption
  ↳ fashion

*Suriname Toad · cicada · Snot Otter · Spanish ribbed newt · parrot fish · fulmar · herring · Zombie worms · Sea cucumbers · hagfish · herring · marabou stork*

This planning was created by a third-grade class in Session 2 of this cycle of shared writing.

Supporting peer conversation takes a lot of patience and practice. Highly scaffolded practices, like shared writing, are great times to model and support this important work. When and how do you teach into partner conversation? How else could you bolster equitable participation during partner turn and talks? How can teachers encourage students to use language that feels authentic and comfortable?

## ✓ Check-Up

Because the goal of shared writing is for students to gain vision of the process of writing, it is not expected that students will immediately go and transfer these processes. You will likely follow up on this cycle of shared writing with explicit teaching of how to do the work you modeled during each session of shared writing. Therefore, simple observations (and/or anecdotal jotting) focused on student participation suffice. You may also decide to ask students what "stuck with them" from this cycle of shared writing and what they look forward to trying on their own.

## ? What Else?

In Session 4, instead of "adding to the writing" by infusing transition words and phrases, you might focus on:

- Creating an interesting hook and/or crafting a satisfying closing.

- Purposefully infusing content-area vocabulary used in the text.

- Adding in a twin sentence (circling back and explaining why a selected example from the text proves the claim).

- Composing a simple counterargument.

- Paraphrasing supportive information from the text versus using a direct quote from the text.

Alternatively, depending on the readiness of class members, you might instead use this text to model summarizing information learned about different animals featured in the book. This could be done through shared writing, as shown here, or through "one and done" interactive writing, where students do small portions of the actual writing, too.

# NURTURING AND SUPPORTING INDEPENDENT PRACTICE

### *GROSS AS A SNOT OTTER* BY JESS KEATING (2019)

Keating prominently highlights key content words in her texts. They are bolded and explained in the text *and* defined in the glossary at the end. In this student-driven learning experience, students work collaboratively to lean on mentor texts (including *Gross as a Snot Otter*) and find inspiration for using domain-specific vocabulary—with minimal teacher interference.

- **Revisit** *Gross as a Snot Otter*, looking for "content words." Find and discuss a few examples.

- **State** that students can be just like Keating and use her thoughtful work as a mentor of how to hold themselves accountable for using the lingo associated with any subject or topic they write on.

- **Invite** students to join together with partners or small groups and spend a few minutes mining this text (and/or other informational texts) and investigating where and how the author includes topic words.

- **Encourage** students to consider the vocabulary associated with a topic they are currently writing about during their independent writing time.

- **Challenge** students to revisit their own writing and find places to include expert vocabulary.

- **Ask** students to share what they did and how it went.

- **Celebrate** a before and after—sharing how infusing content vocabulary improved part of their information writing.

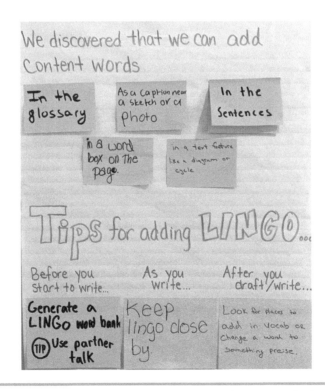

Students in this third-grade class co-created a chart to list (and remember) some of the different places and ways writers include content-area lingo.

## ✔ Check-Up

Check in on the processes students employ and the success they experience with these methods. You may consider:

- Keeping anecdotal notes on what you see and hear as you meet with students.

- Asking students to submit a "before" and an "after" that shows what they tried (or checking revision history on a Google Doc).

- Having students share their work with a partner, providing and receiving peer feedback.

- Having students use a tool (like a checklist or microprogression) to self-assess their results.

## ❓ What Else?

You could ask students to do the same kind of work when they engage in conversation and write in *all* content areas. To provide a few examples, students might work on increasing their:

- Infusion of vocabulary like *character, setting, problem, solution, resolution, infer, theory,* and *evidence* as they write in their reading notebook or when they talk with partners or book clubs.

- Infusion of domain-specific vocabulary as they jot about their math thinking and processes. For example, when working with fractions, they may use lingo like *numerator, denominator, equivalent, simplest form,* and *benchmark* when conversing and writing in math.

- Attention toward using science lingo as they write up lab reports, describing and analyzing what they observed, learned, and believe. For example, while studying buoyancy, they may use words like *buoyant, sink, float, force, density, submerge,* and *displace.*

# NOTES

# Lesson Set Aligned to the Extending Stage

## Featured Text: *Bringing Back the Wolves: How a Predator Restored an Ecosystem* by Jude Isabella (2020)

### 📖 Text Pairings

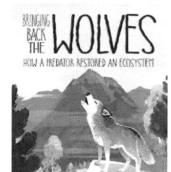

- *Bringing Back the Wolves* is also available as an e-book on the popular online reading platform Epic (www.getepic .com), which makes it accessible to learners in many settings.

- *Scientists Debunk Myth That Yellowstone Wolves Changed Entire Ecosystem, Flow of Rivers* by Michael Kuhne (2019), posted by AccuWeather (online resource)

- *How Wolves Change Rivers* created and uploaded by Sustainable Human (2014a) (online resource)

- *How Whales Change Climate* created and uploaded by Sustainable Human (2014b) (online resource)

### WHAT?

This clear and detailed informational text recounts how, after losing a key part of its ecosystem, Yellowstone National Park became overrun with certain species . . . and how balance was restored by reintroducing the gray wolf. This comprehensive text explores the interconnectedness of nature in a student-friendly, accessible way.

### WHY?

This book is clear and informative and tells an important conservational story. The headings and primary text on each page explain the process of what happened to Yellowstone's ecosystem. The sidebars, illustrations, and student-friendly diagrams go beyond the basics, providing background information and other related information that is sure to engage readers. This book has certain features we expect to see in informational texts (table of contents, headings, bolded words, diagrams, a glossary, etc.), but there are no photographs. This reminds students that when it comes to genre, there are no "absolutes." The index supports teaching different ways to read and use informational texts, too. Finally, the resources shared in the back matter encourage students to learn and discover more. Also check out the *Text Pairings* for short texts and videos that attempt to substantiate, debunk, and extend the information included in this text.

## WHEN?

Just like the other offerings in this chapter, this mentor text slides right into any informational reading or writing unit. It is a natural complement to research units and content-area learning. You may first read this text, over time, as a class read-aloud. Or you may choose to introduce this text in bits and pieces, where and as needed.

 **Content Connections**

- Science: habitats, ecology, animals/wolves, conservation, food chains and webs, and so much more!
- Art: landscape drawing, animal drawing and painting, nature drawing and painting, texture studies
- Personal and Community Wellness: the interconnectedness of a community, the importance of inclusion, conservationism

# INVESTIGATING IDEAS
# THROUGH INQUIRY

### *BRINGING BACK THE WOLVES: HOW A PREDATOR RESTORED AN ECOSYSTEM* BY JUDE ISABELLA (2020)

In this inquiry, students hone their research skills, specifically focusing on the credibility of information from different sources. They read and view texts on one topic that share different information and different perspectives. Students are encouraged to critically contemplate what they access and consume before coming to their own conclusion.

**Guiding Inquiry:** *What really happened in Yellowstone?*

- **Remind** students of previous learning about the wolves in Yellowstone by holding up the book and using the cover to activate prior knowledge.

- **Ask** students to share what they remember. Make a quick sequence map to summarize key information provided within the book. For example: *The government encouraged people to hunt wolves → no wolf packs remained → environment impacted → wolves reintroduced → elk population reduced → plants began to grow → bears had berries to eat; insects and birds had safe habitats . . .*

- **View** the *Text Pairings* video by Sustainable Human (2014a) and read the article by Michael Kuhne (2019). Pose the questions, *What does each author/creator believe? Do you think these sources are credible? What do you believe?*

- **Investigate** ideas. Students will work collaboratively to read different accounts, compare facts, and determine their stance.

- **Discuss** gained understandings and positions as a class community.

- **Summarize** the importance of researching widely and comparing information across multiple sources before drawing any one conclusion.

> **NOTE:** Depending on the interests and readiness of the class, you might choose to engage in whole-class research or use any combination of individual, partner, or small-group research pods during this mini-inquiry.

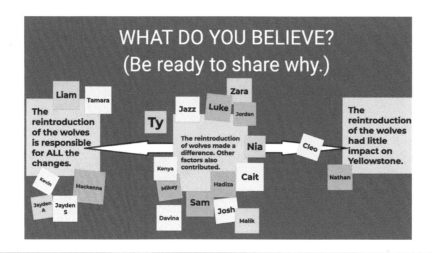

This artifact shows what different members of a seventh-grade class concluded after accessing and consuming information from different sources.

### ✔ Check-Up

Depending on your prioritized goals, you might choose to:

- Keep anecdotal notes on what you observe as students work and discuss ideas.

- Use a checklist to evaluate conversation and/or collaboration (see online resources at resources.corwin.com/mttm).

- Ask students to write up a short reflection sharing what they learned and took away from this spark research inquiry.

- Ask students to share how they will replicate and apply aspects of this experience when they engage in their own research.

### ? What Else?

You could follow up on the fully described inquiry by:

- Having students do some reflective writing to share their own perspective.

- Engaging in caucus-rich debates to encourage students to use researched findings to try to convince others that *their* stance is the accurate one.

You might *instead* choose to view the *How Whales Change Climate* video (Sustainable Human, 2014b) listed in the *Text Pairings* and ask, "What other examples can we find that show the impact of the loss or introduction of a species on an ecosystem?"

# BUILDING VISION VIA MODELED AND GUIDED PRACTICE

*BRINGING BACK THE WOLVES: HOW A PREDATOR RESTORED AN ECOSYSTEM* **BY JUDE ISABELLA (2020)**

Jump-start focus for this cycle of shared writing by exploring the cover of *Bringing Back the Wolves* and activating prior knowledge. Discuss what students remember.

Each session in this cycle of shared writing will likely last 5 to 15 minutes.

## Session 1: Generate ideas.

- **Share** that the class will be collaborating to summarize the information presented in this text. Explain that the intended audience is younger students and the purpose is to teach a younger audience about the reintroduction of wolves to Yellowstone National Park. To begin, the class will need to choose a structure that matches their purpose.

- **Model** identifying and considering different feasible structures, such as *descriptive*, *sequential*, and *cause and effect*.

- **Invite** partnerships to discuss the merits and drawbacks of each structure. Ask a few students to share their thoughts.

- **Choose** the structure that the class feels is the best match for the intended audience and purpose for writing.

## Session 2: Create a plan.

- **Review** the work from Session 1.

- **Model** how to choose a planning method that matches the intended structure (e.g., box and bullets for descriptive, flow chart for sequence, two-column chart for cause and effect).

- **Invite** students to gather thoughts. Provide a few minutes for partnerships to rehearse for writing.

- **Elicit** student ideas and use their input to jot notes on the planning chart.

- **Summarize** the work done and state the necessity of taking time to rehearse and plan before actually writing.

## Session 3: Begin drafting.

- **Review** plans from the previous session.

- **Invite** students to share different ideas for an enticing lead with a partner. Listen as volunteers share ideas with the class.

- **Compose** a lead using one student idea or a hybrid of different shared ideas.

- **Encourage** students to look back to planning from Session 2 and select facts to include. Write what students share.

- **Elicit** more feedback on how to close the piece. Add those thoughts to the class piece.

- **Remind** students that using planning while drafting helps writing to stay focused and organized.

## Session 4: Reread and check for clarity.

- **Review** work from Session 3.

- **Revisit** the intended purpose and prospective audience.

- **Reread** the class-composed piece with that lens.

- **Invite** students to share where clarification is necessary and how to enhance understanding for this younger audience.

- **Revise** the piece, using student suggestions.

- **Remind** students of the importance of keeping an intended audience in mind throughout the process of writing.

## Session 5: Reread and edit.

- **Review** the work that's been done in this cycle of shared writing.

- **Remind** students of one or two recently taught spelling patterns, word parts, or emphasized conventions (syllabification, a studied affix or root, subject–verb agreement, consistent verb tense, etc.).

- **Reread** the class piece, looking for one language concept at a time. Ask students to locate any included examples and improve as needed.

- **Remind** students to consistently apply knowledge of taught spelling and grammar concepts whenever they write.

## ✔ Check-Up

Shared writing is a "show" (I go/we go) component and not meant to explicitly teach students the process of the work. Therefore, simple observing and/or anecdotal jotting is sufficient (check out the templates available online at resources.corwin.com/mttm). You may also decide to ask students what "stuck with them" from this cycle of shared writing and what they look forward to trying on their own.

## ? What Else?

You will notice that the plan for this cycle of shared writing does not only work with this featured book. You can use this same plan to do similar work with another text or topic. You might also:

- Choose to write a similar piece, but change the anticipated audience. Help students see how that changes both the composition and word choice. This can be done as a cycle of shared writing or as a single session of interactive writing.

- Choose to change your purpose for writing. For example, you could share and support the perspective students concluded was "correct" during the outlined inquiry lesson and use information from the book to support this perspective. Again, this could be done through either shared or interactive writing.

# NURTURING AND SUPPORTING INDEPENDENT PRACTICE

### BRINGING BACK THE WOLVES: HOW A PREDATOR RESTORED AN ECOSYSTEM BY JUDE ISABELLA (2020)

After using this text in supported class lessons and experiences, make it available for students to refer to as they write. Here, students support one another in using a mentor text while writing. This student-driven experience reminds teachers to step back and make space for students to step up.

- **Invite** students to revisit this text and identify a craft move that they hope to use in their own writing.

- **Encourage** students to use found inspiration, trying something similar in their own writing.

- **Explain** that classroom writers can contribute to the community by supporting and teaching one another.

- **Invite** students to prepare to teach one another. Specifically, students will share what inspired them, why they appreciated this craft move, where they applied this in their own writing, and how others can do the same.

- **Celebrate** class contributions. Provide time for students to lead and visit expert stations. (Check out Chapter 10 for more details and guidance on this kind of peer teaching.)

> **NOTE:** Two class sessions is *plenty* of time—this is meant to be not a "big" project but instead a natural method of reflecting on learning and contributing to the success of others. Most likely, students will identify a writing move, try it in their own writing, and prepare to teach it in the first designated period. In the second session, students can alternate between facilitating peer teaching and visiting expert stations led by their classmates.

 **Check-Up**

You may:

- Talk to students about their ideas and processes as they prepare to teach classmates. If necessary, offer or coach them on a specific teaching method they might want to try.

- Visit expert stations yourself and see what students teach, how they teach it, and how ready their classmates are to take on that work themselves.

- Use speaking and listening standards to guide a more formal assessment of student presentations.

- Ask students to submit peer assessments on the stations they visited.

## ? What Else?

Instead of expert stations, you could use a similar idea in a much quicker, informal way. For example, once or twice a week, remind students of a strategy you taught using a mentor text and ask students to share with a partner when, where, and how they applied that concept as they worked (in reading, writing, word study, or grammar). Student partnerships can provide on-the-spot feedback and support to one another. They can use any additional minutes to work together to continue to practice that strategy (in other books they are reading, in other pieces of writing, etc.).

# BRINGING BACK THE WOLVES (& MORE)

| Found | Found By | | | DAY TEACHING/ SHARING |
|---|---|---|---|---|
| Creative chapter titles & headings | Cleo | Davina | Ty Malik | 1 |
| LONGER sophisticated sentences <not runons> | Aidan | Jack | Kati | 2 |
| Expert Lingo → explained | JOSH | Jordan Kevin | DYMOND | 1 |
| COOL "other" features (not photo/captions) | Kevin | Keira | Ava | 2 |
| Openings that HINT at author's opinion | Kenya | Tamara | Nathan | 1 |
| STORYTELLING in an info text | | | Alexis Maddie | 2 |

# DAY 1 SESSIONS

| WHAT | WHY | WHO | WHERE |
|---|---|---|---|
| Expert Lingo | Info writers need to sound credible. | Toni & Emily | Zoom link here |
| Features That SHOW Provided Information | It's important to help your reader understand new information. | Julia & Heather | Zoom link here |
| Features That ADD TO & ENHANCE Provided Information | Use all you can to teach readers! | Josh & Chris | Zoom link here |
| Index Searching | Info writers need to research efficiently. | Mike & Tomás | Zoom link here |
| Figurative Language | No one wants to read BORING info writing. | Aimee & Jason | Zoom link here |

The chart at the top was co-created with sixth graders. It shares what they found, tried, and offered support in doing. The virtual posting below the chart was co-created by a seventh-grade class that was working in a fully remote setting.

# STRETCH UP AND BACK SUGGESTIONS: WRITING

By now, I hope it has become clear that every page of every book offers a wide variety of teaching and learning opportunities. The *Stretch Up and Back Suggestions* act as a reminder that one method does not work for everyone. When teachers offer multiple strategies or methods to go about new work and encourage students to discover their own processes, it disrupts traditional teaching methods.

Here I intend to honor that idea and jump-start initial thinking around multiple avenues to work on different *writing* skills. Because this chapter highlighted informational texts, the strategies listed are specific to information writing. Some of these strategies are simpler, and some are more sophisticated. Please also note that similar work can be done with other genres of writing!

Skills and "Stretchable" Strategies to Support Information Writers

| CORE SKILL | ALIGNED STRATEGIES |
|---|---|
| **Information writers choose topics to explore by . . .** | • Talking about, thinking of, and/or listing places they have been<br>• Talking about, thinking of, and/or listing things they do<br>• Talking about, thinking of, and/or listing topics they know about and care about<br>• Talking about, thinking of, and/or listing what they have learned in school<br>• Talking about, thinking of, and/or listing topics they know a bit about . . . and are curious to find out more about<br>• Thinking of their audience and listing topics that will appeal to these readers<br>• Thinking of their purpose and listing items aligned to that purpose<br>• Considering topics they have recently explored as a reader (writer, mathematician, scientist, musician, athlete, etc.) |
| **Information writers hook their readers by . . .** | • Naming their topic and why it matters<br>• Identifying the topic and previewing what's to come (subtopics)<br>• Asking a question related to the topic<br>• Creating a riddle where the answer is the topic<br>• Telling a *brief* story related to the topic<br>• Asking the audience to imagine (e.g., *Picture this . . .*, *Imagine that . . .*)<br>• Including a relevant and interesting quote related to the topic<br>• Shocking readers with a wow fact or statistic |

| CORE SKILL | ALIGNED STRATEGIES |
|---|---|
| **Information writers support reader understanding by . . .** | • Turning sketches into teaching pictures/diagrams (by labeling)<br>• Including text features that show (and/or extend) what they are teaching about<br>• Organizing and grouping facts by subtopic<br>• Creating twin and triplet sentences to say more about a fact<br>• Using "push prompts" to explain more about a fact (e.g., *This means . . .*, *This is important because . . .*)<br>• Making a comparison to something familiar (e.g., *This is like . . .*, similes, metaphors)<br>• Using precise and descriptive words that create a clear picture in the reader's mind<br>• Using appropriate transitions to help readers see connections and bridges between ideas<br>• Thinking about the teaching structure that makes the most sense for each part of the information (compare/contrast, sequential, cause/effect, etc.) |
| **Information writers support readers with content vocabulary by . . .** | • Showing the word in a visual on the page (sketch or text feature)<br>• Including a word box on the page<br>• Bolding the word and including it in a glossary<br>• Including a definition sentence<br>• Sharing the meaning in reader-friendly language<br>• Making a connection or comparison to something readers likely already know<br>• Using an appositive to say more about the meaning<br>• Using parentheses to explain the definition |
| **Information writers close their writing by . . .** | • Reminding the reader of the topic<br>• Reminding the reader why the topic matters<br>• Asking the reader a "lingering question"<br>• Suggesting an action the reader can take after reading the piece<br>• Reminding the reader of the most important facts and takeaways<br>• Sharing information for where to go to find out more about the topic<br>• Hinting at their own perspective on the topic |

# CHAPTER 8

· · · · · · · · · · · · · · · · · · · · · · · · · · · · · · · · · · · · · · · · ·

# Poetry

"We need poetry. We really do. Poetry promotes literacy, builds community, and fosters emotional resilience. It can cross boundaries that little else can" (Aguilar, 2013, para. 1).

Poets are linguistic artists, carefully choosing words while simultaneously composing sound and rhythm. No matter how *you* classify the many different subgenres, I believe that each and every traditional poem—or nursery rhyme, chant, novel written in verse, or song from any musical genre—employs a purposeful and intentional craft technique that plays with sounds and produces rhythm when read, recited, or performed. And it is precisely because of this careful attention to composition that exciting (and far-reaching) learning opportunities result!

Poetry is incredibly adaptable; it can comprise an entire unit of study, and it can be woven into all units of study. Poetry has always helped me teach concepts connected to reading, writing, language, grammar, vocabulary, and spelling. It has been an integral part of supporting speaking and listening skills. When teachers share poetry, they model the appreciation of words, language, imagination, and ideas. The topics of and techniques within poems frequently celebrate personal identities and foster emotional resiliency. And have I mentioned fluency?

The inquiry work within this chapter focuses on writer's craft, figurative language, and word choice. These explorations feel particularly playful! Across this chapter, shared reading is used to model integrated literacy learning. Maria Nichols (2008) wrote that this component enables students "to develop an awareness of the decisions the teacher has been making on their behalf and gradually begin to shoulder some of the responsibility themselves" (p. 71). As such, the forthcoming cycles of shared reading intend to guide students through prioritized skills and strategies. This is followed up with more independently driven learning where students study the craft inherent within these mentor texts. By reading with their writer's eyes, students become ready to try out some of the moves they notice and appreciate (regardless of the genre they are currently composing). When it comes to poetry, not only is there plenty to teach; there is also a lot to love!

*If you finish Part II and are looking for more lesson sets, check out the bonus chapter available in the online companion (resources.corwin.com/ mttm). It features emerging, developing, and extending lesson sets for fantasy fiction.*

**NOTE:** Remember to always first enjoy featured texts and/or poems as a community of readers. Then *revisit* the text, repurposing it as a mentor text for any number of instructional priorities and goals.

# Lesson Set Aligned to the Emerging Stage

## Featured Text: *A Stick Is an Excellent Thing: Poems Celebrating Outdoor Play* by Marilyn Singer (2012)

### 📖 Text Pairings

- *Just Like Me* by Vanessa Brantley-Newton (2020)

- *Wonderful Words: Poems About Reading, Writing, Speaking, and Listening* by Lee Bennett Hopkins (2004), with art by Karen Barbour

- *All Are Welcome* by Alexandra Penfold (2018), with art by Suzanne Kaufman

- *Feel the Beat: Dance Poems That Zing From Salsa to Swing* by Marilyn Singer (2017), with art by Kristi Valiant (audiobook also available)

- *Forest Has a Song* by Amy Ludwig VanDerwater (2013), with art by Robin Gourley

- *The Day You Begin / El día en que descubres quién eres* by Jacqueline Woodson (2018), with art by Rafael López

### WHAT?

The poems included in this text highlight so many fun ways to imagine and connect outdoors. Jovial friends playing all kinds of games fill each page of this energetic anthology.

### WHY?

This collection contains so many of my favorite things: poetry, play, creativity, and imagination. The book feels nostalgic for adult readers—a reminder of days spent outside turning a little something into a whole lot of fun. For younger readers, it sparks a renewed interest in finding great pleasure in the simple things. The settings portrayed are reminiscent of urban, suburban, and rural communities. The lighthearted feel of the colored pencil and ink illustrations further motivates readers to embrace imaginative and creative play.

This text is a natural fit in poetry units (both reading and writing). It also aligns with reading units that emphasize any foundational skills, such as self-monitoring, decoding, and fluency. The strategies employed by the author and illustrator can be appreciated and practiced in virtually any kind of writing unit. Poetry fits into all units—and works with all genres.

## Content Connections

- Science: nature, outdoors, natural resources and materials

- Social Studies: types of communities (rural, suburban, urban)

- Physical Education: movement, outdoor games

- Personal and Community Wellness: play as a human right, source of joy, and method of learning; nurturing imagination; collaborating with others

# INVESTIGATING IDEAS THROUGH INQUIRY

### *A STICK IS AN EXCELLENT THING: POEMS CELEBRATING OUTDOOR PLAY* BY MARILYN SINGER (2012)

In this mini-inquiry, classroom learners explore word choice. Be prepared to highlight the poem titled "Bubbles."

**Guiding Inquiry:** *How do authors create such clear and vivid images in our minds?*

- **Read** the poem aloud.

- **Discuss** the poem. Provide a bit of time for students to share a few of the bubble stories they undoubtedly will want to tell and hear.

- **Invite** students to wonder alongside you as you introduce and contemplate the guiding inquiry.

- **Ask** students to close their eyes and visualize the poem as you read it a second time.

- **Encourage** students to talk with a partner about what they saw in their minds during this reading of the poem.

- **Read** the poem again, this time asking students to look at the poem and identify the words that helped to create the vivid images they just envisioned. Highlight or list these words.

- **Discuss** connected concepts. For instance, if students talk about the bubble being a *ginormous* size, you can name and discuss adjectives. If students name the lines with similes, comparing the bubbles to plates and planets, you may talk about similes and/or hyperbole.

- **Explore** the concept students seem to feel most excited about.

- **Summarize** the experience, naming takeaways and offering that poetry always invites readers to take time to wonder about and appreciate the words included.

 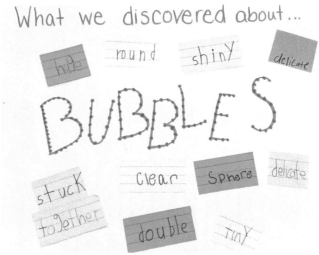

After listening to and envisioning this poem, first graders went outside to blow bubbles. Students then recalled these experiences as they brainstormed words that describe bubbles.

### ✓ Check-Up

- As you listen to and observe students, pay careful attention to the language they use. Are students speaking using a few words? Phrases? Complete sentences? Do they concisely state their ideas? State and explain their ideas?

- Note what you see students doing and prepare to coach students on ways to embrace and use their full linguistic repertoires to say more, share more, and explain more.

### ? What Else?

- Carry out the inquiry as explained here, and then follow up by having students read other poems from this text and exploring the words used in those poems.

- Extend this inquiry by asking students to investigate other poems, looking for the parts of speech and/or language concepts they noticed and appreciated most during this inquiry (adjectives, similes, etc.).

- Other contextualized inquiry experiences could focus on the following wonders:
  - *How does the punctuation a poet uses influence how we read their work?*
  - *How do the words a poet uses create specific feelings in readers?*
  - *What do we notice about words that rhyme?*

- You might choose to use this text to spark an investigation into different forms of play, various games children play, or the vast benefits of play.

# BUILDING VISION VIA MODELED AND GUIDED PRACTICE

*A STICK IS AN EXCELLENT THING: POEMS CELEBRATING OUTDOOR PLAY* **BY MARILYN SINGER (2012)**

This cycle of shared reading integrates different aspects of literacy . . . all while repeatedly returning to and spotlighting the same poem. Throughout this cycle, the poem "Really Fast!" is centered. Similar concepts can be explored with other poems.

## Session 1: Comprehension (predicting)

- **Read** the title of the poem aloud. Do not (yet) let the students see the words of the poem.

- **Model** how to use the title to warm up your brain and predict what the poem might be about.

- **Invite** students to share their predictions.

- **Read** the poem.

- **Revisit** the initial predictions and see which (if any) were accurate.

## Session 2: Word Work (rhyming)

- **Reread** the poem. Invite interested students to join in.

- **Locate** the first set of rhyming words (*races*, *chases*, *bases*).

- **Ask** yourself, "What else rhymes with these words?" and then generate additional rhyming words (like *laces*, *places*, *traces*).

- **Engage** in word play by repeating this process with the other sets of rhyming words (*dashes*, *crashes*, *splashes* and *blast*, *fast*), having students participate more and more with each round.

## Session 3: Word Work (consonant digraphs)

- **Reread** the poem, inviting students to join in.

- **Review** previous word learning about digraphs.

- **Locate** words with digraphs. Encourage students to go on a scavenger hunt in the poem and find words with "hidden" digraphs. Remind word explorers to investigate the beginning, middle, and end of words.

- **List** out the found words with digraphs.

- **Remind** students to use what they know about consonant digraphs as they read and write.

## Session 4: Fluency (parsing and prosody)

- **Prepare** to read the poem aloud. Before beginning, ask students to listen in and notice how you "group" the words and where you take a break. After reading, ask a few volunteers to share what they noticed.

- **Reread** the poem. This time use echo reading and have students repeat each phrased portion of the poem after you.

- **Repeat** this process, asking students to notice your *intonation* (where your voice goes up and where it goes down).

- **Chorally** read the poem—one last time—emphasizing strong fluency.

- **Remind** students to always do their best to read fluently.

 **Check-Up**

Use informal noticings gathered throughout this cycle of shared reading to plan responsive instruction. Prepare to lead whole-class and/or small-group lessons based on this in-the-moment information collecting.

**?** **What Else?**

During this cycle of shared reading, you could add an additional session or switch out a session to instead focus on:

- Comprehension: Invite students to visualize and/or use their bodies to act out the poem.

- Phonemic Awareness: Segment phonemes in select words using Elkonin (sound) boxes.

- Phonics: Locate and discuss words with other taught features, such as blends (like *sk-*, *-st*), compound words, or short /ă/ and long /ā/ sounds and patterns.

- Vocabulary: Look for words with cognates or generate synonyms and antonyms for a few chosen words.

- Grammar: Review previously introduced concepts (different parts of speech, common nouns vs. pronouns, apostrophes, etc.).

- Conversation: Pose a related question and invite students to chat. For instance, you might ask, "What else goes really fast?" Or, by contrast, "What goes really slow?"

After going on a blend *and* digraph scavenger hunt, this first-grade student led the class in rereading the poem.

# NURTURING AND SUPPORTING INDEPENDENT PRACTICE

### *A STICK IS AN EXCELLENT THING: POEMS CELEBRATING OUTDOOR PLAY* BY MARILYN SINGER (2012)

This lesson prepares students to independently notice something they like in a mentor text—and contemplate how and when they, too, could use that strategy in their own writing. Before beginning, select a couple of poems with features you think may stand out to students. For example, you might choose:

○ *The similes that shine through in poems like "Bubbles."*

○ *The rhyming that adds rhythm to poems like "Really Fast!"*

○ *The repetition featured in poems like "Jump!"*

○ *The playful position of words in poems like "Sprinkler."*

○ *The couplets the author uses in poems like "Statues."*

- **Ignite** interest. Share that the class will reread favorite poems and look out for "cool writing moves" they like and want to try.

- **State** that writers prepare to use what they find and love in a mentor text by imagining where and when they could try that same strategy.

- **Model** the following process using one of the selected poems:

  ○ Reread. Look for and find something interesting (that the poet/author did). TIP: Point to what you like, name it, and put a sticky note on that page.

  ○ Think, "When could I try this? Where could I add this to my own work?"

  ○ Make a plan to try it in your writing.

- **Encourage** students to think about where and when they could try that same strategy.

- **Remind** students that being a copycat is a *good* thing when it comes to noticing something in a mentor text and trying it in their own writing.

- **Invite** students to continue this work. Provide students with different poems to explore. Encourage them to use a sticky note to mark a place where they find something they like. Students may say or jot their plan for trying that strategy. (The included *Language Levers* could support students in this work.)

- **Meet** with students. Coach as needed.

- **Celebrate** finding inspiration in a mentor text by providing time for students to share what they liked and plan to try.

> **NOTE:** This lesson emphasizes identifying, appreciating, thinking, and planning ... not implementing. Follow up—another day—with a lesson on how to implement these plans.

---

 **Language Levers**

Post or co-create stems students can use as they explore poems, talk about what they like, or jot on their sticky notes.

- I like this part where . . .
- I like how the poet . . .
- I noticed that here, the poet . . .
- I will . . .
- My plan is to . . .
- I will add this in by . . .
- The best place to try this out myself is . . .

**SAM**    I liked BUBBLES because I could see the words in my mind. I'm going to add more adjectives to my poems.

**KYLE**    I want to use rhyming words like in REALLY FAST. I will make a list of words that rhyme.

**Sophia**    I noticed the poet SPRAYED the words in SPRINKLER. I'm going to rewrite my poem about the sun in the shape of the sun.

**Isla**    I am going to make my poem rhyme, just like in REALLY FAST. My poem is going to be about soccer.

A second-grade teacher decided to do this lesson with a small group of emerging writers. They co-created this chart to keep themselves accountable.

## ✔ Check-Up

- As you meet with students, look carefully to see if they are able to identify and name a specific strategy they like. This is the precursor to making a plan to try that strategy themselves. You might ask questions like these:
  - *What do you like here? Why do you like this?*
  - *Why do you think the author used this strategy?*
- Provide explicit feedback to students, and coach them as they wonder about when and where they plan to try the identified strategy. The more well-thought-out their plan, the more likely students are to carry it out.
- Try to avoid judging student goals. Instead, work to support students in trying whatever strategy they feel is most interesting and intriguing.

## ? What Else?

You might also decide to:

- Increase self-imposed accountability by having students publicize their plans.
- Create small groups based on the strategies students wish to try. Provide explicit small-group instruction in how to try out each selected strategy.
- Use interactive writing to model implementing a set goal.
- Invite students to tally each time they try a found strategy in their own writing.
- Repeat this lesson in other writing units. This strategy extends to any feature or author craft move in any genre or format.

# Lesson Set Aligned to the Developing Stage

## Featured Text: *Fry Bread: A Native American Family Story* by Kevin Noble Maillard (2019)

📖 **Text Pairings**

- *The Arabic Quilt* by Aya Khalil (2020), with art by Anait Semirdzhyan
- *Ohana Means Family* by Ilima Loomis (2020), with art by Kenard Pak
- *This Day in June* by Gayle E. Pitman (2014), with art by Kristyna Litten
- *Festival of Colors* by Kabir Sehgal and Surishtha Sehgal (2018), with art by Vashti Harrison
- *Too Many Tamales* by Gary Soto (1996), with art by Ed Martinez
- *Off-the-Radar Foods: What Is Frybread? Made in the USA: Episode 7* (Video) by Zagat (2015) (online resource)

### WHAT?

This oh-so-worthwhile selection shares the story of an intergenerational group of family and friends making fry bread.

### WHY?

This Caldecott Honor winner transcends all genre boundaries. Without question, *Fry Bread* engages readers with its dynamic and rhythmic text. The illustrations storytell. The author's note at the end provides context, including additional information about how fry bread became a staple in the diet of many Indigenous people. At the end of the book, there is even an included recipe for fry bread. The endpapers list the names of Indigenous communities and nations. Cover to cover, this is a tremendously heartfelt and powerful text!

## WHEN?

I imagine this text could be a part of almost any unit. It has a lyrical, rhythmic composition that draws readers in. Although it does not follow a typical story structure, the illustrations are deeply steeped in storytelling. The ancillary details and included information round out the hybrid structure of the book, making it an appropriate choice for reading and writing in almost any genre.

## Content Connections

- Social Studies: geography, comprehensive study of the histories of Indigenous people and nations

- Math: measurement, customary conversions, fractions

- Personal and Community Wellness: exploring different aspects of personal identities; celebrating and sharing family and community traditions; respecting different cultures and appreciating the joy inherent in cultural traditions; learning about our own heritage and the multifaceted histories of others, especially those who have been marginalized, improperly depicted, and/or underrepresented

# INVESTIGATING IDEAS THROUGH INQUIRY

### *FRY BREAD: A NATIVE AMERICAN FAMILY STORY* BY KEVIN NOBLE MAILLARD (2019)

This two-session inquiry centers on figurative language. This experience can also be modified to become a single-session inquiry.

**Guiding Inquiries:** *Why do writers use figurative language? What impact does figurative language have on readers?*

## Session 1

- **Gather** to quickly review what students know and remember about figurative language.

- **Share** that today you are going to read *Fry Bread*, and students will be on the lookout for figurative language.

- **Reread** the text, encouraging students to identify and jot the examples they see and hear.

- **Explore** the posed inquiries. First, students will individually reflect. Then, small groups will meet to share found examples and discuss ideas.

- **Summarize** this process, experience, and "academic" takeaways as a class.

## Session 2

- **Review** key reflections and understandings from Session 1.

- **Invite** students to reread other lyrical texts and poems and find additional examples of figurative language.

- **Investigate** examples and discuss personal responses in small groups.

- **Share** thoughts, reactions, and understandings in a whole-class discussion.

 **Check-Up**

Observe students. Listen in and coach small groups. Note observations.

Ask students to share found examples of figurative language and the processes they use to make sense of figurative language while reading.

**?** **What Else?**

Session 2 is optional and could be considered a *What Else?* opportunity.

You could also follow up on this inquiry with a third session: *How could including figurative language in our own writing enhance the reading experience for our intended audience?*

Alternative inquiries include:

- What choices were made about punctuation throughout this book? Why might these choices have been made?

- Do words and illustrations work together to have a "synergistic" effect on readers?

- How does reading poetry crafted by IBPOC authors enhance awareness, learning, and joy? (NOTE: IBPOC = Indigenous, Black, and people of color.)

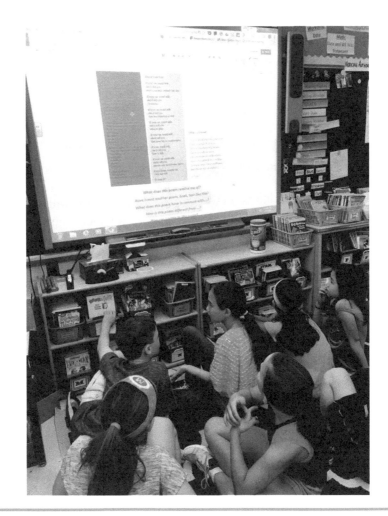

This third-grade class is preparing for small-group collaboration (Session 2). They are investigating and discussing the figurative language found in some of Amy Ludwig VanDerwater's poetry (accessible at www.poemfarm.amylv.com).

# BUILDING VISION VIA MODELED AND GUIDED PRACTICE

*FRY BREAD: A NATIVE AMERICAN FAMILY STORY*
**BY KEVIN NOBLE MAILLARD (2019)**

For this cycle of shared reading, use the two-page spread that begins with the words "Fry bread is sound." Return to these same two pages for each session of this cycle of shared reading. Enjoy the benefits of integrating literacy with such a concise and beautifully composed snippet of text.

## Session 1: Literal Comprehension (synthesis)

- **Read** the words and study the illustrations on these two pages.
- **Model** thinking aloud, naming *some* of what you see and notice.
- **Prompt** students: *What do you* first *see . . . ? What* else *do you notice . . . ?*
- **Cross-reference** shared ideas with the author's note about "Fry bread is sound" at the back of the book.
- **Revisit** the originally featured pages. Synthesize understandings.
- **Summarize** the importance of using all aspects of a text to build a more complete understanding.

## Session 2: Word Work (syllabication)

- **Reread** the two featured pages.
- **Recall** previous work with segmenting words by syllable. Share that when the middle of a word has a doubled consonant, the syllable break usually happens right between those two letters.
- **Locate** examples on the selected pages (*skillet, bubbles, sizzle*). Practice segmenting these words by syllable.
- **Validate** this idea by brainstorming other words with a doubled consonant in the middle. Clap, stamp, or tap out the syllables in each of these words. (OPTIONAL: Consult a resource to

double-check where the syllable break actually lies.)
- **Reiterate** this spelling concept and encourage students to transfer this knowledge when trying to read or write new words.

## Session 3: Grammar (subject–verb agreement)

- **Revisit** the two featured pages.
- **Highlight** the subjects and verbs in this part of the text (e.g., *The skillet clangs . . . The fire blazes . . .*)
- **Investigate** subject–verb agreement. Discover patterns. Hypothesize and work to prove theories.
- **Discuss** why, when, and how students can apply this to their writing.

## Session 4: Studying Craft (word choice, figurative language)

- **Revisit** the two featured pages.
- **State** that one of the many things the author does so well in this book is add sound to writing.
- **Pose** the question, *How did the author enable readers to hear what was happening on this page?*
- **Engage** in brief partner discussions.
- **Invite** students to share what they notice—and the impact word choice had on the reader.
- **Remind** students of the word *onomatopoeia* and generate other examples of onomatopoeia.
- **Discuss** why students would consider using onomatopoeia as they write and how doing so creates a "soundtrack" for their pieces.

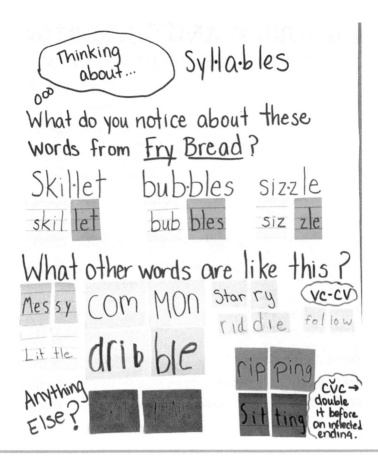

This chart shows how the spotlighted word work (Session 2) was made more concrete and interactive for a third-grade class.

### ✔ Check-Up

Observe students during each session of shared reading and listen in during partner conversations. Informally assess student understanding. In the days and weeks that follow, provide more explicit, process-rich instruction if/as needed.

### ？ What Else?

During a cycle of shared reading, you might also use these two pages to focus on:

- Spelling: Introduce the -el, -le, and -al spelling patterns. Or, if the class is at a different point in their spelling development, review short versus long vowel sounds (especially long/short i patterns and/or long/short o patterns).

- Vocabulary: Locate the verbs on these two pages. Then generate several synonyms for a couple of the verbs. Practice talking using these different words and consider ordering them according to "intensity."

# NURTURING AND SUPPORTING INDEPENDENT PRACTICE

## FRY BREAD: A NATIVE AMERICAN FAMILY STORY
### BY KEVIN NOBLE MAILLARD (2019)

In this lesson, you will encourage readers to develop an ongoing appreciation for the words an author uses. They will also think more deeply about the "why" behind these word choices.

- **Review** previous encounters with *Fry Bread* and how, again and again, the discussion came back to the author's word choice.

- **State** that authors carefully choose words because they hope to create a specific picture, feeling, reaction, or understanding for their readers. Readers notice, react to, and contemplate these choices.

- **Model** one process for doing this, while rereading part of *Fry Bread*.
  - Read alertly and stop when you notice that you see something clearly, feel something deeply, or have learned something new.
  - Pause and ask yourself, "How did the author do this? What words did they use to make this happen?"
  - Think about, say, or jot the "found words" and the impact.

- **Encourage** students to try. Continue reading and ask them to indicate when they clearly see, feel, or understand something. Ask students to look back at the these words and consider how the author "made that happen." Support students as they orally share ideas. (See the *Language Levers* suggestions.)

- **Remind** students that a lot can be gained by reading with their writer's eyes, and by fully appreciating not only what authors wrote but also how they wrote it.

- **Invite** students to continue to practice. Observe and coach as students try this for themselves.

- **Celebrate** the words of authors and poets (and readers taking the time to notice and react to these craft moves) on a consistent basis.

 **Language Levers**

Provide stems (or co-create stems) students could use to share their ideas with others, such as the following:

- *Here, the author wrote . . . It made me feel . . .*
- *When the author wrote . . . I could see . . .*
- *. . . helped me understand . . .*
- *When I read . . . I felt . . .*

 **Check-Up**

Closely observe students during this lesson. Listen in as they try it themselves. After a few days, follow up by doing an informal check of reading notebooks to see if students tried this work and how it went. Alternatively, meet one-on-one or in a small group with students who you feel can use more supported practice to read like a writer.

**?  What Else?**

Connect these reading experiences to writing. Once students get in the habit of noticing and appreciating craft while reading, they will be more apt to use these examples to raise the level of their own writing. Teach one lesson or small series of lessons around doing this work. Prioritized lessons could include teaching and supporting the following strategies:

- Writers set a goal and create an action plan around using mentor texts more frequently during writing.

- Writers look for/identify something interesting in a mentor text they want to try.

- Writers find an appropriate place in their writing to try a "found strategy."

- Writers give feedback to classmates who tried out a strategy they found in a mentor text.

Depending on the readiness shown by class learners, these lessons could happen whole-class, small-group, or one-to-one.

# Lesson Set Aligned to the Extending Stage

## Featured Text: *Out of Wonder: Poems Celebrating Poets* by Kwame Alexander (2017), With Chris Colderley and Marjory Wentworth

### 📖 Text Pairings

- Any other poetry by the 20 poets featured in Alexander (2017)
- *The Poet X* by Elizabeth Acevedo (2018)
- *The Hill We Climb* by Amanda Gorman (2021) (online or print)
- *Thanku: Poems of Gratitude* by Miranda Paul (2019), with art by Marlena Myles
- *Martin Rising: Requiem for a King* by Andrea Davis Pinkney (2018), with art by Brian Pinkney
- *Write! Write! Write!* by Amy Ludwig VanDerwater (2020), with art by Ryan O'Rourke
- Select online videos of spoken word poetry (specifically check out youth and teen poets performing through Get Lit, Brave New Voices, and Poetry Out Loud)

### WHAT?

This collection of incredible poems celebrates and pays tribute to 20 poets from around the globe.

### WHY?

In the preface, Kwame Alexander mentions Lucille Clifton's idea that poetry grows out of wonder. Oh how I love this sentiment! Alexander also shares that the authors of the included poems hope their work will be stepping-stones to wonder, motivating readers to explore more about the poets honored, investigate the poetry in this book, and consider the possible poems readers may decide to write themselves. This book celebrates finding inspiration in the work of others and using that inspiration to fuel our own creativity and craft. Additionally, the mixed-media collage used by Ekua Holmes is simply stunning and enhances the words on each page.

## WHEN?

Please refer to this collection of poetry time and time again, all across the year. Feature this gem in a poetry-focused unit. Drop pieces of this magnificent text into several other units. Not only does the poetry transcend boundaries, but the notes in the back also fuel biographic learning about the featured poets. Even Alexander's preface is a text to be appreciated and studied.

 **Content Connections**

Personal and Community Wellness: cultivating curiosity and wonder in all we do, sustainable gratitude practices, seeking inspiration (especially in the words, voices, and actions of those who have been historically underrepresented in curriculum and learning), harnessing personal inspiration and using it to create and contribute, exploring the power of words and our voices, investigating and celebrating the joy and magic inherent within classic and contemporary poems

# INVESTIGATING IDEAS THROUGH INQUIRY

### OUT OF WONDER: POEMS CELEBRATING POETS
### BY KWAME ALEXANDER (2017)

In this class experience, students begin to think more about poets and poetry.

Before beginning, set up different stations or centers. (See the included Station Suggestions chart for more specific ideas.) Students will rotate from station to station, investigating what poets do. They will discuss ideas and/or leave their thoughts, reactions, and comments at each station. Depending on the size of the class and time available, you might choose to have anywhere from three to five stations. Plan to have students spend 5 to 10 minutes at each station.

**Guiding Inquiry:** *What do poets do?*

- **Share** the inquiry question and spend a few minutes discussing initial responses.

- **Explore** this inquiry further by rotating through different stations. Invite students to read, view, listen, and then think, discuss, and/or jot at each station. You might find it helpful to have the guiding inquiry question (*What do poets do?*) and select *Language Levers* posted at each station.

- **Provide** closure to this experience by spending a few final minutes back together, debriefing the experience and using gained insights to refine responses to the guiding inquiry.

 **Language Levers**

You may choose to post poetry-aligned lingo to support student use of domain-specific vocabulary:

*poem, poetry, poet*

*alliteration, assonance, believe, couplet, figurative language, hyperbole, imagery, line, lyrics, metaphor, meter, onomatopoeia, personification, punctuation, purpose, refrain, repetition, revise, rhyme, rhythm, simile, sonnet, stanza, structure, style, symbol, symbolism, theme, think, verse, wonder*

 **Check-Up**

Observe and listen in as students rotate from station to station. Jot informal notes. Use these noticings as you plan future instruction.

Here is an example of a verse station that was set up by an eighth-grade teacher.

Station Suggestions

| STATION | STATION DESCRIPTION |
|---------|---------------------|
| *Out of Wonder* | Encourage students to wander and wonder at their leisure, exploring and reacting to different poems—or, put a sticky note on specific pages/poems that you want students to focus on. |
| Verse | Set out different texts that are written in verse. Kwame Alexander, Jason Reynolds, Jacqueline Woodson, Elizabeth Acevedo, and Aida Salazar are popular choices. Borrow a few options from the classroom library, school library, and/or local library. |
| Nursery Rhymes and Chants | Set out different poems, chants, and rhymes that may provoke early childhood recollections. Search online (there are a ton for free), check with a primary-grade teacher, or visit a local library. |
| Music | Create a playlist of different songs (any genres) that, for any reason, feel particularly poetic. Provide the opportunity for students to listen and react. Although you can go "classic," I recommend choosing contemporary artists students will recognize and appreciate as relevant. |
| Interview | Set up one or two video texts: This might be an interview with a poet, songwriter, or musician. Rachel Martin's (2017) NPR interview with Kwame Alexander is one such option. |
| Spoken Word Poetry | Feature select videos of performance poetry. There are plenty of videos of talented young poets performing in youth and teen poetry slam competitions online; see *Text Pairings*. |
| Student Work | Set out a range of different examples of student work (permission given and names removed) and/or notebook entries to show "in-process" work. If you do not have in-house student work samples, check online or ask colleagues. |
| Miscellaneous Poetry | Set out different poem anthologies (or select poems) published by favorite authors. See *Text Pairings* and/or borrow from the classroom library, school library, and/or local library. |

## ? What Else?

To simplify this inquiry, you might choose to only put out poems from *Out of Wonder*. Each station could simply be a poem or two from this beautiful mentor text that multitasks. Students could rotate between stations, as described, thinking about the different poems they read and styles of the different poets featured.

# BUILDING VISION VIA MODELED AND GUIDED PRACTICE

### *OUT OF WONDER: POEMS CELEBRATING POETS*
### BY KWAME ALEXANDER (2017)

This cycle of shared reading uses the poem "For Our Children's Children: Celebrating Chief Dan George" (pages 36–37) for each session. During each session, display the poem (ideally using a document camera) so all can see.

## Session 1: Comprehension (structure)

- **Invite** students in, even before reading the poem, by asking a question: *What do we notice about how this poem looks?*

- **Encourage** students to share initial ideas. Support the use of "poetry lingo." For example, if students say the words are broken into five sections, confirm that idea and add that those sections are called stanzas.

- **Read** the poem aloud two times, once where students follow along with their eyes, and once where students close their eyes and envision the words in their minds.

- **Discuss** thoughts about and reactions to the poem. Contemplate structure by imagining why the poet decided to format the poem this way. Take time to nurture initially posed ideas.

## Session 2: Comprehension (synthesis)

- **Remind** students of what was done in the first session. Share that today when you reread the poem, you would like students to connect the words of the poem to the illustration.

- **Reread** the first stanza. Pause and look at the illustration together. Model "finding" the elements mentioned in the illustration and sharing your thoughts about the interplay and relationship between the words and images.

- **Repeat** this process after each stanza, actively including student voices and perspectives.

- **Discuss** overall impressions of the poem and, even more specifically, how the poem and illustration connect.

## Session 3: Word Work (word choice)

- **Reread** the poem.

- **Model** noticing one specific part and thinking about the words the poet chose to use. Share any reactions or feelings you had when reading that part.

- **Prompt** students to also consider word choice. Ask students to share their own ideas with a partner, appreciating a particular line or stanza, mining these words, and considering the impact of these words.

- **Debrief** key takeaways together.

## Session 4: Poem 2 (compare and contrast)

- **Review** previous sessions in this cycle of shared reading.

- **Display** and read a second poem (suggestion: "My Heart Soars" by Chief Dan George).

- **Post** the two poems, side by side.

- **Discuss** both, investigating similarities and differences, and sharing impressions of each.

 **Check-Up**

Continue to notice the language students use as they share their thoughts. Do they include domain-specific vocabulary as they say more about their ideas? If so, how can you celebrate this? If not, how can you support this? Informally note your observations and use these experiences to plan responsive follow-up instruction.

**? What Else?**

During this cycle of shared reading, you might instead decide to focus on:

- Personal responses and reactions to the poem.

- Vocabulary (discussing nuances and/or synonyms and antonyms of select words).

- Identifying and discussing taught spelling patterns (inflected endings, silent letters, syllabification, affixes, or other word parts).

- Recognizing and exploring specific grammar concepts (verb tenses, adverbs, comma usage, conjunctions, or colons).

# NURTURING AND SUPPORTING INDEPENDENT PRACTICE

### *OUT OF WONDER: POEMS CELEBRATING POETS*
### BY KWAME ALEXANDER (2017)

In this lesson, students notice figurative language in a mentor poem and then use this inspiration to enhance their own writing.

- **Recall** previous learning experiences centered on *Out of Wonder*. Briefly review different types of figurative language.

- **State** that writers *use* inspiration found in mentor texts by trying what they see in their own writing.

- **Model** one way of doing this, using a poem from *Out of Wonder*:
  - Reread a favorite poem. Stay on the lookout for examples of figurative language.
  - Ask yourself, "Do I see any examples of figurative language? What do I appreciate and admire about the poet's decisions?"
  - Try it yourself. Tinker with previously written work and/or create a new poem/piece.

- **Encourage** students to join you in imagining where else and how else you can try something similar.

- **Remind** students that mentor texts are incredibly useful tools. Students can always lean on a text as they incorporate increasingly sophisticated craft moves into their writing.

- **Invite** students to try out this work themselves. Make previously featured poems and texts available to students as they practice.

- **Observe** and coach students as they work.

- **Celebrate** efforts by asking volunteers to share small pieces of their writing.

> **NOTE:** You can also decide to zoom out and focus this lesson on *any* appreciated craft move.

 Writing *is* vulnerable work—and if you are asking students to take this risk, then you also need to be ready to do the same. Do you write in front of students? How comfortable are you using your own writing as you lead lessons and meet with students? What value and impact do you see in regularly sharing your words with the class?

### ✔ Check-Up

As you meet with students (one-on-one or in small groups), talk with them about their process. Which parts of this work feel most challenging? Which are most enjoyable? Show and coach "next step" work that is appropriate for different classroom learners. You may want to keep anecdotal notes. The templates online could prove helpful (resources.corwin.com/mttm).

Spiral similar lessons. Continue to support students as they find inspiration in mentor texts and try different craft moves in their own writing.

There are abundant opportunities for informal assessment in the form of kidwatching and conversation. The record-keeping templates available on the companion website bring ease and fluency to this important work.

## ? What Else?

- There are several examples of "place poetry" in *Out of Wonder*, such as "In Every Season" and "The Music of the Earth." Find and share a few examples. Then ask students to consider places they have been and places that are special to them. Encourage students to write poetry about these places, perhaps borrowing strategies they see in the mentor texts shared.

- Build a "poem trifecta." Have students identify a poem they love in *Out of Wonder*.

Then have them research and find an original poem by the author that inspired this poem. Last, students can use the style and elements of these two poems as inspiration as they create their own "tribute" poem. As a possible extension, students can share all three poems with others and explain what craft moves they lifted and tried—and why!

- Students can do a bit of quick research on a favorite poet to learn more about the poet's life, style, and work. They can then use that knowledge and inspiration in their own writing.

# STRETCH UP AND BACK SUGGESTIONS: GRAMMAR

The *Stretch Up and Back Suggestions* are included in each chapter in Part II to help teachers work toward becoming more instructionally inclusive. These suggestions represent ways to honor student readiness, preferences, and choices. Chapter 8 spotlights *grammar* suggestions that are flexible enough to be supported in a wide range of texts. Please note that this is not an exhaustive, all-inclusive list and these stage classifications are not universally agreed upon. It is very possible that some emerging concepts will be introduced to learners in the developing stage—and that some learners who work on extending concepts will not have internalized *every* emerging and developing concept. Use these suggestions in the way that makes the most sense for the students you work with right here and right now.

 Language is closely tied to personal identities. It is also always evolving. One of my prioritized goals of grammar instruction is for students to feel confident and prepared to make thoughtful language choices that reflect their own personal style and voice. Do you agree or disagree? Do you believe there are an *always* and a *never* when it comes to language learning? Why or why not?

## Emerging

- Recognize and print uppercase and lowercase letters.
- Understand basic nouns, verbs, adjectives, interrogatives, and prepositions.
- Identify common, proper, and possessive nouns; regular and irregular plural nouns; and collective nouns.
- Understand simple sentence structure.
- Recognize and use common conjunctions and transition words.
- Capitalize *I*, the first letter of the first word in a sentence, names of people, names of places, names of holidays, and dates.
- Use end-of-sentence punctuation; commas in dates, in greeting and closing a letter, and to separate items in a list; and apostrophes in possessives and contractions.
- Consult references and tools as needed to support correct application of taught concepts and conventions.

Developing (all of the above *plus*)

- Recognize and form simple and compound sentences (and identify and fix up fragments and run-ons).
- Identify adverbs, relative pronouns, relative adverbs, abstract nouns, coordinating conjunctions, and interjections.
- Apply knowledge of regular and irregular verbs and of different verb tenses (simple, perfect, and progressive).
- Recognize and fix up inappropriate shifts in verb tenses.
- Capitalize titles.
- Use commas in quotations and in compound sentences.

Extending (all of the above *plus*)

- Recognize and form simple, compound, complex, and compound complex sentences.
- Ensure subject–verb agreement and pronoun–antecedent agreement.
- Show deepened understanding of proper case (subjective, objective, and possessive) of pronouns.
- Use all prior teaching of verb tenses and skillfully use verb tenses to convey time, sequences, states, and conditions; form and use verbs in active and passive voice.
- Understand subordinating conjunctions, prepositional phrases, italics, clauses, and dangling modifiers.
- Recognize and understand purpose of "other" punctuation such as parentheses, dashes, hyphens, and ellipses.
- Use commas to separate an introductory element.

Ideally, teachers want to build students' knowledge of these concepts *and* understanding of how to apply these concepts. Please remember that this list of concepts is *one way* to support students across the developmental continuum. You may also decide to personalize and revitalize learning by switching out any of the titles featured within this chapter for one of the *Text Pairings* suggestions or another current classroom favorite. Each step you take toward providing student-centered instruction is worthy of your time and effort! As you do so, be sure to also take a moment to reflect on and celebrate the excitement and success that results.

# PART III

# You've Got This!

*Educators need to innovate and create
with specific students in mind.*

Using a few core texts and a small collection of instructional methods to support learning makes sense. It feels feasible. It also yields success. Integrated and aligned instruction helps *students* connect the dots and transfer knowledge from one setting to the next. By strategically rethinking opportunities for integration, *educators* have the time, energy, and opportunity to support the wide range of next steps of classroom learners.

Over the last several chapters, lessons have been presented that use a core set of multitasking mentor texts to integrate literacy. These lessons were designed to be flexible enough to align with different texts and bendable enough to support different students. And yet, tinkering with previously created lessons may not always be enough. This makes sense because I do not personally know the students you work with. Only you are fully prepared to carry out integrated lesson sets that center on current students. In the classroom, the end goal is for students not to simply replicate what is modeled, but instead to use gained experience and knowledge and make it their own. Well, the same goes for teachers! My goal is for you not only to replicate and modify lessons, but also to feel ready to create integrated lesson sets yourself. This is where Part III comes in.

In Part I, the foundation was laid for the *why* and *what* of this work. In Part II, the *how, where,* and *when* were crystalized, and examples were provided. And here in Part III, it's all about feeling prepared and confident to use the ideas presented—and make them your own. Educators need to innovate and create with specific students in mind. Therefore, Chapter 9 provides guidance for deciding what to teach, which texts to use, and how to plan plenty of responsive instruction with just a few texts. Additionally, Chapter 10 shares ideas for getting students more involved in this process so they are truly a part of creating the learning and not simply recipients of instruction. This playful planning process is not a straight line. It zigs, zags, and constantly morphs. These last two chapters intend to help you find joy in the journey. Think of this work like taking on your own inquiry project. Enjoy the experience of exploring and tinkering with ideas—and finding the seemingly magical combination that works best for the learners currently in the room.

# CHAPTER 9

- - - - - - - - - - - - - - - - - - - - - - - - - - - - - - - - - - - - - - - - -

# DIY Processes for Creating Multitasking Lesson Sets

"We have an ethical and moral imperative to ensure that every student receives a humanizing, impactful literacy education" (Morrell, 2017, p. 456).

Teaching is never stagnant. Some say it is a careful balance of science and art. Well-honed repertoires of research-supported practices enable us to mold and adapt instruction to fit the people in the room. As Pedro Noguera (2019) writes, "Anyone who works in public schools knows that students arrive with different needs. . . . Addressing the needs of all students is not easy but that is the goal of equity in education" (para. 3). Teachers consistently reach far above and beyond what is mandated. They strive to learn about the communities where they teach, to listen to students, and to implement instruction that honors, celebrates, and highlights student histories and identities. They work tirelessly to support learning that feels meaningful, relevant, and useful, knowing this changes with each group of students. Units aren't intended to be replicated period to period and/or year to year. Curriculum takes shape when it's carried out *with* students. Because of this, the lessons shared throughout Part II are a great starting place, but they may not always be enough.

My experience *has* equipped me with an ever-growing repertoire of strategies. It has also led me to understand and accept that no one can have all the answers. People are unique. No single lesson set will make sense for all students. This is what makes teaching so beautiful and personal. It is what makes teachers so necessary. To properly plan and facilitate learning for the students currently in the room (or on the Zoom), teachers need to center and celebrate those people. Therefore, lessons in Part II intend to serve as a mentor text for how to use multitasking mentor texts. I hope the lesson sets and text recommendations are useful. I hope that as you implement and adapt the lessons, you become comfortable using a small set of mentor texts in a variety of flexible ways. Now it's time to take that work to the next level.

This chapter names the processes I use to design integrated lessons so that you feel just as comfortable using multitasking mentor texts to create integrated lesson sets on your own. Although it's beyond the scope of this professional text to delve into *every* facet of preparing for and implementing responsive instruction, in this chapter I share a process that works—time and again—for preparing integrated instruction using a core set of multitasking mentor texts. Essentially, it looks like this:

1. Determine instructional priorities.
2. Curate a core set of multitasking mentor texts.
3. Merge instructional priorities and multitasking mentor texts to plan integrated literacy lessons.

Please read on to prepare to enact each of these steps and add them to your own repertoire.

# STEP 1: DETERMINE INSTRUCTIONAL PRIORITIES

Katie Egan Cunningham (2019) wrote, "Literacy learning is full of possibilities for building a sense of awe and wonder in students" (p. 120). I appreciate this sentiment, and I believe that literacy learning does the same for the whole community—teachers included. My respect and admiration for students—and ongoing sense of personal wonder—enable me to experience great joy as I reimagine how to reshape the curriculum to design responsive and relevant instruction.

## TAKE STOCK OF WHAT YOU KNOW—AND SEEK MORE INFORMATION

Teachers need to learn about students, and not only their academic histories. In *Cultivating Genius*, Gholdy Muhammad

(2020) provides reflective questions teachers can ask themselves to learn about students' histories, identities, and literacy and language practices. Muhammad also suggests that educators:

- Respect, listen to, and trust students.

- Reflect on and examine their own teaching practices.

- Get to know families.

- Study the curriculum, specifically to analyze and reimagine how to make it meaningful to students, their families, and their communities.

Through these actions, it becomes clear that no one set way of doing anything will make sense for every group of learners. Learning about students is a necessary precursor to providing responsive instruction. Become curious about students. Learn more about them. Wonder about and contemplate learning experiences that will help students activate their own learning and reimagine their own potential. This "preliminary" work is essential to the success of all that follows.

## LOOK FOR WHAT'S THERE— AND CONSIDER LOFTY YET ATTAINABLE NEXT STEPS

There's a big difference between covering content and teaching students. By using an asset lens and focusing attention on what is already in place, teachers are making the intentional decision to teach students. When adults center and build on student strengths, they are better able to cultivate interest. Additionally, educators attain clarity around what comes next. Motivation and momentum in learning result. Here are actionable steps for noticing assets and connecting these strengths to next-step priorities.

### 1. CURATE A SMALL COLLECTION OF FORMAL AND INFORMAL ASSESSMENTS

There is certainly no shortage of assessment happening these days! Pick an assessment . . . any assessment. Better yet, pick a small range of assessments. For example, in writing, you might look at a formally published piece, an "in progress" draft, and your conferring notes with anecdotal observations. In reading, you may collect a running record, a unit post-assessment, and a self-reflection. Virtually anything works, but having a small collection of artifacts and anecdotes enables teachers to see how students work at different times and in different settings as they take on different tasks.

## 2. INVESTIGATE AND NAME WHAT YOU SEE

As you mine this collection, be observational, not evaluative. Focus on what is there and done well instead of what is missing or done incorrectly. For example, instead of saying to yourself that a student could not answer any inferential questions, you might instead name that the student was able to provide a detailed and well-sequenced retell of the text. Instead of remarking that a student spelled a multisyllabic word incorrectly, you might name the strategy the student *did* use in trying to spell the word. Name asset-based observations or briefly jot what is observable and in place. As I do this work, I find myself using language like *I see . . .*, *I notice . . .*, or *Here, the student . . .*

This kind of asset observing is good practice when teachers are alone, with colleagues, and, of course, with students. During a session at 2020's Leading Equity Virtual Summit, Erica Buchanan-Rivera said, "We can't communicate deficit thinking to kids and expect them not to adhere to it—words matter, language choices matter" (Eakins & Buchanan-Rivera, 2020, 11:35). I believe that teachers need to avoid deficit thinking and deficit language when they speak with students, and also when they speak *about* students. The language teachers choose to use also matters when they are with colleagues and even when they reflect alone. Every student has strengths in place and plenty to celebrate. These assets are the basis for next-step teaching.

## 3. CONNECT OBSERVATIONS TO NEXT STEPS

Use a lens of curiosity and wonder about what comes next. This could sound like "Because the reader has a strong understanding of what is happening in the story, they are ready for strategic instruction in thinking about what the characters are feeling and learning," or "Because the writer has competently used the question lead in their writing, they are ready to expand their repertoire by exploring other kinds of leads." The secret to this work is that what was noticed connects to what comes next.

If I were going to state this *noticing-naming-connecting-prioritizing* work as a concise strategy, it would sound a little like this:

After getting to really know students, teachers glean next steps by mining formal and informal assessments.

1. Collect a few different learning artifacts (formal and/or informal).

2. Ask yourself, "What do I see? What is this student already doing?"

3. Name those observations and brainstorm possible next steps.

If this process feels different from your usual practice, I'll provide some helpful hints. The first is to practice this with colleagues. Look through student work together. This is definitely a situation where two or three heads work better than one! Also, having a fresh set of eyes and a new perspective is often quite valuable. My second piece of advice is to work efficiently. Mining student work and naming a possible next step happens in 30 seconds to 2 minutes. This is not "report card" or "parent-teacher conference" preparation kind of work. The intended audience here is you—and the goal is to *quickly* find out what's going well and consider what comes next. Take the pressure off yourself. There is not one perfect answer or "must" next step. Part of deciding what comes next comes from your gut, based on your experience, knowledge, and understanding of the student. Ideally, this process is ongoing . . . and if you make it too laborious, you won't want to do it (and you won't have the time to do it) on a regular basis. If needed, retrain your brain to focus on assets instead of deficits. Remember that developing this habit will take a little practice—keep at it. And when it comes to deciding next steps, don't overthink it too much. Trust yourself.

Do you find yourself first noticing deficits or assets? What advice could you give someone—including yourself or a colleague—who, although well intentioned, often focuses on perceived deficits instead of students' assets?

## SYNTHESIZE AND GENERALIZE INSTRUCTIONAL PRIORITIES

Once you notice what's going well and decide what comes next for individual students, you are ready to identify patterns within the class. Admittedly, this synthesizing may not feel glamorous. However, it is incredibly important in the process of turning observations into responsive teaching. I can't tell you how often I took the time to jot observations . . . and then filed that information in a cabinet drawer or on a district spreadsheet and never looked back. Essentially, the time I spent contemplating and ascertaining next steps was a waste, because I didn't synthesize that information or have it handy as I planned instruction. Over time, I learned from this mistake. Now I know that synthesizing observations is essential for preparing student-centered instruction. Because I hope to help you avoid this common pitfall, I am sharing tips to build preparedness and tools to amplify efficiency. As you do this work, priorities *will* pop out, and subsequent planning will become more fluent, streamlined, and successful.

Patterns and Priorities That May Emerge From Formal and Informal Assessments

| LITERACY DOMAIN* | A FEW NEXT-STEP PRIORITIES YOU MAY DISCOVER |
|---|---|
| Reading | • Identity and Engagement<br>• Work Habits<br>• Concepts of Print<br>• Decoding and Self-Monitoring<br>• Fluency<br>• Literal Comprehension<br>• Inferential Comprehension<br>• Analytic Thinking and Critical Understanding<br>• Talking and Jotting About Reading |
| Writing | • Identity and Engagement<br>• Work Habits and Using Resources<br>• Meaning<br>• Process<br>• Structure, Focus, and Organization<br>• Development<br>• Craft and Voice<br>• Conventions<br>• Collaborating |
| Language and Words | • Engagement and Work Habits<br>• Phonemic Awareness<br>• Phonics<br>• Spelling Patterns<br>• Word Parts (including roots)<br>• High-Frequency Words and Commonly Confused Words<br>• Vocabulary<br>• Parts of Speech<br>• Capitalization<br>• Punctuation<br>• Figurative Language<br>• Use of Resources and Tools<br>• Transfer |

* Speaking, listening, and conversation are woven into all literacy domains.

We all have different ways of determining these patterns. In fact, I use different tools at different times. What follows are explanations of a few of the different methods I have tried and used successfully. Each method yields the same result: synthesizing observations and identifying current patterns and priorities.

## IN-DEPTH "CLASS AT A GLANCE" GUIDES

When I was new to this work, I didn't totally trust myself. I sought clarity and needed more guidance. Class-at-a-glance forms did the trick! I loved having so much information all on one page. Class-at-a-glance forms provide a great deal of information. Student names are listed across the top, and different learning goals, skills, or concepts are listed along the side, thereby creating a matrix. To complete such a chart, the teacher efficiently notes recent observations, indicating what is currently in place for each student, and small-group patterns and whole-class trends emerge almost instantly. These templates can be utilized at the start of a unit (using pre-assessments) or during a unit (using in-the-moment observations or in-process work).

Several printable reading and writing class-at-a-glance guides are available in the online companion (resources.corwin .com/mttm). Additionally, *several* different word study class-at-a-glance forms are available with the *Word Study That Sticks Companion* book (Koutrakos, 2019).

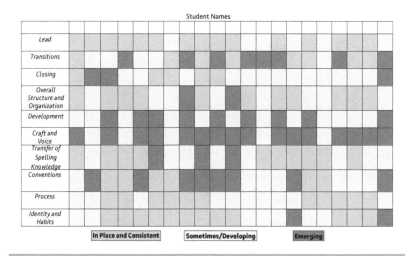

The color-coding within this writing class-at-a-glance chart shows how small-group patterns and whole-class trends easily pop out. In this class, writing identities have been established. The class also has a strong grasp on leads. Using and varying transitions is one possible priority for next-step instruction. Composing closings is another strong possibility for next-step instruction.

## SYNTHESIZED "4-BOXER"

I must admit that I am big fan of the "4-boxer." For years, I found myself folding paper (hot dog and hamburger folds) and keeping that paper close by whenever I administered running record assessments or looked through a pile of writing assessments. I then began walking around with different 4-boxers as I conferred, and I instantly saw small-group patterns emerge in real time. I have created more 4-boxers than I care to admit.

When I create a 4-boxer, I identify four different domains of learning. Essentially, these reflect four different possibilities for prioritized next steps; these could be four different pursuits, for example, from the "Patterns and Priorities" chart shown on page 218. As I mine assessments or observe students as they work in class, I first notice what's in place. Then, I add their names to the quadrant that specifies a connected next step. If over 50% of the class falls in one domain, that is clearly a whole-class priority. Additionally, small-group patterns and individual goals are easily unearthed.

Several downloadable and printable reading and writing 4-boxers are available in the online companion (resources.corwin.com/mttm). These ready-to-go templates are available across the emerging, developing, and extending stages. Each document spotlights four domains that are often prioritized in that stage of learning.

**Mentor Texts That Multitask READING "4-Boxer"**
**Developing**

| Engagement and Work Habits | Foundational Skills |
|---|---|
| Shanna<br>Paul<br>Devon | Ashley<br>Sha'Rey<br>John<br>Abe<br>Destiny<br>David |
| **Literal Comprehension** | **Inferential Comprehension** |
| Laura<br>Deniz<br>Sami<br>Lewis<br>Chris<br>Carla<br>Cole<br>John | Christina<br>Sophia<br>Daphne<br>Charlie<br>Marion<br>Darshi<br>Dylan<br>Layla |

This reading 4-boxer was created while working in a second-grade classroom. Shanna, Paul, and Devon are ready to explore their reading identities and work on building work habits. Ashley is part of a group that is prepared to work on solidifying foundational reading skills.

If we are going to keep things real, there have been many times when even a 4-boxer felt a bit too formal. Before family communications were sent out digitally, I often saved the extra flyers and used the backs to jot in-the-moment thoughts as I walked around the room and chatted with students. Similarly, I would often reach for a piece of that thin manila drawing paper to scribble next-step notes as I worked my way through a pile of assessments. Although this method was incredibly informal, for me, it was just as effective as any class-at-a-glance form or 4-boxer in helping me efficiently discover patterns and trends within and across the class.

Of course, there are no printable and reproducible versions of *this* online, but I encourage and applaud anyone who finds comfort in repurposing and reusing whatever is handy!

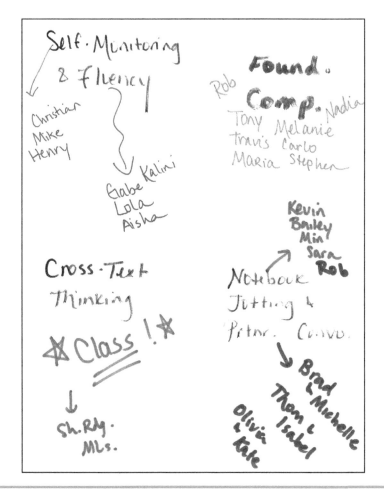

This in-the-moment example shows some of my thinking while working in a fourth-grade collaborative teaching classroom. While it may look a bit disorganized, it made perfect sense to me! I used these jots to guide my preparation of responsive learning experiences.

Although I admit that "using assessment formatively" or "formatively determining instructional priorities" has a stuffy sound to it, I hope the information and examples provided here show you that it is really anything but! As a reminder:

1. Take stock of what you know—and seek more information.
2. Look for what's there—and consider lofty yet attainable next steps.
3. Synthesize information to identify instructional priorities.

This process is happening all the time in classrooms around the world. It is never one and done; it happens naturally and consistently. It becomes a habit. The process I described here is one option for doing this work . . . but, of course, there are plenty of other valid ways. The most important takeaway is that no matter how it is done, determining instructional priorities through formative assessment needs to happen. Remember that with practice, this process becomes easier and more efficient. As you build this routine, remind yourself that the effort put forth here often saves a ton of time on the back end.

## STEP 2: CURATE A CORE SET OF MULTITASKING MENTOR TEXTS

In Part I, I shared different expert perspectives on what a mentor text is and how to select a mentor text. I also added some of my own ideas! Throughout Part II, I named names and outlined lessons featuring fabulous texts that fit the previously mentioned criteria. Because I am a book lover (and indecisive), I also included abundant *Text Pairings* options for use in conjunction with spotlighted texts and/or as replacements for these highlighted texts. Now, let's clarify the process for curating a core set of multitasking mentor texts that can be used in ways that matter.

### IS IT A HIGH-QUALITY TEXT?

There are so many amazing texts out there. Often, the hardest part is choosing which ones make their way into text sets. In keeping with the less-is-more theme woven throughout this book, remember that a small stack of multitasking mentor texts does the trick!

In Chapter 1, I shared what makes a worthy classroom mentor text. If you need a refresher, please look back and skim that section. To briefly summarize, when considering a prospective text, make sure it offers multiple gateways and entry points for students. Furthermore, mentor texts should reflect the interests of *current* students. Teachers need to choose books that are relatable for today's student population, not their own personal favorites from 20, 30, or 40-plus years ago. Yes, there are still times I choose to share a classic or neo-classic, but I also prioritize selecting and highlighting new books on a regular basis. I urge you to consider doing the same. During his Leading Equity Virtual Summit session, Dee Lanier emphasized the need for teachers to build connection points with students and resist the urge to discredit their interests (Eakins & Lanier, 2020). This means that even if I prefer music from my own glory days, I will still seek and select more current options to use as part of a lyrical poetry unit. It is also essential to consistently include and feature the work of IBPOC authors, illustrators, and creators. These points of consideration will enable you to strategically layer high-quality texts and create "short stacks" of multitasking mentor texts.

A couple of helpful hints:

(1) When curating a text set, variety is an asset. Whenever I build a small stack of texts in preparation for teaching, I layer texts that complement one another. Sometimes this means that the text set I plan to use for the next few weeks consists of an image, a short video, a picture book, and a poem. Sometimes this means that a unit text set is comprised of an informational text, a website, an article, and a podcast.

(2) Remember that not every mentor text has to be a formally published text. Almost every time I create a new text set, there is also a sample or two that was written by a teacher (me!). After all, I can't ask students to do the work that I have not done myself. Additionally, I almost always include a student-written sample in my stack. (Please keep in mind that whenever I use student work, I always ask permission and remove names *before* sharing.) The authenticity and accessibility of a student-created sample can't be overstated. These texts show students how someone their age has done this work. I find that as much as students love the formally published texts spotlighted, they love learning from the "homegrown" samples, too.

## HOW MANY WAYS COULD I USE THIS TEXT?

After selecting a few high-quality mentor texts that reflect student interests, cross-check each option to decide if the text aligns with curricular goals and current learning priorities. To that end, you may ask yourself these key questions:

- Does this text offer multiple entry points for engagement and interaction? Will it support instruction for students with different areas of readiness?

- Does this text offer a wide range of learning opportunities? What opportunities do I see on each page/in each part?

- How does this text fit with the units I am about to teach? Does it align well with all literacy domains? Can it also be used in other parts of the day?

- Which student-centric instructional priorities can be supported with this text? Is it "enough" to make the cut and become a truly multitasking mentor text?

- What "heart work" can be done with this text? How can this text invite the class to celebrate aspects of their own identities, learn about others, connect, and/or contribute to the community?

As I wander through mentor texts, I look for the concepts I plan to spotlight in upcoming instruction. When I see a page, a part, or even a sentence that is a match, I place a sticky note on that page and write what I plan to teach. For example, if I plan to teach classroom writers to develop their stories by adding dialogue through speech bubbles and a page of a book has a speech bubble, I write "speech bubble" on a sticky note and put it right on that page! Similarly, if I am preparing to teach informational readers to mine the openings and closings of texts to try to ascertain the author's perspective and I come across an informational text that has an opening or closing that can be used as an example, I write "hint at author perspective" on a sticky note and place it on that page. Thankfully, *every* page of any text offers seemingly endless opportunities to support foundational skills, delve into spelling patterns, identify grammar concepts, and explore vocabulary. The key is to focus on what you see that aligns to prioritized learner goals and upcoming teaching. Try not to get caught up in everything that's possible; stay focused on looking for and marking the places that you can use in the coming weeks.

I'd like to offer a couple of final words of wisdom. First, when curating a small set of multitasking mentor texts, this partnering of "high-quality text criteria" and "matches current priorities" reminds us that, sometimes, even a favorite book may not be the best choice for this class this year. That's okay. What can initially feel like a mismatch or setback is actually a chance to discover and fall in love with a brand-new mentor text! Second, it is important to clearly state that although transforming a mentor text into a multitasking mentor text fuels deep learning that transfers, *overusing* a text can do the opposite. When

I curate a new text set, I typically use this short stack (across the literacy block) for a few weeks. Think 3-4-5-6: Having three to four strategically layered multitasking mentor texts helps teachers confidently prepare responsive and connected instruction for about five to six weeks. Thoughtfully curated text sets provide abundant opportunities for relevant, authentic, and contextualized learning. Yes, there are times I stretch these numbers *just a bit*. But, I know that by creating different text sets throughout the year, I am also cultivating engaged learning—from the first day of school through the last.

# STEP 3: MERGE INSTRUCTIONAL PRIORITIES AND MULTITASKING MENTOR TEXTS TO PLAN INTEGRATED LITERACY LESSONS

Once you know students and have a feel for the class dynamics (*who*), have decided on learning priorities (*what*), and have collected a core set of multitasking mentor texts (*where*), it is time to flesh out the *when* and *how*.

Chapter 2 outlined different instructional practices that support mentor text multitasking. This is where I introduced integrated literacy and explained inquiry practices and gradual release practices, too. Teaching methods and structures like interactive read-aloud, shared reading, shared writing, interactive writing, minilessons, strategy groups, and conferring were described. (For a quick reminder of each of these instructional structures, check out the chart on pages 30–32.) The lessons in the Part II chapters showed these structures in action— merging learning priorities, multitasking mentor texts, and instructional methods.

Now let's step into how you can design lesson sets for the learners you currently support.

## DECIDE WHICH INSTRUCTIONAL METHODS TO USE

As you formulate action plans for using mentor texts to carry out instruction, you will want to select the structure(s) that offer the level of support most appropriate to introduce, reinforce, or spiral spotlighted concepts. The accompanying graphic provides a reminder of which structures represent the most highly supported learning experiences, and which intend students to take on more of the responsibility.

**Teaching Methods That Strategically Build Student Independence**

| Heavier Scaffold | Lighter Scaffold |
|---|---|

Interactive Read-Aloud
    Shared Reading and Shared Writing
        Interactive Writing
            Whole-Class, Small-Group, and 1:1 Mentoring
                Partner and Club Work
                    Independent Practice

Note: Inquiry-based learning ranges from heavily scaffolded to lightly scaffolded to completely student-initiated and -directed.

Choose methods of instruction carefully. Gradual release only makes sense when the scaffolds are removed and students learn to do more and more of the work themselves. This means that many skills and concepts are successfully taught not through "one and done" lessons but instead over time. For example, you may *first* introduce and model a reading strategy in an interactive read-aloud, *then* teach students *how* to do this reading work through a whole-class lesson, and *continue to support* this practice as you work with small groups of learners. Or you may *first* introduce and provide vision of a grammar concept during a session of shared reading and *then* explicitly teach into this convention using a cycle of mentor sentence inquiry (Anderson & LaRocca, 2017). You can *continue to support* transfer and application of this learning through one-to-one conversations during writing. Students can also support one another in checking for correct application during peer conferences.

 Take some time to reflect. Be honest: Do you tend to over-scaffold? Are there times you are more reticent to remove scaffolds? Is there a subset of classroom learners for whom you tend to provide more scaffolded instruction? What steps can you take to intentionally design instruction that (appropriately) puts more of the grappling responsibility on learners?

In a blog written for Collaborative Classroom, Zaretta Hammond (2020) reminds teachers, "Instructional equity happens when the teacher is scaffolding learning to the point that *the scaffold at some moment falls away, so that the student becomes independent.*" What Hammond warns teachers against is over-scaffolding and "permanent instructional crutches." Remember that the end goal is for students to internalize these cognitive routines and to be ready, willing, and able to do this work (and related work) independently. Students benefit from the opportunity to delve into rich, complex work. Successfully working through moments of productive struggle propels motivation, engagement, and learning.

# PLAN WITH PRIORITIES IN MIND

It is possible to efficiently prepare integrated lessons that meet mandates and align to current student priorities. Make a tentative plan for how an upcoming unit could go. Please note that this plan is always flexible because a week or two in, you may realize that your anticipated pacing or priorities need some readjusting. The Unit Planning Template provides a bird's-eye view for an upcoming unit. A downloadable and reproducible version of this unit template is available on the companion website (resources.corwin .com/mttm). There is also a version for writing available online.

### *Mentor Texts That Multitask*: Unit Overview (Reading)

Reading Unit: THEME STUDY

| Reading Unit Goals: | Mentor Texts: |
|---|---|
| • Readers develop theories about the author's perspective, intentions, and message(s).<br><br>• Readers consider different themes.<br><br>• Readers compare themes across texts.<br><br>• Readers use conversation to deepen thinking.<br><br>**Prioritized Class Goals:**<br><br>• Cross-text Thinking<br><br>• Literate Conversation | • *Mango Moon*, Diane de Anda (2019)<br><br>• *Dreamers*, Yuyi Morales (2018)<br><br>• *They Call Me Güero: A Border Kid's Poems*, David Bowles (2018)<br><br>• Collection of teacher and student reading notebook entries |

| Immersion | Early Unit Work | Mid-Unit Work | End-of-Unit Work | Conclusion |
|---|---|---|---|---|
| **Plan:**<br><br>• Interactive Read-Alouds: *Mango Moon and Dreamers*<br><br>• Cycle of Shared Reading: 3 Poems from *They Call Me Güero* . . . | **Plan:**<br><br>• Readers develop theories about the author's perspective, intentions, and message(s).<br><br>* Literate Convo *<br><br>* Jotting in Notebook * | **Plan:**<br><br>• Readers consider different themes.<br><br>• Readers use conversation to deepen thinking.<br><br>* Literate Convo *<br><br>* Jotting in Notebook * | **Plan:**<br><br>• Readers compare themes across texts.<br><br>* Literate Convo *<br><br>* Jotting in Notebook * | **Plan:**<br><br>• Readers compare themes across texts.<br><br>Collaborative Performance Task |
| **Mentor Texts:**<br><br>*Mango Moon*<br><br>*Dreamers*<br><br>*They Call Me Güero* . . . | **Mentor Texts:**<br><br>*Mango Moon*<br><br>Teacher and student reading notebook entries | **Mentor Texts:**<br><br>*Dreamers*<br><br>Teacher and student reading notebook entries | **Mentor Texts:**<br><br>*Mango Moon*<br><br>*They Call Me Güero* | **Mentor Texts:**<br><br>*Mango Moon*<br><br>*Dreamers*<br><br>*They Call Me Güero* |

Using the Unit Overview Planning Template helped me see how and when I could infuse my short stack of mentor texts into a middle school reading unit where theme was explored. This "tiny yet mighty" multitasking text set was used across the literacy block for about six weeks.

When I plan with priorities in mind, I *may* instead think about how I can introduce, teach, and support students' acquisition of a prioritized skill or concept. I *might* also ponder all the ways I could use one mentor text to support a range of current class priorities. The Learning Concept Planning Template and Text-Specific Planning Template (both available online at resources .corwin.com/mttm) provide easy ways to plan with priorities in mind.

### *Mentor Texts That Multitask*   LEARNING CONCEPT PLANNING TEMPLATE

**PRIORITIZED SKILL/CONCEPT:** READING, WRITING, and PUNCTUATING DIALOGUE

**MENTOR TEXT(S):** *Islandborn* BY JUNOT DIAZ and LEO ESPINOSA

| | **Planning Notes:** | | **Check-In** |
|---|---|---|---|
| **Investigating Ideas Through Inquiry** | GRAMMAR INQUIRY - WHERE DOES THE PUNCTUATION ( . , ! ? ) GO IN DIALOGUE?<br>• FIND DIALOGUE<br>• INVESTIGATE WHERE PUNCTUATION GOES<br>• DEVELOP A THEORY AND CHECK THEORY<br>• SHARE IDEAS | | CONVERSATION AND COLLABORATION CHECKLIST |
| **Building Vision Via Modeled and Guided Practice** | Cycle of Shared Reading<br>Cycle of Shared Writing<br>Interactive Read Aloud<br>Interactive Writing<br>Other | **Planning Notes:**<br>OTHER MENTOR SENTENCE STUDY:<br>"I'm going to put in the pyramids," said Dahlia.<br>INTERACTIVE WRITING:<br>• Elicit ideas – – – dialogue<br>• Students dip in to add quotation marks and punctuation marks | **Check-In**<br>INFORMAL NOTICINGS |
| **Nurturing and Supporting Independent Practice** | **Planning Notes:**<br>WRITING MINILESSON: Writers check for clarity by confirming how they punctuate dialogue.<br>PARTNER FIND AND FIX GAME: Reread each other's work to check for dialogue punctuation. | | **Check-In**<br>PARTNERS SHARE FIND AND FIX EXAMPLES |

While working with a third-grade class, I wanted to teach dialogue in reading, writing, and grammar. The Learning Concept Planning Template enabled me to see how I could use one text to introduce, teach, and nurture this skill.

MENTOR TEXT: *Islandborn* by Junot Diaz & Leo Espinosa

| Domain | Embedded Opportunities (Student-Specific) | Embedded Opportunities (Curriculum) | Planning Notes |
|---|---|---|---|
| **Personal and Community Wellness** | Exploring heritage and traditions | SS ⟶ discussion | 'Speed dating' conversation ⟶ speaking and listening |
| **Reading** | Identifying lessons and discussing takeaways | Interactive Read Aloud | The lesson might be . . . because . . . I now . . . because . . . |
| **Writing** | Development Techniques *setting details *dialogue | Minilessons | Writers dev. stories by * adding setting details * adding dialogue |
| **Phonemic Awareness Phonics and Spelling Vocabulary** | -ed and irregular past tense verbs | Interactive Writing *Partner game* | I.W. DIP IN FOCUS Partner game ⟶ FIND AND FIX |
| **Grammar Other Language** | DIALOGUE | Minilessons *Partner game* | ↓ SAME ! *Also . . . mentor sentence study* |
| **Other** | Check for transfer and application during conferring conversations | | |

The Text-Specific Planning Template helped me to expand my view. By using this tool, I identified different times and places I could strategically use one mentor text, enabling it to multitask.

Once you curate a short stack of multitasking mentor texts, prepare to use it flexibly. Revisit it at different times and for different purposes. Use each selected text in your set to connect and integrate instruction. Select and use the lesson planning form(s) that feel most comfortable for you. Of course, you will also need to consider district guidelines, as different schools have different requirements for the planning templates staff use. All the templates described and shown here are available online (resources .corwin.com/mttm), and I invite you to try them out as you play around with different ways of making mentor texts multitask.

A synthesized version of the processes described in this chapter is shown in the following chart.

DIY Process for Creating Mentor Text Lesson Sets

| DETERMINE INSTRUCTIONAL PRIORITIES | CURATE A CORE SET OF MULTITASKING MENTOR TEXTS | MERGE INSTRUCTIONAL PRIORITIES AND MULTITASKING MENTOR TEXTS TO PLAN INTEGRATED LITERACY LESSONS |
|---|---|---|
| What do I know about these learners?<br><br>What do I see them doing?<br><br>What next steps make sense?<br><br>How does this line up with the curriculum?<br><br>What will I address whole-class? Small-group? Individually? | Which high-quality texts will these learners be interested in reading and returning to time and time again?<br><br>Which high-quality texts offer many entry points so that everyone can grapple with rich and rigorous concepts?<br><br>Which high-quality texts will enrich and extend our classroom community?<br><br>Where do I see opportunities to prepare instruction around current class and curricular priorities?<br><br>How many opportunities do I see to integrate relevant learning experiences? Which parts could support readers? Writers? Word and language explorers? Conversationalists? | Which instructional structures will I use?<br><br>Which skills and concepts will I prioritize?<br><br>How else could I integrate learning?<br><br>How could I foster regular practice?<br><br>How will I streamline this work, connecting content areas and promoting consistent application and transfer? |

# CHAPTER 10

# Stepping Aside: Student-Initiated Learning With Multitasking Mentor Texts

"Students are not dependent on us for thought" (Anderson, 2007, p. 13).

I've said it before, and I'll say it once more: The goal is not "you go"—instead, it is "you go because you choose to and feel ready to do so." Effective instruction prepares students to deeply understand and manipulate taught information and processes. If the goal is for students to transfer learning, then multitasking mentor texts are the bridge to this student-initiated practice. As teachers step back, these tools step up, supporting students as they jump-start their own learning and enhance collective class learning.

The mentor texts teachers model using flexibly are the same tools students can use to feel more confident as they practice. These multitasking resources support students as they grapple and provide "teacher-free" guidance for getting themselves unstuck. Multitasking mentor texts enable students to make thoughtful choices and informed decisions as they work. Furthermore, students can use these cornerstone texts during peer learning experiences. Trust in students. They can and will step up. This final chapter is dedicated to this worthy pursuit: placing the learning into students' hands by showing them how to use multitasking mentor texts as they take the reins.

If you think about it, Part II was a multitasking mentor text for you, providing the foundation of what integrated literacy (with a core set of multitasking mentor texts) looks like, sounds like, and feels like. It provided the experience necessary for then doing this work yourself, innovating and creating lesson sets from the ground up. Similarly, when you carry out the lessons in Part II and those you create using the guidance provided in Chapter 9, you are doing the same thing for students. The methods of instruction you utilize model different processes for learning—and the role multitasking mentor texts play in each of these pursuits. When you use these texts as you facilitate classroom experiences, you teach students *how* to embark on these kinds of adventures so they are ready to take off on learning journeys of their own. Partnerships and clubs, expert stations, and edcamps are powerful vehicles for student-facilitated learning. You can amplify the success of these collaborative learning structures by incorporating multitasking mentor texts.

## PARTNERSHIPS AND CLUBS

It is important to prioritize time for partners and clubs to work together on a regular basis. Ellin Keene (2018) writes, "Engagement is deepened by perspective blending—engaged children are aware of how others' knowledge, emotions, and beliefs shape their own. When children talk and write about their beliefs, they are more engaged; they have a stake in learning" (p. 127). Students can be completely engaged without a teacher (or any adult) present. And they are often intrinsically motivated to initiate and facilitate peer-to-peer experiences. It makes sense to capitalize on what works.

Partnerships and clubs cultivate peer learning. This happens across all grades and all subjects. When partnerships and clubs are established and sustained, students always have someone to share, think, ponder, or explore ideas with. However, it is important to point out that partners and clubs don't always experience immediate success. Cultivating relationships and building new habits takes some practice and patience. It is widely accepted that when something is new or difficult, a tool usually helps. Multitasking mentor texts are tools for helping students become focused, productive, and successful during these peer learning experiences.

Here are a few tips for jump-starting successful partnerships and clubs:

- Set up partnerships and clubs with great intention. This may be done sometimes by the teacher and other times by students themselves.

- Purpose is a key driver of how partners and clubs come together. Also, consider personalities, dispositions, and personal learning goals.

- Keep established partnerships and clubs consistent for a certain duration of time—and then change these pairings and groupings at periodic intervals throughout the year.

Once partnerships and clubs are established, teachers continue to provide ongoing support and feedback. Students also rely on multitasking mentor texts as supports in this important work. The "Roles" chart shares how multitasking mentor texts can lead to more dynamic and effective partner and club learning.

What are your go-to strategies for cultivating respectful and productive partnerships and clubs? How do these efforts affect student relationships and readiness to work? What else could you consider or try when it comes to creating and sustaining this kind of peer work?

## Roles in Supporting Partnerships and Clubs

| TEACHERS | MULTITASKING MENTOR TEXTS |
|---|---|
| Support budding partner and club work by asking students to sit together when the class gathers for read-alouds, minilessons, shared reading and shared writing, and other work. By practicing turning and talking in this more scaffolded setting, students are better able to sustain independent conversation when you are not present. | When you spotlight flexible use of multitasking mentor texts during whole-class learning, students begin to understand the wide range of learning opportunities within these texts. Students see a clear and effective model for how to refer to, use, and lean on mentor texts. This prepares them to do the same during partner and club time. |
| Provide instruction in the logistics: where to go, what to bring (mentor texts), how to decide who goes first, how to plan and use time well. This guidance makes a huge difference! If you teach into these kinds of protocols, the students will likely experience greater long-term success. | Multitasking mentor texts are a necessary resource in being prepared for partner and club meetings. Celebrate when you see students prepared (multitasking mentor texts brought and readily available) for these sessions. |
| Model and coach students as they learn to provide respectful and meaningful feedback for one another. | Students of all ages and in all settings benefit from leaning on texts during collaborative work. Multitasking mentor texts are tools partners and clubs use as they seek inspiration, explain their ideas, find examples, provide feedback, and try new work together. |

# EXPERT STATIONS AND EDCAMPS

It is also fun to have students do the actual teaching. That's where expert stations and edcamps come in. Expert stations are fully planned. Students take on the role of both expert and teacher. Edcamps are more authentic, in-the-moment, student-facilitated learning experiences. They are only partially planned.

I have used expert stations in all grades and settings and have facilitated edcamps in Grades 3 and up. It's important to share that multitasking mentor texts have a central role in each of these processes. Here, I explain the role multitasking mentor texts play in these kinds of student-initiated learning experiences.

## EXPERT STATIONS

There are many times when single-session expert stations make sense. These kinds of expert stations often come at the end of an informational reading or writing unit or any unit that involved research. Students commemorate and share learning by sharing what they discovered. They refer to mentor texts as they recount and report what was learned. These celebratory events work well for students of all ages, especially young learners.

At other times, single-session expert stations are based on anything *you* might typically teach. On occasion, I have had students ask me if they could lead a whole-class lesson or a small-group lesson to share something they recently learned. For instance, students have taught classmates how to use a word wall while writing or how to apply phonics knowledge and accurately decode while reading. At other times, students have created short videos (using platforms like Seesaw, Flipgrid, or Screencastify) to share a tip or a workaround. The common denominator: Students demonstrate this work with a multitasking mentor text.

Teachers may also set aside more time for a class community to prepare for and implement expert stations. In this model, students sign up for what they want to model, prepare their lessons and materials, and then teach others in the class or community. These more carefully prepared experiences work with students of all ages, but are most appealing to students with previous expert station practice. Very often, these multisession events look a lot like this:

## Session 1: The class community reflects and decides on teaching topics.

- Gather the class together to reflect on recent learning. Identify and celebrate areas of growth. Invite students to consider how recently acquired skills are useful and which should be shared with others.

- Support students in narrowing down possible teaching topics and publicizing one concept they want to teach to their classmates. Sometimes, students lead an expert station alone, and other times they do so collaboratively.

- Session 1 often takes 10 to 20 minutes.

## Session 2: Students prepare to teach others.

- Ask students to pinpoint the strategy they plan to teach and think through a process associated with this strategy (how *they* like to do it).

- Provide time for students to prepare (or create) teaching tools. *This is where multitasking mentor texts come in.* Students will lean on a selected text as they model the concept they plan to teach and encourage peers to try out the work.

- This session often lasts about 15 to 30 minutes. Sometimes it is extended by doing a "trial run" with a partner.

## Sessions 3 and 4: Students facilitate and visit expert stations.

- During Session 3, half the students stay at their station to teach while the other half of the class visits different stations to learn. During Session 4, the class members switch roles: Yesterday's teachers are today's learners. Students do not get to visit every station. Instead, they choose the stations they feel will be most beneficial.

- These two sessions often last about 20 to 30 minutes. However, there is quite a bit of movement. Each teaching session/rotation takes about 5 to 10 minutes.

- I often conclude expert stations by inviting students to reflect, celebrate, and make plans for when they will try what they learned.

Multitasking mentor texts play a featured role in these expert stations. The following charts show a few of the *most popular* literacy-themed expert stations and the role these mentor texts play in each.

## The Role of Multitasking Mentor Texts in Reading-Themed Expert Stations

| FOCUS OF STATION OR SESSION | USE OF MULTITASKING MENTOR TEXTS |
|---|---|
| • How to figure out tricky words<br>• How to clarify the meaning of an unknown word<br>• Ways to preview a text<br>• Methods for remembering details and retelling<br>• A tried-and-true process for figuring out the main idea<br>• How to create different kinds of reading notebook entries<br>• How to select a book you will love<br>• Ways to stay motivated and engaged while you are reading<br>• Book talk stations | Students will teach and provide feedback to one another using mentor texts. They will show and tell the process of these skills by using these already read, practiced resources. This may sound like . . .<br><br>• Watch me as I reread this page of X and figure out how to say this new, tricky word.<br><br>• Let's work together to try to find the main idea in this section of X.<br><br>• I am going to use this book, X, as I model how I decide if it is something I will love to read. |

## The Role of Multitasking Mentor Texts in Writing-Themed Expert Stations

| FOCUS OF STATION OR SESSION | USE OF MULTITASKING MENTOR TEXTS |
|---|---|
| • What to do when you feel like you don't have any good ideas<br>• Tips for keeping your writing folder or notebook organized<br>• Ideas for building writing stamina<br>• Setting a writing goal and making an action plan<br>• How to:<br>  ○ *Craft a strong hook*<br>  ○ *Expand and develop one part*<br>  ○ *Use sensory details*<br>  ○ *Think of and choose interesting words*<br>  ○ *Create believable characters*<br>  ○ *Keep writing focused*<br>  ○ *Create a satisfying ending*<br>  ○ *Decide what to revise*<br>  ○ *Proofread your own work*<br>  ○ *Provide feedback to a partner* | Mentor texts provide the context for expert station teaching and feedback. Students will show and tell the process of these skills by using these comfortable and flexible resources. This may sound like . . .<br><br>• My writing notebook is a great mentor text. I can use it to show you so many cool things writers do. Today, I will use it to help you see how you can keep your work organized.<br><br>• When we first read X, the first page really stuck out to me. I'm going to show you how we can use a mentor text to help us try on leads in our own writing.<br><br>• I noticed that in your writing, you . . . . Since you already did that part, would you like to try . . . ? There's a great example in X we can use as we work on this together. |

The Role of Multitasking Mentor Texts in Word and Language-Themed Expert Stations

| FOCUS OF STATION OR SESSION | USE OF MULTITASKING MENTOR TEXTS |
|---|---|
| • How to use a certain tool or resource<br><br>• Various decoding strategies (how to figure out a tricky word)<br><br>• The *why* behind different phonics features or spelling patterns<br><br>• Introduction of a word part or root<br><br>• Introduction or spiraled review of a range of different grammar concepts<br><br>• Noticing and fixing up fragments and run-ons to create complete sentences<br><br>• Playful ways to explore and tinker with sentence structure<br><br>• Creating a certain feel or tone to writing by making choices about words and conventions<br><br>• Noticing and understanding figurative language<br><br>• Proofreading strategies | Words and conventions are thoughtfully chosen and conventionally used in selected mentor texts. As such, these are effective resources for showing and telling the process of student-selected skills. As students lean on these flexible resources, it may sound like . . .<br><br>• There's an example right here in X. Do you see how this word looks long and scary? But, it's not, because if we look at each part . . .<br><br>• Mrs. K is always telling us to use what we learned in spelling. Let's look and see how the author of X used words with vowel teams in their writing. Then, I'll teach you how you can do that, too.<br><br>• When I am trying to write longer sentences that aren't run-ons, it can be tricky. So, I sometimes find a sentence I like, and use the structure of that sentence to help me write a new, fancier sentence. Today, I will show you how I do that (using X for inspiration and support). |

# EDCAMPS

Edcamps require less formal planning and more in-the-moment collaborating, teaching, and learning. These resemble the professional edcamps you may have attended and taken part in, but with some small tweaks. Due to time constraints and daily schedules, the classroom edcamps I have taken part in often occur over two or three sessions instead of on one single day.

### Session 1: Planning Day

- Come together to reflect on recent learning. Provide time for students to think about what they have learned and where they have grown.

- Co-create a list of the connected topics the students want to investigate or continue to explore.

- This session often takes about 10 to 20 minutes. Before Session 2, create a schedule for the edcamp.

### Session 2: Edcamp Day

- During Session 2, three to five groups run simultaneously. Students attend the session they are most interested in. Every student's voice and expertise is a valuable part of the learning. The goal is for conversation to be synergistic. In each group, the ideas, insights, and perspectives shared by different students grow everyone's understanding. Multitasking mentor texts are out and available as students collaborate; the "Common Ways" chart shows how to use multitasking mentor texts in edcamps. This exploratory part of the session also often lasts 20 to 30 minutes.

- The groups then reconnect. Volunteers from each group share out pieces of their conversations. Often, students refer to and use multitasking mentor texts as they debrief and celebrate their collaborative experience. This takes another 10 to 20 minutes.
  NOTE: This reflective sharing can be saved for a third session.

#### Common Ways Multitasking Mentor Texts Are Centered in Edcamps

| READING | WRITING | WORDS AND LANGUAGE |
|---|---|---|
| Multitasking mentor texts are often used to investigate: | Multitasking mentor texts are often used to investigate: | Multitasking mentor texts are often used to investigate: |
| • The different works of a specific author<br><br>• A topic of interest<br><br>• The characteristics of a genre<br><br>• Reactions to ideas in a text<br><br>• Methods for jotting thinking while reading<br><br>• Practices of a skilled researcher | • The characteristics of a genre<br><br>• Organizational structures<br><br>• Flow of writing<br><br>• Different leads, openings, closings, and conclusions<br><br>• Show-don't-tell details<br><br>• Creating a feeling (tone)<br><br>• Word choice | • Patterns, affixes, word parts, and roots<br><br>• Interesting vocabulary and strategic word choice<br><br>• Tone and mood<br><br>• Relevant conventions |

As students engage in edcamps, they lean on multitasking mentor texts as they collaboratively contemplate and investigate:

- *What's our plan for this study?*

- *What are we finding?*

- *How do these discoveries make us feel?*

- *What's most important?*
- *Will we try/use this?*
- *Where and when will we try/use this?*
- *How could we try/use this?*
- *What different possibilities exist for next steps?*

During the reflective and celebratory component of edcamps, students use these and similar inquiries to add to the *big potential* (Achor, 2018) of collaborative learning. They will likely reference multitasking mentor texts as they share sentiments such as the following:

- *We studied and investigated . . .*
- *We analyzed . . .*
- *We came to believe . . . because . . .*
- *There were some different thoughts about this, and some of our perspectives included . . .*
- *After this experience, we plan to . . .*
- *We have a few suggestions for you. Here's how to use this as you read/write/explore words or language . . .*

There are endless options for edcamps!

Prioritizing time and opportunities for students to lead matters. When students are not only partners in learning but drivers of learning, they are more engaged, committed, and successful. Mentor texts can multitask in the hands of students. No teacher needed! This is such a worthy goal as we embark on this student-centered, text-supported journey.

# Epilogue

I am persistent in my pursuit to become a better version of myself. I imagine this drive came from my parents. Every day of their (way too short) lives, my parents exemplified what it meant to consider others, contribute to your community, and give "110%" to all you do. Their daily actions reflected their core values and beliefs. Many times, the gestures of collegiality and kindness they offered others had ongoing ripple effects. I was also raised to listen, act, and do my part to make the most of today . . . and take another step forward tomorrow.

I'm grateful that as an educator, I have the chance to enact this mindset each day. This work is complex. It is creative. It is challenging. And it is incredibly important. Teachers contribute. They create necessary change. I stand in awe of all teachers do, and I am honored to do this work alongside you.

I see and appreciate all that is already being done in classrooms. In this book, I have not tried to create a new program or completely novel approach to learning. Instead, I hope the pages of this book prompted mid-reading nods and recollections of methods you know, believe in, and trust. I hope you walk away with a reminder that classroom work doesn't have to be draining or depleting. Teachers can find energy and joy in a recommitment to tinkering with and reimagining some of the "great stuff" already in place. Essentially, it's also important to use an asset-based approach to what *teachers* do each day! This is a sustainable way of moving forward. So much has already been learned about what does work. Let's continue to cultivate these seeds (and already blooming plants), revitalizing and rejuvenating literacy learning. Making this choice often includes quiet moments of reflecting and wondering, "What if?" and "What else?" These contemplations often lead to answers that begin with "I can," "I will," and, eventually, "I do."

I hope that across these pages you have found accessible, practical, and actionable ways to share your love of texts, genuine respect for students, and enthusiasm for teaching and learning. My hope is that through thoughtful text selection and instructional choices, you continue to find fulfillment and joy in exploring questions like these:

- *How can I connect students with great texts and affirming learning experiences?*

- *How can I integrate learning so it feels more cohesive and connected?*

- *How can I support students in asking relevant questions and leading learning quests themselves?*

- *What small shift can I make today?*

- *What else can I try tomorrow?*

I can't wait to hear about where these explorations take you.

*Pam Koutrakos*

Pam Koutrakos
Twitter: @PamKou
Instagram: @Pam.Kou

# References: Featured Texts

Alexander, K. (with Colderley, C., & Wentworth, M.). (2017). *Out of wonder: Poems celebrating poets*. Candlewick.

Anderson, A. (2018). *Neither*. Little Brown Books for Young Readers.

Boynton-Hughes, B. (2019). *Brave Molly*. Chronicle Books.

Craft, J. (2019). *New kid*. Quill Tree Books.

de Anda, D. (2019). *Mango moon*. Albert Whitman.

Denise, A. A. (2019). *Planting stories: The life of librarian and storyteller Pura Belpré*. HarperCollins.

Hatke, B. (2015). *Little robot*. First Second.

Isabella, J. (2020). *Bringing back the wolves: How a predator restored an ecosystem*. Kids Can Press.

Keating, J. (2019). *Gross as a snot otter*. Knopf Books for Young Readers.

Lee, Y. H. (2019). *Dragon pearl*. Disney Book Group.

Ludwig, T. (2013). *The invisible boy*. Knopf Books for Young Readers.

Maillard, K. N. (2019). *Fry bread: A Native American family story*. Roaring Book Press.

Muhammad, I. (with Ali, S. K.). (2019). *The proudest blue: A story of hijab and family*. Little, Brown.

Patel, S. (Director). (2015). *Sanjay's super team* [Film]. Pixar Animation Studios.

Pimentel, A. B. (2020). *All the way to the top: How one girl's fight for Americans with disabilities changed everything*. Sourcebooks Explore.

Portis, A. (2019). *Hey, water!* Neal Porter Books.

Robinson, C. (2019). *Another*. Atheneum Books for Young Readers.

Roselló, J. (2019). *Red panda and moon bear*. Top Shelf Productions.

Roselló, J. (2020). *Panda roja y oso lunar* [Spanish ed.]. Top Shelf Productions.

Sanders, R. (2018). *Pride: The story of Harvey Milk and the rainbow flag*. Random House Books for Young Readers.

Singer, M. (2012). *A stick is an excellent thing: Poems celebrating outdoor play*. Clarion Books.

Underwood, D. (2015). *Interstellar Cinderella*. Chronicle Books.

# References: Text Pairings and Other Instructional Resources

The Ability Center of Greater Toledo. (2020, July 30). *Young advocate webinar: Jennifer Keelan* [Video]. YouTube. https://www.youtube.com/watch?v=3BIvsxZRZ3w

Acevedo, E. (2018). *The poet X*. HarperTeen.

Aguirre, J. (2012). *Giants beware!* First Second.

Ahmed, R., & Burrington, S. (2020). *Mae among the stars*. HarperCollins.

Al Abdullah, Q. R. J. (with DiPuccio, K.). (2010). *The sandwich swap*. Little, Brown Books for Young Readers.

Andreae, G. (2001). *Giraffes can't dance*. Orchard Books.

Annable, G. (2019). *Peter and Ernesto: The lost sloths*. Macmillan.

Anno, M. (1997). *Anno's journey* (Paperback ed.). Puffin Books.

Argueta, J. (2001). *A movie in my pillow [Una pelicula en mi almohada]*. Children's Book Press.

Associated Press (adapted by Newsela staff). (2020). *Merriam-Webster declares "they" its 2019 word of the year*. Newsela. https://newsela.com/read/they-word-of-year/id/2000003785/

Authors Everywhere! (2020, March 9). *Drawing demo: Draw ANYTHING and EVERYTHING with Jarrett Lerner!* [Video]. YouTube. https://www.youtube.com/watch?v=eCh2Zm6GkoM

Barillaro, A. (Director). (2016). *Piper* [Short film]. Pixar Animation Studios.

Barnes & Noble. (2018, July 25). *Graphic novels vs. comic books* [Video]. YouTube. https://www.youtube.com/watch?v=eHcOvoBM0VY

Bates, A. J. (2018). *The big umbrella*. Simon & Schuster.

Becker, A. (2013). *Journey*. Candlewick.

Becker, A. (2014). *Quest*. Candlewick.

Birdsong, B. (2019). *I will be fierce!* Roaring Brook Press.

Boyle, P. (2019). *Queer icons from gay to z: Activists, artists, and trailblazers*. Smith Street Books.

Brantley-Newton, V. (2020). *Just like me*. Random House Children's Books.

Brooks, A. C. (2019, November 24). *Opinion: By being kind, we can all become better people*. Newsela. https://newsela.com/read/ela-more-kindness/id/2000001694/

Brosgol, V. (2018). *Be prepared*. Macmillan.

Buitrago, J. (2015). *Two white rabbits*. Groundwood Books.

Byers, G. (2018). *I am enough*. Balzer + Bray.

Camerini, V. (2019). *Greta's story: The schoolgirl who went on strike to save the planet* (M. Giovannoni, Trans.). Aladdin.

Cervantes, J. C. (2018). *The storm runner*. Rick Riordan Presents.

Cherry, M. A., Downing, E., Jr., & Smith, B. W. (Directors). (2019). *Hair love* [Short film]. Sony Pictures Animation.

Choi, Y. (2001). *The name jar*. Knopf.

Chokshi, R. (2018). *Aru Shah and the end of time*. Rick Riordan Presents.

Chung, A. (2018). *Mixed: A colorful story*. Henry Holt.

Climo, S. (1992). *The Egyptian Cinderella*. HarperCollins.

Climo, S. (1996). *The Korean Cinderella*. HarperCollins.

Cohen, M. (1967). *Will I have a friend?* Macmillan.

Craft, J. (2020). *Class act*. Quill Tree Books.

Deer, B. (2019). *The fox wife*. Inhabit Media.

Denise, A. A. (2019). *Sembrando historias: Pura Belpré: bibliotecaria y narradora de cuentos*. HarperCollins Español.

dePaola, T. (2002). *Adelita: A Mexican Cinderella story*. G. P. Putnam's Sons Books for Young Readers.

Diaz, A.-C. (2020, July 30). Nike's "You can't stop us" wins Cannes film Grand Prix. *Ad Age*. https://adage.com/creativity/work/nike-you-cant-stop-us-cannes/2271211

Díaz, J. (2018). *Islandborn*. Dial Books.

Eaton, M., III. (2012). *The flying beaver brothers and the evil penguin plan*. Penguin Random House.

Farley, C. J. (2015, October 2). "Sanjay's super team": The backstory [Video]. *The Wall Street Journal*. https://www.wsj.com/video/anjays-super-team-the-backstory/37F1B86B-0537-43D3-8F0E-7FD2242DB36F.html

Forsyth, K. (2017). *Vasilisa the wise and tales of other brave young women*. Serenity Press.

Gerson, M.-J. (2018). *Fiesta femenina: Celebrating women in Mexican folklore*. Barefoot Books.

Gorman, A. (2021). *The hill we climb: An inaugural poem for the country*. Viking Books.

Hale, S. (2017). *Real friends*. First Second.

Hale, S. (2019). *Best friends*. First Second.

HarperCollins Publishers. (2021). *Meet the "new kid" in this trailer for the graphic novel by Jerry Craft*. https://www.harpercollins.com/blogs/harperkids/new-kid-trailer-graphic-novel-by-jerry-craft

Henkes, K. (1987). *Sheila Rae, the brave*. HarperCollins.

Henkes, K. (2000). *Wemberly worried*. HarperCollins.

Hoban, T. (2003). *I wonder*. Clarion Books.

Holm, J. L. (2019). *Sunny rolls the dice*. Graphix.

Hopkins, L. B. (2004). *Wonderful words: Poems about reading, writing, speaking, and listening*. Simon & Schuster Books for Young Readers.

Jamieson, V. (2016). *The great pet escape: Pets on the loose!* Holt Books for Young Readers.

Jamieson, V., & Mohamed, O. (2020). *When stars are scattered*. Penguin Random House.

Johnson, C. (1955). *Harold and the purple crayon*. Scholastic.

Johnson, R. K. (2012). *The shark king*. TOON Books.

Kaling, M., & Fisher, L. (Creators). (2020). *Never have I ever* [TV series]. Kaling International.

Keating, J. (2016). *Pink is for blobfish: Discovering the world's perfectly pink animals*. Knopf Books for Young Readers.

Keating, J. (2017). *What makes a monster?: Discovering the world's scariest creatures*. Knopf Books for Young Readers.

Keating, J. (2018). *Cute as an axolotl: Discovering the world's most adorable animals*. Knopf Books for Young Readers.

Khalil, A. (2020). *The Arabic quilt: An immigrant story*. Tilbury House.

Khan, H. (2020). *Like the moon loves the sky*. Chronicle Books.

Krosoczka, J. J. (2018). *Hey, kiddo*. Graphix.

Kuhne, M. (2019, July 1). *Scientists debunk myth that Yellowstone wolves changed entire ecosystem, flow of rivers*. AccuWeather. https://www.accuweather.com/en/weather-news/scientists-debunk-myth-that-yellowstone-wolves-changed-entire-ecosystem-flow-of-rivers/349988

Kunkel, A. B. (2020). *Digging for words: José Alberto Gutiérrez and the library he built*. Random House Children's Books.

Lại, T. (2011). *Inside out and back again*. HarperCollins.

Lehman, B. (2004). *The red book*. Clarion Mariner.

Lehman, B. (2011). *The secret box*. Clarion Mariner.

Levy, D. (2019). *Becoming RBG: Ruth Bader Ginsburg's journey to justice*. Simon & Schuster Books for Young Readers.

Library of Congress. (2020, August 19). *Carmen Agra Deedy: Family stories from a master storyteller* [Video]. YouTube. https://www.youtube.com/watch?v=Q7k7ZrYCB18

Lin, G. (2005). *The year of the dog*. Little, Brown Books for Young Readers.

Lin, G. (2010). *Ling and Ting: Not exactly the same!* Little, Brown Books for Young Readers.

Lindstrom, C. (2020). *We are water protectors.* Roaring Book Press.

Loomis, I. (2020). *Ohana means family.* Neal Porter Books.

Louie, A.-L. (1996). *Yeh Shen: A Cinderella story from China.* Puffin Books.

Martin, R. (1998). *The rough-face girl.* Puffin Books.

Mbalia, K. (2019). *Tristan Strong punches a hole in the sky.* Rick Riordan Presents.

Messner, K. (2017). *Over and under the pond.* Chronicle Books.

Mills, D. (2018). *La frontera: El viaje con papá [My journey with papa]* (Spanish and English ed.). Barefoot Books.

Morales, Y. (2018). *Dreamers.* Neal Porter/ Holiday House.

Mosca, J. F. (2017). *The girl who thought in pictures: The story of Dr. Temple Grandin.* The Innovation Press.

Naujokaitis, P. T. (2017). *Dinosaurs in space: Out of this world!* Blue Apple.

Nielsen, J. A. (2016). *The scourge.* Scholastic.

Patel, S. (2015). *The art of Sanjay's super team.* Chronicle Books.

Paul, M. (2019). *Thanku: Poems of gratitude.* Lerner Publishing Group.

Pearlman, R. (2018). *Pink is for boys.* Hachette Book Group.

Pearson, L. (2015). *Hilda and the troll.* Flying Eye Books.

Penfold, A. (2018). *All are welcome.* Knopf Books for Young Readers.

Pett, M., & Rubenstein, G. (2011). *The girl who never made mistakes.* Sourcebooks Jabberwocky.

Pinkney, A. D. (2018). *Martin rising: Requiem for a king.* Scholastic Press.

Pitman, G. E. (2014). *This day in June.* Magination Press.

Public Radio International (adapted by Newsela staff). (2019, January 17). *California teen leads legal efforts to allow immigrants to remain in U.S.* Newsela. https://newsela.com/read/California-teen-leads-immigration-lawsuit/id/48767/

Random House Kids. (2018, June 1). *Pride: The story of Harvey Milk and the rainbow flag: Rob Sanders* [Video].

YouTube. https://www.youtube.com/watch?v=iI29LssHqU4

Read Riordan Staff. (2018, December 11). *Rick, Yoon, and Dragon Pearl (Exclusive interview).* Read Riordan. https://www.readriordan.com/2018/12/11/rick-yoon-and-dragon-pearl-exclusive-interview/

Reynolds, P. H. (2004). *Ish.* Candlewick.

Robertson, J. (2019). *Nibi emosaawdang [The water walker]* (S. Williams & I. Toulouse, Trans.). Second Story Press.

Robeson, T. (2019). *Queen of physics: How Wu Chien Shiung helped unlock the secrets of the atom.* Sterling Children's Books.

Rosenthal, A. K. (2013). *Exclamation mark.* Scholastic.

Runton, A. (2004). *Owly: Vol. 1. The way home and the bittersweet summer.* Top Shelf Productions.

San Souci, R. D. (1997). *Sootface: An Ojibwa Cinderella story.* Dragonfly Books.

San Souci, R. D. (1998). *Cendrillon: A Caribbean Cinderella.* Simon & Schuster Books for Young Readers.

Santat, D. (2011). *Sidekicks.* Arthur A. Levine Books.

SciShow Kids. (2015, March 11). *The world's ugliest animal* [Video]. YouTube. https://www.youtube.com/watch?v=A7LU5Wxc_0Y

Sehgal, S., & Sehgal, K. (2018). *Festival of colors.* Beach Lane Books.

Sell, C. (2018). *The cardboard kingdom.* Penguin Random House.

Sicardi, A. (2019). *Queer heroes: Meet 52 LGBTQ heroes from past and present.* Wide Eyed Editions.

Simon, S. (2001). *Animals nobody loves.* Chronicle Books.

Singer, M. (2017). *Feel the beat: Dance poems that zing from salsa to swing.* Dial Books.

Solnit, R. (2019). *Cinderella liberator.* Haymarket Books.

Soto, G. (1996). *Too many tamales.* Penguin Young Readers Group.

Sotomayor, S. (2019). *Just ask!* Philomel Books.

Spires, A. (2009). *Binky the space cat.* Kids Can Press.

Springer, K. (2019, February 6). The writer's block: An interview with Jerry Craft. *Middle-Grade Mojo*. https://middlegrade mojo.com/2019/02/06/the-writers-block-an-interview-with-jerry-craft/

Stewart, M. (2014). *Water*. Scholastic.

Sturm, J., Arnold, A., & Frederick-Frost, A. (2015). *Sleepless knight*. First Second.

Sustainable Human. (2014a, February 13). *How wolves change rivers* [Video]. YouTube. https://www.youtube.com/watch?v=ysa5OBhXz-Q

Sustainable Human. (2014b, November 30). *How whales change climate* [Video]. YouTube. https://www.youtube.com/watch?v=M18HxXve3CM

Telgemeier, R. (2019). *Guts*. Scholastic.

Thompson, L. A. (2015). *Emmanuel's dream: The true story of Emmanuel Ofosu Yeboah*. Schwartz & Wade.

Thomson, B. (2010). *Chalk*. Two Lions.

Thomson, B. (2013). *Fossil*. Two Lions.

Time. (2015, June 29). *This is the history of the rainbow flag* [Video]. YouTube. https://www.youtube.com/watch?v=TWZMLzkdzxg

VanDerwater, A. L. (2013). *Forest has a song*. Clarion Books.

VanDerwater, A. L. (2018). *With my hands: Poems about making things*. Clarion Books.

VanDerwater, A. L. (2020). *Write! Write! Write!* Wordsong.

Venable, C. A. F., & Yu, S. (2010). *Hamster and Cheese*. Graphic Universe.

Wang, J. (2019). *Stargazing*. First Second.

Warga, J. (2019). *Other words for home*. HarperCollins.

Washington Post (adapted by Newsela staff). (2019, October 15). *Immigrant children face risky road to better opportunities in U.S.* Newsela. https://newsela.com/read/migrant-kids-hope/id/2000000025/

WeAreTeachers. (2019, January 24). *Storytime video: Planting stories: The life of librarian and storyteller Pura Belpré* [Video]. YouTube. https://www.youtube.com/watch?v=rAefwxYCydk

Winter, J. (2002). *Frida*. Arthur A. Levine Books.

Woodson, J. (2018). *The day you begin [El día en que descubres quién eres]*. Penguin Young Readers Group.

Yamada, K. (2016). *What do you do with a problem?* Compendium.

Yamada, K. (2018). *What do you do with a chance?* Compendium.

Yoon, S. (2016). *Be a friend*. Bloomsbury.

Yorio, K. (2020, January 27). Jerry Craft breaks barriers with historic 2020 Newbery win. *School Library Journal*. https://www.slj.com/?detailStory=Jerry-Craft-Breaks-Barriers-with-Historic-2020-Newbery-Win-books-libraries

Yue, J. (2019, October 30). *Sprinter Marissa Papaconstantinou on what it means to be an influencer on and off the track*. Athletics Canada. https://athletics.ca/papaconstantinou-wpa-2019/

Zagat. (2015, April 15). *Off-the-radar foods: What is frybread? Made in the USA, Episode 7* [Video]. YouTube. https://www.youtube.com/watch?v=Trcxxhzhg-o

Zietlow Miller, P. (2018). *Be kind*. Pan Macmillan.

# References

Achor, S. (2018). *Big potential: How transforming the pursuit of success raises our achievement, happiness, and well-being.* Currency.

Afflerbach, P. (2016). Reading assessment: Looking ahead. *The Reading Teacher, 69*(4), 413–419. https://doi.org/10.1002/trtr.1430

Aguilar, E. (2013, April 8). Five reasons why we need poetry in schools. *Edutopia.* https://www.edutopia.org/blog/five-reasons-poetry-needed-schools-elena-aguilar

Ahmed, S. (2018). *Being the change: Lessons and strategies to teach social comprehension.* Heinemann.

Anderson, J. (2005). *Mechanically inclined: Building grammar, usage, and style into writer's workshop.* Stenhouse.

Anderson, J. (2007). *Everyday editing: Inviting students to develop skill and craft in writer's workshop.* Stenhouse.

Anderson, J., & LaRocca, W. (2017). *Patterns of power: Inviting young writers into the conventions of language, grades 1–5.* Stenhouse.

Ansley, B. M., Meyers, J., McPhee, K., & Varjas, K. (2018, March 2). The hidden threat of teacher stress. *The Conversation.* https://theconversation.com/the-hidden-threat-of-teacher-stress-92676

Bear, D. R., Invernizzi, M., Templeton, S., & Johnston, F. (2004). *Words their way: Word study for phonics, vocabulary, and spelling instruction.* Pearson/Merrill/Prentice Hall.

Beers, K., & Probst, R. E. (2017). *Disrupting thinking: Why how we read matters.* Scholastic.

Bishop, R. S. (1990). Mirrors, windows, and sliding glass doors. *Perspectives, 1*(3), ix–xi.

Briceño, A., & Klein, A. F. (2019, March/April). A second lens on formative reading assessment with multilingual students. *The Reading Teacher, 72*(5), 611–621. https://ila.onlinelibrary.wiley.com/doi/abs/10.1002/trtr.1774

Bryan, T. A. (2019). *The art of comprehension: Exploring visual texts to foster comprehension, conversation, and confidence.* Stenhouse.

Busby, E. (2019, February 25). Teachers suffer more stress than other workers, study finds. *The Independent.* https://www.independent.co.uk/news/education/education-news/teachers-stress-professionals-mental-health-workload-national-foundation-educational-research-a8795691.html

Chall, J. S. (1983). *Stages of reading development.* McGraw-Hill.

Chávez, A. F., & Longerbeam, S. D. (2016). *Teaching across cultural strengths: A guide to balancing integrated and individuated cultural frameworks in college teaching.* Stylus.

Clay, M. M. (2016). *Literacy lessons designed for individuals* (2nd ed.). Global Education Systems.

Cooper, R., & Murphy, E. M. (2016). *Hacking problem based learning: 10 easy steps to PBL and inquiry in the classroom.* Times 10.

Culham, R. (2016). *Dream wakers: Mentor texts that celebrate Latino culture.* Stenhouse.

Cunningham, K. E. (2019). *Start with joy: Designing literacy learning for student happiness.* Stenhouse.

Daniels, H. (2017). *The curious classroom: 10 structures for teaching with student-directed inquiry.* Heinemann.

Daniels, H. S., & Ahmed, S. K. (2015). *Upstanders: How to engage middle school hearts and minds with inquiry.* Heinemann.

Dorfman, L., & Dougherty, D. (2014). *Grammar matters: Lessons, tips, and conversations using mentor texts, K–6.* Stenhouse.

Dorn, L., & Soffos, C. (2011). *Interventions that work: A comprehensive intervention model for preventing reading failure*. Allyn & Bacon.

Dorn, L., & Soffos, C. (2017). *Teaching for deeper comprehension*. Stenhouse.

Duke, N. K. (2004, March 1). The case for informational text. *Educational Leadership, 61*(6), 40–44. http://www.ascd.org/publications/education-al-leadership/mar04/vol61/num06/The-Case-for-Informational-Text.aspx

Eakins, S., & Buchanan-Rivera, E. (2020, January 2). *Unpacking identity-affirming schools with Dr. Erica Buchanan-Rivera* [Webinar]. Leading Equity Center Virtual Summit. https://www.leadingequitycenter.com/products/leading-equity-virtual-summit-2020-all-access-pass/categories/1940497/posts/6517482

Eakins, S., & Lanier, D. (2020, January 3). *Finding the connection point with Dee Lanier* [Webinar]. Leading Equity Center Virtual Summit. https://www.leadingequitycenter.com/products/leading-equity-virtual-summit-2020-all-access-pass/categories/1903934/posts/6376115

Ehrenworth, M., & Vinton, V. (2005). *The power of grammar: Unconventional approaches to the conventions of language*. Heinemann.

Eisner, W. (2008). *Comics and sequential art: Principles and practices from the legendary cartoonist*. Norton.

España, C., & Herrera, L. Y. (2020). *En comunidad: Lessons for centering the voices and experiences of bilingual Latinx students*. Heinemann.

Faulkner, R. T. (2015, October 23). Why children should be encouraged to read fantasy and science fiction. https://medium.com/@RodFaulkner/why-children-should-be-encouraged-to-read-fantasy-science-fiction-1c1a8acc7fa3

Ferlazzo, L. (2019, December 16). The importance of focusing on students' assets. *Education Week*. http://blogs.edweek.org/teachers/classroom_qa_with_larry_ferlazzo/2019/12/the_importance_of_focusing_on_students_assets.html

Fisher, D. B., Hattie, H., & Frey, N. (2016). *Visible learning for literacy, grades K–12: Implementing the practices that work best to accelerate student learning*. Corwin.

Gentry, J. R. (1982). An analysis of developmental spelling in GNYS AT WRK. *The Reading Teacher, 36*, 192–200.

Goldberg, G. (2015). *Mindsets and moves: Strategies that help readers take charge*. Corwin.

Goodman, Y., & Owocki, G. (2002). *Kidwatching: Documenting children's literacy development*. Heinemann.

Hammond, Z. (2015). *Culturally responsive teaching and the brain: Promoting authentic engagement and rigor among culturally and linguistically diverse students*. Corwin.

Hammond, Z. (2020, January 22). A conversation about instructional equity with Zaretta Hammond. *Collaborative Circle*. https://www.collaborativeclassroom.org/blog/a-conversation-about-instructional-equity-with-zaretta-hammond-part-1/

Harvey, S., & Daniels, H. S. (2015). *Comprehension and collaboration: Inquiry circles for curiosity, engagement, and understanding*. Heinemann.

Herman, K. C., Hickman-Rosa, J., & Reinke, W. M. (2017, October 6). Empirically derived profiles of teacher stress, burnout, self-efficacy, and coping and associated student outcomes. *Sage Journal, 20*(2), 90–100. https://doi.org/10.1177/1098300717732066

Horace Mann Educators Corporation. (2020). *The hidden impact of COVID-19 on educators: Rising health concerns, lower risk tolerance and benefit gaps: Insights from the Horace Mann Educators Health and Well-Being Study—November 2020*. http://www.horacemann.com/~/media/documents/supplemental/The%20Hidden%20Impact%20of%20COVID-19%20on%20Educators.pdf

Keene, E. O. (2018). *Engaging children: Igniting a drive for deeper learning*. Heinemann.

Koutrakos, P. (2018). *Word study that sticks: Best practices K–6*. Corwin Literacy.

Koutrakos, P. (2019). *The word study that sticks companion: Classroom-ready tools for teachers and students K–6*. Corwin Literacy.

Krutkowski, S. (2017). A strengths-based approach to widening participation students in higher education. *Reference Services Review, 45*(2), 227–241. https://doi.org/10.1108/RSR-10-2016-0070

Lopez, S. J., & Louis, M. C. (2009). The principles of strengths-based education. *Journal of College and Character, 10*(4). https://doi.org/10.2202/1940-1639.1041

MacKenzie, T. (2019). *Inquiry mindset: Nurturing the dreams, wonders, and curiosities of our youngest learners.* Elevate Books Edu.

Mahnken, K. (2017, October 31). 61% of teachers stressed out, 58% say mental health is not good in new national survey. *The 74.* https://www.the74million.org/61-of-teachers-stressed-out-58-say-mental-health-is-not-good-in-new-national-survey/

Martin, R. (2017, July 27). *Getting kids interested in poetry* [Audio]. NPR. https://www.npr.org/2017/07/27/539682661/getting-kids-interested-in-poetry

McGee, P. (2017). *Feedback that moves writers forward: How to escape correcting mode to transform student writing.* Corwin Literacy.

Meehan, M. (2019). *Every child can write: Entry points, bridges, and pathways for striving writers.* Corwin.

Minor, C. (2019). *We got this: Equity, access, and the quest to be who our students need us to be.* Heinemann.

Mitchell, K. L. (2018). *Experience inquiry: 5 powerful strategies, 50 practical experiences.* Corwin.

Morrell, E. (2007). *Critical literacy and urban youth: Pedagogies of access, dissent, and liberation.* Routledge.

Morrell, E. (2017, September). Toward equity and diversity in literacy research, policy and practice: A critical, global approach. *Journal of Literacy Research, 49*(3), 454–463.

Muhammad, G. (2020). *Cultivating genius: An equity framework for culturally and historically responsive literacy.* Scholastic.

Munsch, R. (1980). *The paper bag princess.* Annick Press.

Nichols, M. (2008). *Talking about text: Guiding students to increase comprehension through purposeful talk.* Shell Education.

Noguera, P. (2019, July 8). *Equity isn't just a slogan. It should transform the way we educate kids.* The Holdsworth Center. https://holdsworthcenter.org/blog/equity-isnt-just-a-slogan/

NYU Steinhardt School of Culture, Education, and Human Development. (2018, October 29). *Teacher education reinvented: Supporting excellence in teacher education.* https://teachereducation.steinhardt.nyu.edu/an-asset-based-approach-to-education-what-it-is-and-why-it-matters/

Obama, M. (2018). *Becoming.* Crown.

Pearson, D., & Gallagher, M. (1983). The instruction of reading comprehension. *Contemporary Educational Psychology, 8*(March), 317–344.

Ritchhart, R. (2011). *Making thinking visible: How to promote engagement, understanding, and independence in all learners.* Jossey-Bass.

Ritchhart, R. (2015). *Creating cultures of thinking: The 8 forces we must master to truly transform our schools.* John Wiley & Sons.

Robb, L. (2016). *Read, talk, write: 35 lessons that teach students to analyze fiction and nonfiction.* Corwin.

Scholastic. (2019, October 3). *Jason Reynolds on the power of story* [Video]. YouTube. https://www.youtube.com/watch?v=TRGjaOiIdnU

Souto-Manning, M. (2018). Foreword. In C. L. Ryan & J. M. Hermann-Wilmarth (Eds.), *Reading the rainbow: LGBTQ-inclusive literacy instruction in the elementary classroom* (pp. ix–xi). Teachers College Press.

Vygotsky, L. S. (1978). *Mind in society: The development of higher psychological processes.* Harvard University Press.

Walther, M. (2018). *The ramped-up read aloud: What to notice as you turn the page.* Corwin.

Westman, L. (2018). *Student-driven differentiation: 8 steps to harmonize learning in the classroom.* Corwin.

Wilhelm, J. D., Bear, R., & Fachler, A. (2019). *Planning powerful instruction, grades 6–12: 7 must-make moves to transform how we teach—and how students learn.* Corwin.

Wiliam, D. (2011). *Embedded formative assessment.* Solution Tree Press.

# Index

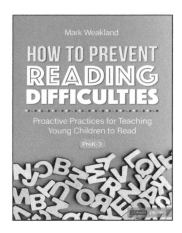
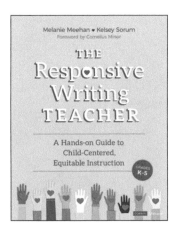
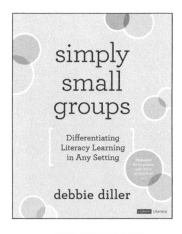

At Corwin Literacy we have put together a collection of just-in-time, classroom-tested, practical resources from trusted experts that allow you to quickly find the information you need when you need it.

**DOUGLAS FISHER, NANCY FREY, NICOLE LAW**

Using a structured, three-pronged approach—skill, will, and thrill—students experience reading as a purposeful act with this new comprehensive model of reading instruction.

**PAM KOUTRAKOS**

Packed with ready-to-go lessons and tools, this user-friendly resource provides ways to weave together different aspects of literacy using one mentor text.

**REBECCA G. HARPER**

Customizable strategies turn students' informal writing into a springboard for daily writing practice in every content area—with a focus on academic vocabulary, summarizing, and using textual evidence.

**MELANIE MEEHAN, CHRISTINA NOSEK, MATTHEW JOHNSON, DAVE STUART JR., MATTHEW R. KAY**

This series offers actionable answers to your most pressing questions about teaching reading, writing, and ELA.

**CORWIN**

**CORWIN** A SAGE Publishing Company

Helping educators make the greatest impact

**CORWIN HAS ONE MISSION:** to enhance education through intentional professional learning.

We build long-term relationships with our authors, educators, clients, and associations who partner with us to develop and continuously improve the best evidence-based practices that establish and support lifelong learning.